The Black Arch...

SCREAM OF THE SHALKA

By Jon Arnold

Published March 2017 by Obverse Books

Cover Design © Cody Schell

Text © Jon Arnold, 2017

Range Editor: Philip Purser-Hallard

Jon would like to thank:

Phil Purser-Hallard for asking me back

Simon Clark, James Goss, Jonathan Clements, Paul Scoones and Paul Driscoll for their much appreciated assistance

Mark Donovan, for the Withnail *joke*

Carolyn and Eddie, for patience

Jon Arnold has asserted his right to be identified as the author of this Work in accordance with the Copyright, Designs and Patents Act 1988.

Also available

The Black Archive #1: Rose by Jon Arnold

The Black Archive #2: The Massacre by James Cooray Smith

The Black Archive #3: The Ambassadors of Death by LM Myles

The Black Archive #4: Dark Water / Death in Heaven by Philip Purser-Hallard

The Black Archive #5: Image of the Fendahl by Simon Bucher-Jones

The Black Archive #6: Ghost Light by Jonathan Dennis

The Black Archive #7: The Mind Robber by Andrew Hickey

The Black Archive #8: Black Orchid by Ian Millsted

The Black Archive #9: The God Complex by Paul Driscoll

Coming soon

The Black Archive #11: The Evil of the Daleks by Simon Guerrier

The Black Archive #12: Pyramids of Mars by Kate Orman

The Black Archive #13: Human Nature / The Family of Blood by Naomi Jacobs and Philip Purser-Hallard

For Carolyn, for reasons that would take several lifetimes to explain

CONTENTS

OVERVIEW

Serial Title: *Scream of the Shalka*

Writer: Paul Cornell

Director: Wilson Milam (animation by Cosgrove Hall)

Original UK Webcast Dates: 13 December 2003 – 18 December 2003

Running Time: Episode 1: 14m 37s

Episode 2: 10m 16s

Episode 3: 12m 13s

Episode 4: 14m 37s

Episode 5: 12m 41s

Episode 6: 15m 5s

Regular Cast: Richard E Grant (The Doctor), Sophie Okonedo (Alison), Derek Jacobi (The Master)[1]

Guest Cast: Craig Kelly (Joe), Andrew Dunn (Max), Anna Calder-Marshall (Mathilda), Conor Moloney (Dawson / Greaves), Ben Morrison (McGrath / Caretaker), Diana Quick (Prime), Jim Norton (Kennet)[2]

Antagonists: Prime, the Shalka

---

[1] No further stories were made with this cast, but future plans involved Alison and the Master as regulars alongside the Doctor.
[2] David Tennant's lines as a caretaker in episode 5 are uncredited.

Novelisation: *Scream of the Shalka* by Paul Cornell. BBC Books, 2004.

Sequels and Prequels: 'The Feast of the Stone' by Cavan Scott and Mark Wright

Responses:

'Cornell's approach was to assume that everyone watching already knew what **Doctor Who** was all about. That may be why it often feels like **Doctor Who** fan fiction instead of the real thing. It's not helped by a serious problem at the heart of the whole thing: Richard E Grant, who admitted at the time that he wasn't all that interested in science fiction and knew nothing about **Doctor Who** going in.'

[Christopher Bahn, 'Doctor Who (Classic): Scream of the Shalka', AV Club, 21 December 2013]

'*Shalka* stands up as a successful experiment nixed only by the return of **Doctor Who** to television.'

[Mark Clapham, Eddie Robson and Jim Smith, *Who's Next: An Unofficial and Unauthorised Guide to Doctor Who*]

SYNOPSIS

Episode 1

At a meteorite impact site in New Zealand, two researchers see worm-like creatures, and succumb to paralysis. Some time later, an aloof and embittered **Doctor** arrives in a strangely deserted English town centre. From **Alison Cheney**, who works behind the bar in the local pub, her boss **Max**, and **Mathilda**, a homeless woman, he learns that the town has been cut off for three weeks, with the terrified populace under a form of mind control. Subterranean creatures punish excessive noise by compelling the locals to immolate themselves in lava spilling from cracks across the town – into one of which the TARDIS has fallen.

Angry at whichever agency has sent the TARDIS here, the Doctor at first refuses to become involved, but changes his mind after Mathilda dies in a sonic attack. Recognising Alison as one of the few locals willing to fight back, he calls on her and her GP boyfriend **Joe**. Refusing to be afraid of monsters, he continues to make noise until some monsters arrive.

Episode 2

The Doctor learns that the creatures are made of 'bioplasma', which they harden into temporary bodies. He incapacitates his attackers, first by reflecting their sonic screams at them, and then with an improvised bomb that blows up a hardware shop, and incidentally Alison and Joe's house. The noise stuns all the aliens, apparently breaking their control over the town.

Beneath the Earth's surface, their leader uses sonic technology to enter the TARDIS. At the console is **the Master**, who repels her with a force field. The Doctor calls on the help of the United Nations to find the TARDIS. To his annoyance the military arrive under **Major Kennet**, and begin to evacuate the town. Alison and Joe's convoy is attacked by the creatures, who forcibly extract Alison.

Episode 3

The Doctor tricks Kennet, **Sergeant Greaves** and their men into blocking their access to the local caves with a rockfall. Safely inside, he hijacks a colony creature made up from multiple aliens, used as a guard-dog, and has it take him to their leader: **Prime**, the War Chief of the aggressively imperialist **Shalka** Confederacy.

Prime threatens Alison until the Doctor readmits the Shalka to the TARDIS, and shuts down what turns out to be the Master's android body. The Doctor is angry at Alison for exposing his vulnerability. Alison (now wounded in the forehead) reveals that she dislikes Lannet, where she lives with Joe, and has been thinking of leaving them both. Believing that the Shalka have learned the principles of the TARDIS, Prime reconfigures a wormhole gateway to their homeworld into a black hole, and has the Doctor thrown into it.

Episode 4

Reactivating himself, the android Master attempts to bargain with the Shalka, explaining that the Doctor had him conceal the TARDIS's true systems from them.

As he falls, the Doctor resigns himself to death, believing he has doomed Alison. However, remembering that his mobile phone is part of the TARDIS, he is able to reconfigure it into a doorway to the console room. He expels the occupying Shalka into the black hole and returns, energised, to Kennet's base. He learns from a captured Shalka that the creatures are vulnerable to pure oxygen.

The aliens return Alison, but her head wound is troubling her, and like most of the evacuees – and Greaves, who was briefly alone with the captive Shalka – she has a sore throat. The Shalka reassert their control over the Lannet diaspora, including Alison, Joe and Max, and direct them to a wood in the Pennines. A miniature Shalka emerges from Alison's forehead.

Episode 5

Across the world, communities like Lannet, controlled though Shalka conduits like Alison's, are assembling. Their vocal cords have been manipulated to emit sonic signals, which will generate gases causing Earth's atmosphere to resemble the Shalka's subsurface conditions, leading to extreme weather and (according to the Doctor) the extinction of humanity within an hour.

Arriving in the Pennines with Kennet and his men, the Doctor removes Alison's conduit. Over Kennet's and Joe's protests he takes her to the Shalka's headquarters. Prime explains that subterranean Shalka inhabit most of the worlds in the universe, particularly those whose civilisations are thought to have committed ecological suicide. On the surface, chaos is spreading as the atmosphere changes.

Episode 6

By swallowing the conduit he took from Alison, the Doctor is able to reprogram it and connects both himself and Alison to the interconnected exchange of information that is the Shalka's scream. They destroy Prime's acolytes and reconfigure the wormhole as a black hole again, sucking Prime in. The Doctor causes the rest of the Shalka on Earth to vaporise, freeing their slaves before Alison can use them to repair the damage they have caused. The Earth begins to heal itself nonetheless.

The Master explains some of their history to Alison: he helped when the Doctor lost his last companion, and in return the Doctor saved him from a lingering death. Now they are exiles, forever sent into danger by 'those who punish us', though the Master himself cannot leave the TARDIS. At his prompting, Alison says goodbye to Joe. The Doctor promises to drop her off with her mother in the recent past, but when Joe phones her home she is not there. She leaves with the Doctor, even so.

INTRODUCTION

Doctor Who was dead, to begin with. There was no doubt about that. It had ended on 6 December 1989 and, despite the optimistic final declaration of having work to do[3], had only subsequently returned for a couple of charity sketches and as a TV movie co-produced with Fox[4]. Although the latter was optimistically seen as a pilot for a putative ongoing series, its US reception effectively meant this was stillborn[5].

The years between 1989 and 2005 have subsequently been termed by **Doctor Who** fandom as 'the Wilderness Years'[6]: the period when the show was not an ongoing presence on television. This phrase is actually a huge disservice to those engaged in producing new **Doctor Who** stories during the period; with the Virgin Books **New Adventures** range (1991-97), the BBC **Eighth Doctor Adventures** (1997-2005), *Doctor Who Magazine*'s comic strip and later Big Finish's eighth Doctor audios, there were a wealth of stories seeking to present themselves as the direct continuation of the television series[7]. And, from the same publishers and producers,

---

[3] *Survival* episode 3.
[4] *Dimensions in Time* (1993), *The Curse of Fatal Death* (1999) and *Doctor Who* (1996), respectively.
[5] The broadcast conflicted with both a significant episode of **Roseanne** (1988-97) and an NBA playoff game featuring arguably the sport's most popular player of all time and biggest box-office draw, Michael Jordan.
[6] For example, the issue of the fanzine *In-Vision* dealing with this period is named 'The Wilderness Years'.
[7] The term 'the Wilderness Years' derives from the idea of television being **Doctor Who**'s primary medium, ahead of, for

there were stories of past Doctors which often sought to simply recreate the ambience of the era of the show in which they were set, but sometimes sought to tell new types of stories featuring these Doctors – chiefly Virgin's **Missing Adventures** (1994-97), the BBC **Past Doctor Adventures** (1997-2005) and the bulk of Big Finish's output[8]. Producers such as Reeltime, BBV and Dreamwatch Media also produced unlicensed stories featuring monsters or characters from the show[9], and even characters and concepts originating in print or audio sustained their own spin-off lines[10]. For all that new **Doctor Who** on television was limited to one new

---

example, radio or literature. On the Resonance FM podcast 'Book List: Novelising **Doctor Who**', Paul Cornell suggested that the amount of exciting new stories made in this period meant that they would be better termed 'the Theme Park Years' (Fitch, Alex, 'Book List: Novelising **Doctor Who**', Resonance FM Podcast, 12 December 2013)

[8] This debate between whether **Doctor Who** was better served stretching the format or retreading past glories was boiled down to the binary 'rad' versus 'trad' (i.e. 'radical' versus 'traditional'). In truth, a book or audio story which was a pure example of either was rare; it's better to understand the concept as a spectrum which at one end simply seeks to recreate the television series and at the other seeks to stretch the boundaries of what may be attempted in a **Doctor Who** story in its chosen medium.

[9] These often amounted to **Doctor Who** with the serial numbers unsubtly filed off: Colin Baker and Nicola Bryant played 'The Stranger' and 'Miss Brown' in one BBV range and Sylvester McCoy and Sophie Aldred played 'The Dominie' and 'Alice' in another. (Rees, Dylan, *Downtime: The Lost Years of Doctor Who*, 2017.)

[10] For example Bernice Summerfield, Faction Paradox and Iris Wildthyme, all of whom have sustained well over a decade of their own adventures across various publishers.

episode and a pair of charity sketches, in a wider sense **Doctor Who** was in rude creative health.

However, all of these attempts to construct an ongoing story for the Doctor were limited in that the terms of their licence dictated that they use extant television Doctors[11]. They could not introduce a new Doctor as an ongoing lead in the series. The first three attempts to produce **Doctor Who** as a web-only animated series, *Death Comes to Time* (2001-02), *Real Time* (2002) and *Shada* (2003), emphasised this[12]. *Death Comes to Time* told an apparently final **Doctor Who** story using Sylvester McCoy's seventh Doctor and Sophie Aldred's Ace; *Real Time* starred Colin Baker's sixth Doctor; and *Shada* retold Douglas Adams's aborted 1979 script with a narrative framing device allowing it to feature Paul McGann's eighth Doctor. Hindsight makes all three of these efforts look primitive: audio plays with largely static pictures illustrating the action, and any movement achieved by alteration of the viewpoint of the picture, chiefly rotation or zoom-ins. This reflects contemporary technological limitations of connecting to the

---

[11] Virgin Publishing mooted regenerating the Doctor in the mid-90s but were forbidden from doing so – he would have been modelled on David Troughton (Ortiz, Julio Angel, 'Throwback Interview: Paul Cornell', 2002). The **Doctor Who** comic strip *Wormwood* (1998) included a fake regeneration that was not flagged as such, and included a false Doctor modelled on Nicholas Briggs, who'd played the part in the amateur **Audio-Visuals** series.

[12] Whilst *Death Comes to Time* was a BBCi production, *Shada* and *Real Time* were produced by Big Finish (and later released by the company on CD). *Death Comes to Time* was notable for being the first BBC drama made for an online audience: **Doctor Who**'s pioneering spirit remained intact.

internet more than a lack of ambition; with the vast majority of internet connections being dial-up and extremely slow by modern standards, a fully animated episode would take a long time to load and would be subject to delays and the possibility of the connection dropping[13].

This changed in 2002. With no new TV series apparently imminent, BBCi producer James Goss pitched a new web-only series of **Doctor Who**; one which would not only seek to be the first in an ongoing story but also to introduce an entirely new Doctor[14]. This was initially a hard sell, despite the **Doctor Who** section being one of

---

[13] Appropriately for **Doctor Who**, another reason was apparently a lack of budget. On the DVD commentary for *Scream of the Shalka* James Goss mentions that it was the first BBCi **Doctor Who** animation that actually had an animation budget at all. He describes their previous productions as either having 'a tiny, tiny budget or in one case a genuinely non-existent budget.'

[14] According to the essay 'The Making of *Scream of the Shalka*' accompanying the BBC Books novelisation, Big Finish's **Unbound** series (a series of six 'What if?' plays) alerted BBCi that the BBC 'in general' were no longer worried about regenerating the Doctor. The principal objections to new Doctors had come from BBC Films, who had apparently been pursuing a film deal based on the series for 'many years' and were worried that any new Doctor would spoil any casting announcement of theirs. Given that Big Finish's **Unbound** Doctors were explicitly alternative incarnations, this may have been based on (or taken advantage of) a generous interpretation of what constituted a 'new' Doctor; particularly with the intention of *Scream of the Shalka* being the first of a new series. (Cornell, Paul, *Scream of the Shalka*, p196.)

the most popular parts of the BBC website[15] and *Death Comes to Time* attracting 100,000 viewers[16]. **Doctor Who** was perceived as an outdated relic[17]. However, the success of the webcasts[18], combined with the quality of animation produced for the BBCi webcast *Ghosts of Albion* (2003)[19], meant that Goss and executive producer Martin Trickey were able to overcome resistance to the idea of BBCi producing their own original **Doctor Who** story[20]. It was produced and broadcast to coincide with the show's 40th anniversary, a birthday otherwise marked only perfunctorily by the

---

[15] According to the 'Interweb of Fear' feature on the *Scream of the Shalka* DVD, only the news and weather sections of the BBC site ranked ahead of it at the time of *Scream of the Shalka*'s production.

[16] Figure stated in the 'Interweb of Fear' feature.

[17] Goss recounts his head of department remarking that **Doctor Who** 'only had a year left in it' in 2003, and a colleague cattily suggesting that they 'should just be doing **Blake's 7**' (episode 3 DVD commentary). Hindsight puts such remarks in similar context to those who dismissed the motor car or internet as passing fads.

[18] Cornell cites the *Shada* webcast in his essay; however, as this was only broadcast in May and June of 2003 the dates don't make sense. Given that he cites an anecdote on p204 regarding the Gallifrey One convention, which takes place every February, it can safely be assumed that any commission was based on the success of *Death Comes to Time* and *Real Time*.

[19] This was an animated drama serial original to the BBC Cult website, but which was tied into their **Buffy the Vampire Slayer** section due to being co-written by Amber Benson (who played Tara Maclay on the series) and Christopher Golden (author of multiple **Buffy** tie-in novels). Benson also directed the initial story.

[20] Goss phrased this as 'people finding 99 reasons to say no before they'll say yes'.

BBC[21]. Significant acting talent would headline the cast: Richard E Grant, Derek Jacobi and the soon-to-be-Oscar-nominated Sophie Okenedo. Paul Cornell, one of the leading writers of the **Doctor Who** novel lines and a successful writer outside the small world of **Doctor Who** fiction, provided the script. Plans for further stories were advanced to the point of a further script being partially written.

And yet Grant's Doctor was effectively dead before broadcast; relegated to a sideline that meant his only other appearance would be in a short story for the BBC Cult website. Any oxygen of publicity the webcast might have generated was sucked away by the September announcement of the new **Doctor Who** television series overseen by Russell T Davies; the 'indefinite shelving' announced in February 2004 was merely confirming the obvious. *Scream of the Shalka* had been relegated to an oddity before it was shown; at best it was something to tide fans over before the show's big return to its original medium. Not so much the road not taken, as a shady dead-end side street just before a far more attractive destination.

This isn't about **Doctor Who**'s triumphant return. It's the story of something equally interesting; a glimpse of what might have been.

---

[21] The only other contender for an official anniversary story was *Deadly Reunion*, a BBC Books third Doctor novel whose celebratory nature seemed restricted to reuniting 1970s Script Editor Terrance Dicks and Producer Barry Letts as co-authors. Otherwise celebration was limited to an official Panopticon event, a souvenir hardback (*Doctor Who: The Legend* by Justin Richards) and a natty logo which incorporated the figure 40 into the 'H' and 'O' of 'DOCTOR WHO'.

CHAPTER 1: 'AN EMOTIONAL ISLAND'

The Character

Any new Doctor has several parents: the creative team behind the series (in the 20th century usually a combination of script editor and producer; in the 21st century the executive producer designated as showrunner); the lead actor; and to a certain degree the costume designers who set the tone of the outfits the character wears. Each Doctor's character derives from a combination of such elements.

There are essentially two approaches taken on those occasions where a new Doctor has coincided with key creative changes behind the scenes. These are invariably occasions where the series has been reshaped; often this involves refreshing the backstory. For example, Patrick Troughton's arrival is the last stage in Innes Lloyd and Gerry Davis moving the Doctor from observing to actively interfering[22]; whereas the coincidental near simultaneous arrival of Hinchcliffe, Holmes and Tom Baker turns the Doctor from Earth-based scientist to intergalactic wanderer[23]. These are fundamental reshapings of the show's format from the prior production team's vision; however, they are content to proceed in terms of story continuity with the previous format – they move on with a new actor providing a different energy to the series, but don't change the facts we think we know about the Doctor. Other occasions have seen production teams introduce new information about the Doctor's background to suit their version of the show. Troughton's

---

[22] *The Power of the Daleks* (1966).
[23] Starting with *Robot* (1974-75).

departure and Pertwee's arrival see the Doctor's background being filled in and the show almost entirely reformatted[24]; and once Andrew Cartmel had time to think about a creative direction for the series, he introduced what became known as 'the Cartmel Masterplan' which overwrote the facts we thought we knew about the Doctor and imposed an almost mythic background on him[25]. More relevantly to *Scream of the Shalka*[26], *Doctor Who* (1996), with its status as a de facto pilot, and *Rose* (2005), as an attempt at a mass-market relaunch, seek to impose entirely new histories on the main character.

Of all the incarnations of the Doctor, the *Shalka* Doctor[27] is the least explored; with the anniversary minisode 'The Night of the Doctor' (2013) even Paul McGann's Doctor had a greater number of onscreen appearances, even before audios and novels are considered[28]; the War Doctor made two appearances[29] and

---

[24] *Spearhead from Space* (1970).

[25] None of this background mythology is directly stated onscreen, instead being limited to such instances as the Doctor's line 'Oh Davros, I am so much more than just another Time Lord' in *Remembrance of the Daleks* episode 4 and Lady Peinforte's threatened revelations in *Silver Nemesis* episode 3 (both 1988). Much of it was only teased out in the **New Adventures** novels, with the full revelations occurring in Marc Platt's *Lungbarrow* (1997).

[26] Hereafter, generally, '*Shalka*'.

[27] By convention, Grant's (supposedly ninth) Doctor is known by this title to avoid confusion with Christopher Eccleston's 'ninth' Doctor.

[28] At the time of writing the eighth Doctor has appeared in 94 audio plays (with more announced), 73 novels, three novellas, a 50th anniversary novella and, numerous short stories. By this token, far

spawned his own spin-off novel and a Big Finish audio series. By contrast, the *Shalka* Doctor appeared only once more, in a short story published on the BBC Cult website[30]. There is no beginning to his story, no indication as to how he regenerated from his previous body; and while we can get a good sense of the events that shaped him, these events are not explained onscreen or in the novelisation[31]. In a real sense this Doctor exists only to battle the Shalka; the life principle to oppose the Shalka's death principle.

The first important decision with regards to the Doctor was that he should be introduced 'mobile, himself and whole from moment one.'[32] This went against a trend dating back to *Spearhead from Space* (1970) where the new Doctor had spent some proportion of his debut disoriented before settling down into character. It reached a nadir with *The Twin Dilemma* (1984) where we're uncertain even at the end of the story if the Doctor has fully recovered from his regeneration.

This adherence to using a regeneration story to introduce a new Doctor had caused narrative problems for *Doctor Who* (1996). Whilst including Sylvester McCoy in order to maintain continuity with where the show had ended in 1989 was an admirable aim, it

---

from being the shortest-serving Doctor, he may well be the most extensively explored Doctor of them all.

[29] *The Name of the Doctor* and *The Day of the Doctor* (both 2013) plus a brief cameo in 'The Night of the Doctor'.

[30] 'The Feast of the Stone' by Cavan Scott and Mark Wright (see Appendix 2).

[31] They can, however, be found on the infotext on the *Scream of the Shalka* DVD and are discussed in Chapter 4.

[32] Cornell, *Scream of the Shalka*, p208.

meant that Paul McGann's new Doctor did not appear until half an hour into his initial story and acted in a deliberately disorienting way until the final scenes. For a story attempting to introduce the Doctor to an American audience (and reintroduce him to a British one) this was creatively a disastrous decision. It requires an audience to accept the character, further accept his ability to regenerate and then to accept him all over again inside less than 90 minutes. For a show explicitly aiming to be a pilot episode for a new series, this is asking a lot of the audience and you can see why new viewers might have picked something less confusing such as **Roseanne** or a basketball game.

Scream of the Shalka would have a shorter running time than *Doctor Who* (1996) (the DVD sleeve gives a running time for *Shalka* as approximately 78 minutes, including six sets of opening and closing credits, whereas *Doctor Who* (1996) runs for 89 minutes in the US and Canada and 85 minutes in the UK[33]), and therefore a regeneration would consume a large chunk of the narrative. Given that the narrative would be compressed into episodes of no longer than 15 minutes, it also meant that dealing with regeneration would make the character of the Doctor the focus rather than the adventure. Doing without a regeneration scene means at a stroke that there is no need to explain the Doctor nor any more-than-human abilities he has in his initial adventure. The show, as Steven Moffat has said it should be, is about the new adventure rather

---

[33] The difference in running times is due to different frame rates between the US system and PAL broadcast system used in the UK.

than the aftermath of a past story[34]. Essentially this is the same lesson Russell T Davies would apply to introducing the Doctor in *Rose*[35].

The key to the development of this Doctor was the tonal decision to have him influenced by what Cornell termed the 'gothic romanticism'[36] of the Doctor's character in the Jon Pertwee and Tom Baker eras, the **Doctor Who** he had watched as a child:

> 'When I was a kid, I almost found the character of the Doctor as scary as the monsters, and the TARDIS and everything else about the show. Here was [...] a man who specialised in monsters, and a vast magical box that might contain more of them. He came from that world of threat and terror, even if he was a good force within it. The unpredictability and anger of a man who wasn't reassuring or comfortable was something I wanted to bring to the ninth Doctor.'[37]

'Gothic' is a term rarely associated with the Pertwee era of the show[38]; generally in regards to **Doctor Who** it's used solely to refer

---

[34] Cook, Benjamin, 'The DWM Interview: Steven Moffat', Doctor Who Magazine (DWM) #502, September 2016, p20.

[35] *Scream of the Shalka* does, however, assume the audience has a familiarity with the concept of the TARDIS.

[36] Cornell, *Scream of the Shalka*, p 209. For further discussion of the use of the influence of the **Doctor Who** brand of gothic in this story, see Chapter 4.

[37] Cornell, *Scream of the Shalka*, p 209.

[38] However, several serials in this period are influenced by the post-Gothic strand of science-fiction Hammer productions, as discussed in Chapter 2 of Bucher-Jones, Simon, *The Black Archive 5: Image of*

to the period of the show produced by Philip Hinchcliffe and Robert Holmes. Cornell seems to be using it specifically to refer to aspects of the often autocratic and abrupt manner of Pertwee's Doctor; a 'natural authority'[39] often characterised by his being 'impatient with those whose intellect does not match his own, he treats authority figures with contempt.'[40] This disdain for authority figures (often including the Brigadier and extending to public servants such as Chinn and Trenchard[41]) asserts the character as beyond human authority: all that's preventing him from becoming a monster is his own sense of morality[42]; he could easily be guilty of 'unscrupulous or potentially rapacious behaviour' which often characterises the heroes of gothic romanticism[43]. Essentially he's often the man who bullies the bullies because he regards himself as the highest authority[44]. This disrespect in the character for what would

---

the Fendahl (2016), so there are traces of a modern Gothic influence in this era.

[39] Chapman, James, Inside the TARDIS: The Worlds of Doctor Who – A Cultural History (2006), p79.

[40] Chapman, Inside the TARDIS, p78.

[41] In The Claws of Axos (1971) and The Sea Devils (1972) respectively.

[42] Cornell's childhood uncertainty toward the Doctor may well account for his suggestion in his **New Adventures** novel Timewyrm: Revelation (1991) that an alternative third Doctor became the dictator of the alternative Earth in Inferno (1970).

[43] Hughes, William, Historical Dictionary of Gothic Literature (2012), p224.

[44] This opposition to bullying is central to Cornell's conception of the character; the original outline has him 'angry at cruelty' (p210) and a passage in the novelisation emphasises this character's belief that 'Knowledge would always conquer force' and 'cleverness beats

normally be regarded as authority figures continues into Tom Baker's era – the period where the gothic romantic nature perceived by Cornell is matched by the overarching aesthetic of the series. This Doctor of the 1970s may be a hero, but he's not in any sense a conventionally reassuring breed of hero; it's aptly summed up by a quote regarding Aslan from *The Lion, The Witch and the Wardrobe*: 'Safe? [...] Who said anything about safe? 'Course he isn't safe. But he's good.'[45]

With this in mind it's easy to see the *Shalka* Doctor as a direct throwback to the Doctors of this era, bypassing the development of the character in the 1980s[46]. We first meet him raging at unknown superiors for not being where he's supposed to be; this harks back to the Pertwee Doctor's continued frustration with the Time Lords during his exile, or even more directly to the opening scenes of *The Brain of Morbius* (1976) which feature the Baker Doctor raging at the unseen Time Lords who have diverted the TARDIS from its course. It's further reflected in the design of the Doctor's outfit:

---

fists' (both p170). Cornell also recounts a conversation where he confesses to wanting to write **Doctor Who** thanks to being bullied in the playground (p208). Bullying is clearly an important theme for Cornell; it's the subject of his forthcoming novel *Chalk* which he describes as 'incredibly personal and 'the novel I've always wanted to get into print' (Harris, Lee, 'Back to School with Paul Cornell's *Chalk*').

[45] Lewis, CS, *The Lion, The Witch and the Wardrobe* (1950), p75.

[46] Though the sixth and seventh Doctors are both an unpredictable, unsafe breed of hero to different degrees they don't quite have the authority that Pertwee and Baker brought to their performances.

Cornell originally envisioned the costume as 'a sombre Edwardian[47] suit, in black or dark brown, with boots and a waistcoat'[48], whilst Cosgrove Hall added the cape when animating the character – perhaps wisely, as this then gives the Doctor a distinctive silhouette. Whilst it does immediately spark a visual comparison to the clichéd image of Dracula (drawn largely from Christopher Lee's performance of the role for Hammer Productions[49]), it's also reflective of character in the same way as the Christopher Eccleston ninth Doctor's leather jacket; it acts as a protective shell for someone who doesn't want to let the world in.

The parallel with Dracula is one that bears further scrutiny: the comparisons with this Doctor aren't limited to simple appearances. Cornell's stated aim of drawing on gothic romanticism as a basis for his Doctor means that a parallel between the characters is almost inevitable: for all that Dracula is painted as a malign influence in Stoker's novel, his charismatic sway over the female characters Lucy Westenra and Mina Harker (nee Murray) means there is a dark romantic element to him.[50] There are generic similarities between the characters – both have a functional immortality and an ability to amend their form; both seem able to exert a fascination on young humans (particularly female) and both come from a decadent aristocratic tradition. The emphasis on this

---

[47] This is frequently used as shorthand for the Doctor's outfit; an indication that Cornell's thinking in creating this Doctor was perhaps too confined by his knowledge of the show's past.
[48] Cornell, *Scream of the Shalka*, p211.
[49] Starting with *Dracula* (1958) and continuing into many sequels.
[50] An element strongly played up in *Bram Stoker's Dracula* (1992), which featured Richard E Grant as Dr Seward.

Doctor's hauteur and emotional coldness makes it easy to see why Cosgrove Hall might have imposed a more vampiric appearance on the Doctor than Cornell originally intended. This Doctor is arguably a mirror image of Dracula; they share a certain similarity of appearance but whereas Dracula is a clearly necrotic influence, the Doctor looks to preserve life; the two characters use their similar powers to very different ends.[51]

The other fictional antecedent for this Doctor is also drawn from Victorian literature: Sherlock Holmes. This was explicit from the initial press release in which Grant described his interpretation of the role as 'Sherlock Holmes in Space'[52]. This may well have been a familiar reference point he drew on when creating his interpretation of the Doctor; when interviewed for *Doctor Who Magazine* he protested that he had never seen **Doctor Who** and knew nothing about it[53]. Given the role and the material the script provided him with, it therefore made sense to draw on a British character from a similar tradition with which he was already familiar.[54] Physically, Grant has the tall, thin build typical of Sherlock Holmes from Sidney Paget's illustrations for *The Strand*; once he has drawn the parallel the comparison is irresistible. It's also clear where he found encouragement from the script; this

---

[51] The Master is perhaps a better conventional parallel; he has stolen the life force of others and forced them to act against his will. In this story he can also be seen as undead, albeit in SF terms.
[52] BBC, 'Grant Takes On **Doctor Who** Role'.
[53] Cook, 'No One Can Hear You Scream', p15.
[54] Grant had played both Sherlock Holmes (in *The Other Side*, an episode of the 1992 BBC drama series **Encounters**) and his brother Mycroft (in the 2002 TV Movie *Sherlock*, aka *Case of Evil*).

Doctor is capable of deducing where he is simply from the smell of the air[55] and spends much of the first two episodes piecing together what's going on from minor details such as the quietness of the town on a Saturday night or a wisp of steam from a manhole cover. He's also capable of locating Alison by apparently miraculous deduction, which is later revealed to be more a case of sharp observation (he read her address from her payslip). When these actions are linked with the unemotional nature of this version of the character, Holmes seems an obvious source in both the writing and acting. Cornell may have consciously been looking to **Doctor Who** of the 1970s for his inspiration but his drawing on 'gothic romanticism' and Edwardiana meant that he was perhaps influenced by deeper traditions than he originally thought[56].

The parallels with the 1970s Doctors are more visible in one of the key relationships he forms in the story, with Major Kennet. The Doctor demonstrates a habit of barging into situations and asserting his authority; he does this upon meeting Alison in the pub and also when he enters Alison and Joe's flat. This assumption of authority becomes something of a running gag after the military's arrival, with Kennet expressly telling the Doctor, 'You don't give my men orders' and the Doctor defying this, to Kennet's eventual

---

[55] Episode 1.

[56] That Cornell may have been influenced by Holmes is supported by his use of Holmes in subsequent work – namely the story 'The Deer Stalker' for the BBC Cult website (also reprinted in his collected short stories volume *A Better Way To Die)*, the episode *You've Got Me, Who's Got You?* for CBS's contemporary update of Holmes, **Elementary** (2012-) and the third novel in his **Shadow Police** sequence, *Who Killed Sherlock Holmes?* (2016).

frustration[57]. This is a point at which the decision to avoid continuity references pays dividends; it would have been all too easy to have UNIT arrive at this point, potentially with the Brigadier, but instead the Doctor has to build a new relationship with the military[58]. By the story's conclusion this has settled down into an almost Doctor-Brigadier relationship; the Doctor has proved himself by dealing with the Shalka (and in Kennet's utilitarian phrasing, kept casualties to 'thousands, not millions'[59]), and thus earned the military's approval as someone who will take necessary action to foil a threat. He's even sharing a joke with Kennet and Greaves at the story's end, indicating that he's opened up a little – it's not only his decision to bring a new companion on board the TARDIS which shows his character development. He may essentially be the gentleman amateur[60], but he's earned their trust through competence.

Personifying this Doctor as a well-bred dilettante leads to perhaps the most striking trait of this Doctor; the way he plays up the aristocratic nature of the role[61]. When discussing Christopher Eccleston's portrayal, Gareth Roberts characterised his predecessors as 'lordly Edwardian philanthropists, stepping in from

---

[57] Episode 3.

[58] Although UNIT is referenced briefly in episode 2, this is a passing mention to explain why the regular army is deployed instead.

[59] Episode 6.

[60] A trait perhaps most obvious during the Pertwee era, where he's often seen to be tinkering with elaborate contraptions in the equivalent of his shed.

[61] For further discussion of this, see Chapter 3 of Millsted, Ian, *The Black Archive #8: Black Orchid* (2016).

a position of privilege to help the little people.'[62] This was successfully subverted by Davies with the casting of Christopher Eccleston[63], but it's something that's played up here by the writing and the casting. Cornell's initial notes cast him as 'an intellectual', with 'a great degree of civilisation and kindness'[64] and compounds this aristocratic vision of the Doctor with the Edwardian outfit which includes a Keble College scarf[65]. The interior of the TARDIS is described in the novelisation as 'a study befitting some ancient Oxford professor'[66]. Where Davies's version read *Heat* magazine (and indicated familiarity with subjects of the articles) this Doctor seems to have no interest in modern popular culture: before the end of episode 1 he's referenced Pachelbel and the D'Oyly Carte[67]. everything about the character of this Doctor is designed to emphasise the 'Lord' in Time Lord.

---

[62] Roberts, Gareth, 'Guess Who?', *Doctor Who Companion: Series 1*, DWM Special Edition #11, July 2005, p7.

[63] Even the David Tennant incarnation, which plays up to the Doctor's lordly nature to a greater extent than Eccleston's, affects a working-class accent.

[64] Cornell, *Scream of the Shalka*, p210.

[65] Keble being an Oxford college currently best known for its scientific courses. (Though the novelisation suggests that the Doctor attended Keble in the 1930s, which just predates the change of emphasis from theology to science. Perhaps that change was the Doctor's influence...)

[66] Cornell, *Scream of the Shalka*, p47.

[67] He also claims to have known Andy Warhol (episode 6), and the novelisation indicates he studied fencing to an Olympic standard (p172). He's a world class namedropper in the true Pertwee style.

This leads to the scene with Mathilda, the homeless lady, in episode 1 being a tad problematic. Whilst he's obviously trying his best to empathise with her, and he's obviously troubled by her situation, the line about him being 'a homeless person myself' comes across as a little patronising and disingenuous. At this point we don't know enough to guess what might have happened to Gallifrey. Instead, the instant thought of the viewer is that he has a home – the TARDIS – and as one recent novel described it, its dimensionally transcendental nature makes it more akin to a 'billion-square-foot mansion'[68]. At best it's a clumsy attempt at empathy; were you being unkind you could characterise it as a parody of a *Guardian* reader: concerned but ending up patronising despite their best intentions.

These impressions are reinforced by the casting. It's intriguing to speculate how the role might be played differently had the alternative casting come off. Eddie Izzard was offered the role[69], and whilst the speech patterns may not have differed greatly, his tendency to subvert roles may have offered a more chaotic Tom-Baker-style performance. The genuinely intriguing possibility, however, would have been Robbie Williams – according to Paul Cornell on the DVD commentary, this was a distinct possibility. This casting would have been completely against the aristocratic emphasis; Williams was the biggest pop star in the country at the

---

[68] Colgan, Jenny T, *In the Blood* (2016), p74.
[69] According to James Goss on the DVD commentary to episode 3; given how the animations are closely based on likenesses, this raises the intriguing possibility of the first transvestite Doctor. According to the infotext on the DVD Douglas Henshall was also considered.

time *Shalka* was made and known more as a light entertainment variety of pop star[70]. This would not only have made for excellent publicity, but been more in line with the casting of the defiantly non-aristocratic Christopher Eccleston as the televised ninth Doctor a few months later[71]. It might also have pushed the conception of this Doctor to a more interesting area, away from the comfort zone of making him more like he had been on television. The casting of Richard E Grant, however, meant that, if anything, this Doctor would the most aristocratic incarnation of them all.

The Performance

Scream of the Shalka was not the first time Richard E Grant had played the Doctor. In the 1999 charity sketch *The Curse of Fatal Death* he briefly played the 10th incarnation of the Doctor ('cute, sexy and lick-the-mirror handsome'[72]), as part of a scene where the Doctor burns through his last four regenerations in a matter of minutes[73]. Grant's 90-second cameo there is energetic, almost

---

[70] Williams had partaken in animated drama before in *Hooves of Fire* (1999). However, this was narration rather than an acting role.

[71] In class terms, not in terms of acting ability. In his essay in the novelisation, Cornell also mentions that a British musician who was a closet **Who** fan nearly persuaded his 'Hollywood actress girlfriend' to take part (p207). The obvious inference to draw here would be that these were Chris Martin and Gwyneth Paltrow, but this remains unconfirmed.

[72] Which he proceeds to demonstrate enthusiastically. And you thought David Tennant's incarnation was vain...

[73] This includes a miraculous last-second reprieve for an apparently dying Doctor; as the first broadcast **Doctor Who** written by Steven Moffat and, at the time, potentially the only story he'd ever write for the show, it's got just about everything he wanted to do in

cavalier in nature, and the manic performance perhaps demonstrates perhaps his strongest suit as a lead actor[74]. For an actor who later claimed that he'd never seen the show and knew nothing about it[75], it's a remarkably Doctorish performance with charisma, confidence, an instant ability to take charge of any situation and a cutting wit. This might be down to any number of factors: the production team filling him in on the nature of the character, simply playing the lines as written or putting in the sort of standard heroic performance he'd reprise a year later in the BBC adaptation of **The Scarlet Pimpernel** (1999-2000)[76].

---

under 20 minutes. This didn't stop him reusing a hell of a lot of it when he got control of the show: the list includes the Doctor marrying (*The Wedding of River Song* (2011), probably); a character repeating a torturous ordeal (*Heaven Sent* (2015)); a gender-swapping regeneration (*Dark Water / Death in Heaven* (2014), *Hell Bent* (2015)), a flirtatious Doctor-Master relationship (*Dark Water / Death In Heaven* et al), a Doctor confused by physical affection (Matt Smith and, to a lesser extent, Peter Capaldi's incarnation) and foiling plans by fiddling with time (*The Day of the Doctor*). Not all of this is original or even unique to Moffat's work, but it's pretty much all you need to give anyone as a primer on Moffat's **Doctor Who**.

[74] The extent to which Grant plays up his adopted aristocratic nature could be seen to an almost parodic degree when he popped up on the BBC coverage of Elizabeth II's Diamond Jubilee River Pageant in an outfit Straight Outta Downton with Union Jack accessories.

[75] Cook, Benjamin, 'No One Can Hear You Scream', DWM #336, p13.

[76] Whilst Cornell deliberately avoided watching *The Curse of Fatal Death* when writing the Doctor, he did watch **The Scarlet**

Grant's performance in *Shalka* has come in for much criticism; Russell T Davies describing his performance as 'terrible' and 'lazy'[77] and Philip Sandifer describing him as 'absolutely awful', wanting 'the most one-note interpretation of the Doctor imaginable and 'not doing anything but reading the lines out with generically dramatic inflection'[78]. There's no denying that Grant's performance lacks energy, but the fact that he's far from the only performer to suffer in this regard indicates that this may not be a function of his performance. It's also at odds with the descriptions given of him during recording, at the time and with hindsight:

> 'He bounded round the studio, whirling props above his head, hooting, roaring, running and pounding tables with what my mum would call vim. No take was ever quite the same. Take One may have been angry excitement, Take Two would be casual boredom, Take Three would end with him leaning over and licking Sophie.'
>
> [James Goss] [79]
>
> 'One of the things Richard added to this [...] was a lot of small improvisations. He would come out with an extra line suddenly.'
>
> [Paul Cornell][80]

Pimpernel to see how Grant might play the role. Cornell, *Scream of the Shalka*, p217
[77] Cook, Benjamin, 'Tooth and Claw', DWM #360.
[78] Sandifer, Philip, 'You Were Expecting Someone Else 19 (Scream of the Shalka)'.
[79] Quoted in Cornell, *Scream of the Shalka*, p223.

This isn't consistent with those simple dismissals of his performance, nor do those compliments ring of people covering up a poor creative decision[81]. Instead, the problem with the performance lies in something that's down to either a necessity of this animated form, directorial decision or a combination of both. The problem is that each line is delivered clearly and in full before the next line begins; everyone politely waits for the other person to fully finish speaking before they begin their line. As *Who's Next's* verdict on Shalka notes, this feeling of the 'in-the-room intimacy of a radio drama [...] sits oddly when you're watching pictures on a screen at the same time.'[82] Conversations therefore rarely develop the energy of genuine interaction between two people, and instead feel like two people speaking in the same place and same time but not actually communicating. Whilst animation ameliorates this to a degree by the simple use of close-ups and characters facing each other, it drains the energy and emotion from performances; we don't get proper reactions to build a scene.

Shalka gains energy and momentum from the action sequences, with the actions of the Shalka driving the story forward, but it's perhaps overly ambitious to attempt a story which requires both Doctor and companion to undertake significant emotional journeys in this medium. It can be demonstrated in how flat scenes such as those between Alison and Joe at home in episode 1 feel, or how

---

[80] Episode 1 DVD commentary.
[81] Though Cornell does concede in his DVD commentary that Grant was perhaps uncomfortable in the role.
[82] Clapham, Mark, Eddie Robson and Jim Smith, *Who's Next: An Unofficial and Unauthorised Guide to Doctor Who* (2005), p390.

the joke between Kennet and Graves about getting a tan in episode 6 doesn't quite work. None of the performances are particularly poor, and the script gives them something to work with, but the flaw is one of being a little too ambitious about what the animated medium might achieve within the technological limitations of the internet at the time[83]. Perhaps, outside live-action **Doctor Who**, Muirinn Lane Kelly's suggestion of taking the Doctor 'on a journey'[84] weakened the production rather than, as with conventional storytelling wisdom, strengthening it.

This lack of reaction ends up being particularly problematic for the role of the Doctor. The Doctor is naturally the protagonist and the main person that the rest of the cast react to; the character who drives the story. Therefore, when Grant tries to inject some energy by interacting with other characters – for example in any of the scenes with Kennet when he begins to order troops around, or when he angrily strides into Alison and Joe's flat in episode 1 – the reactions to the emotions he's conveying aren't quite there. They're overly polite. It's not that he's not gelling with the other actors, nor necessarily that they're providing inappropriate reactions, it's more that the sense of the lines as performed, rather

---

[83] The style of animation used in *Shalka* is fairly stiff compared to Disney films or the general style of Japanese anime; these more fluid styles (and bigger budgets) are more adept at conveying emotion by emphasising character expressions. It's notable that neither of the two subsequent Doctor Who animations, *The Infinite Quest* (2007) and *Dreamland* (2009), have made this mistake; they've minimised the emotional content and concentrated on action to give the productions an energy.

[84] 'Carry On Screaming', Scream of the Shalka DVD extra.

than what might be considered realistic, means that the character reactions feel unnatural. Angry, frightened or excited people wouldn't simply wait for someone else to finish speaking like this. There's never a real sense that anyone's truly excited or scared to see the Doctor, whether he's barging into a pub dressed strangely, talking to a homeless woman or blowing up Alison and Joe's home. It's an issue compounded by the relative lack of movement in faces – expressions rarely change during a scene, except for a regular blinking. Every scene is therefore played out on one emotion for every character. Consequently, we react in the way the production and presentation of the story tells us the characters are reacting: uncertainly. We know this is a **Doctor Who** story and we're supposed to empathise with the hero but we remain, to a large degree, unengaged by him.

This lack of engagement is actually initially of benefit to the character. In the series, each new Doctor we meet is essentially a stranger and, with only two exceptions[85], we're reliant on already familiar characters to frame our reactions to each Doctor. Ian and Barbara, who are set up as our initial point of view and coded as relatively ordinary characters, are our viewpoint when meeting the first Doctor[86]; the second is made acceptable to the audience through Ben and Polly's responses, and so forth[87]. With this Doctor the slightly stilted nature of the production means we're unable to

---

[85] With the exception of *Doctor Who* (1996), the only Doctor not introduced through an initially established viewpoint character or pre-existing companion is Matt Smith's incarnation (*The Eleventh Hour* (2010)).
[86] 'An Unearthly Child' (*An Unearthly Child* episode 1, 1963).
[87] *The Power of the Daleks*.

form an emotional view through Alison's or Kennet's eyes as there's no real way to convey the necessary emotion or attachments. As the character at the beginning of the story is deliberately 'alienated and cut off and distant from the world'[88], this reinforces the initial impression of the character we're meant to form. He's at a distance from us. Although by the end of the story he's comfortable enough to namedrop to Alison and to share a joke with Kennet and Greaves, it's difficult to convey the sense of him having changed too much. Alison's line about him still being 'an emotional island' in Episode 6 only reinforces this.

What *Shalka* undeniably ends up doing well is in establishing its lead character in line with Cornell's original conception. The casting and animation reinforce the aristocratic, gothic nature he aimed for[89]. Grant's performance is in keeping with a Doctor traumatised by recent, undefined events, who gradually (though not entirely effectively) warms toward humanity by the end of the episode. It looks to make the lead character a dramatic presence with recognisable emotions rather than simply an eccentrically dressed dramatic function who battles monsters with no emotional consequences. Ultimately though, the need to make the Doctor a character who can function in an ongoing 21st-century drama series ends up hampered by the caution of trying to use prior incarnations as a role model; the Doctors of the 1970s were

---

[88] Cornell, episode 1 DVD commentary.
[89] Though not Byronic: he might be mad and dangerous to know, but he's explicitly not bad in the Byronic way. Certainly not until Russell T Davies and Steven Moffat introduce the possibilities of sex and romance to **Doctor Who**.

designed for a different age and model of television and end up as performance pieces for the actor's own personalities as much as fleshed-out characters. This Doctor, haunted by recent events and not quite connecting with humans, is similar in conception to the post-2005 Doctor[90]; the presentation of the character, though, is distinctly and deliberately old-school **Doctor Who**. He's a little too cold to be the hero who could persuade viewers that they want to travel with him. If he asked the Eccleston question 'D'yer wanna come with me?'[91], it would not only be more formally phrased but you'd have to think twice about it. It's a version of the character that's **almost** there, **almost** right for the time, but not quite.

---

[90] Certainly there's an emphasis on the Doctor as a character that appears absent from Mark Gatiss', Gareth Roberts' and Clayton Hickman's pitch from 2001 (Kibble-White, Graham, 'Doctor Who 2001', DWM #500).

[91] From the trailer for the 2005 season.

CHAPTER 2: 'OR ARE YOU JUST THE SAME AS ALL THE OTHER SHEEP?'

'Alison Cheney is an everywoman [...] someone for you and me to identify with while the Doctor is being mysterious and difficult.'

[Paul Cornell][92]

The idea of the everywoman (or everyman) companion became somewhat lost from **Doctor Who** with the departure of Sarah Jane Smith. The show had veered between companions contemporary to the time of broadcast (Ian and Barbara, Dodo, Ben and Polly, Liz Shaw and Jo Grant) and periods where the companions had no relation to the time period (the period between Ian and Barbara's departure and Dodo's arrival and the Troughton era following Ben and Polly's departure[93]), but had settled on having a companion providing a contemporary point of view for all 1970s stories up to *The Hand of Fear* (1976). Following a single companionless story, there then wasn't a companion who could reasonably be called an identification figure for the main intended audience (the British viewing public) until the show's original run finished in 1989. Leela was a savage from the far future; Romana a Time Lord; Adric from another universe entirely; Tegan and Peri from different countries; Nyssa and Turlough were aliens and Ace, whilst contemporary, came with a convoluted backstory that meant she was first

---

[92] Quoted in Cook, 'No One Can Hear You Scream', p16.
[93] From 'The Planet of Decision' (*The Chase* episode 4 (1965)) to 'Bell of Doom' (*The Massacre* episode 4 (1966)) and from *The Evil of the Daleks* (1967) to *The War Games* (1969), respectively.

encountered on an ice planet light years from home. Grace and Chang Lee may be seen as attempts at giving the main (American) intended audience a viewpoint character, but given their appearance is limited to a single story and neither boards the TARDIS at the end of the adventure, it's tough to class them as companions in anything like the way it's applied to those who accompany the Doctor on his adventures[94].

Alison is the first companion in 27 years who comes with a straightforward British background; prefiguring the **Doctor Who** of Russell T Davies and Steven Moffat, which has consistently prioritised the Doctor having a companion contemporary to broadcast accompanying him[95]. Like the other versions of **Doctor Who** proposed in the 21st century, much of what we see in *Scream of the Shalka* is a reaction to the perceived mistakes the makers of **Doctor Who** made in the 1980s[96]; there are few better illustrations of this than the role of the companion.

---

[94] Plus, the small matter of Grace's profession, her love of opera and her conveniently sitting on the board of major scientific projects means she's not exactly designed for mass appeal.

[95] *Voyage of the Damned* (2007), *The Next Doctor* (2008), *The Waters of Mars* (2009), *The Snowmen* (2012) (where the real Clara Oswald appears briefly, but never interacts with the Doctor), *Heaven Sent* and *The Husbands of River Song* (2015) are the only stories not to feature the Doctor with companions from near-contemporary 21st-century Earth – although it's easy to argue, particularly with the Ponds and Clara, that the convoluted backstory which accrues around them makes them less successful as viewpoint characters as time goes on.

[96] For further discussion, see Chapter 4.

We first meet Alison working in a pub. Like Rose 14 months later this is intended as a deliberately archetypal profession: a relatively low-paying job indicative of someone uncertain of where they might want to go in their career, or who has become trapped in a mundane existence. Alison holding an ordinary job was always an important component of her character; even in the original outline she was working in a cinema.

As originally envisaged there would have been a further parallel with Rose; she would be yet to leave home, although in her case she would have been taking a year out to be in a better financial position for university. The latter point leads to an important distinction between the viewpoint characters of Cornell and Davies; Cornell's character sees education as a route out of the small town of her youth ('waiting for someone amazing to come along at university; she's set her sights on the unobtainable'[97]); she knows there are opportunities to realise her potential and works towards them. She has either a good general knowledge or an appreciation of art: she knows who Gaudi is[98]. Rose doesn't even know that these opportunities exist; she doesn't know or look for a route out of a comfortable but unsatisfying existence of living at home, drifting along in a relationship both partners seem to take for granted; muddling along in a retail job which seems not to provide obvious career development opportunities. In short, Alison is

---

[97] Cornell, *Scream of the Shalka*, p211.
[98] As originally envisioned, her heroes would have included the unlikely figures of Napoleon and Churchill; perhaps this is a tad less likely than Clara's claim in *Deep Breath* (2014) to have had a pin up of Marcus Aurelius on her wall.

designed as an aspirational middle-class character, whereas Rose is working-class (in *New Earth* (2006) the snobbish Cassandra goes so far as to term her a 'chav'). In this sense Alison is more of a forerunner of Rose's successor Martha: she shares her higher level of education, and the main difference in character appears to be Martha's focus on her medical career as opposed to Alison becoming distracted by a relationship. Both Rose and Alison offer broadly recognisable situations to an audience; both are designed to appreciate the wonders of the universe but it's Davies's character who, in retrospect, is better designed for mass appeal.

The shift from having Alison live with her family to living with her boyfriend was simply a decision of economy in terms of narrative and budget[99], yet it renders her a stronger character. As initially conceived she's waiting for something to happen; as she appears on screen she's made a decision to give up on the opportunities promised by education in pursuit of the potential happiness of a long-term relationship[100]. She ends up in Lannet of her own volition; this gives her a degree of agency. It also gives her a reason to remain with Joe; she's staked a lot on this relationship even though tensions are apparent from their first scene (the muted argument about the TV remote). This is a relationship as rotten

---

[99] 'It took Muirinn to say that the family, including a small child who had two lines, were a waste of resources, and that Alison could just as easily talk to a single character...' (Cornell, *Scream of the Shalka*, p215).

[100] As stated in the contemporary **Doctor Who** reference book *Doctor Who: The Legend*: 'Alison gave up her degree to live with her boyfriend, Joe.' Richards, Justin, *Doctor Who: The Legend*, (2003) p392.

under the surface as Rose and Mickey's is; it takes the arrival of the Doctor and the promise of seeing the wonders of the universe to make both women see that the situation they have ended up in isn't particularly attractive after all. The difference is that Alison is aware of this, but not admitting it to herself, whereas Rose's horizons are limited. This ultimately leads to very similar climactic scenes where they decide to board the TARDIS; both women explicitly reject their lovers to travel with the Doctor.

This is another example of how *Shalka* is what Cornell described as 'kind of like [...] John the Baptist'[101] for Davies's version of the show; previously the most that any companion willingly gave up to travel with the Doctor was a job.[102] The idea of the troubled relationship came from James Goss, with the suggestion that Alison's boyfriend (originally named Dean)[103] accompany her and the Doctor in the TARDIS; however Paul Cornell resisted this on the basis that the audience wouldn't care for 'unhappy, miserable

---

[101] DVD commentary for episode 1. Whilst this may seem egocentric, he does also acknowledge on the commentary that much of this is simply to do with the model of writing drama at the time.

[102] Jamie forgoes his role as piper; Zoe boards the TARDIS rather than continuing in her role on the Wheel, and Sarah seems to have a very understanding editor – the rest are a mixture of kidnaps and situations where their first meeting with the Doctor has ended with an irreversible upheaval to their previous domestic situation. The choice of giving up family or lovers to travel with the Doctor is never made in the original series; instead it's more common for companions reject the Doctor for domestic contentment (Jo in *The Green Death* (1973), Leela in *The Invasion of Time* (1978)).

[103] Infotext for episode 4.

people, constantly bickering'[104], and resolved this by having Dean die by being covered in lava and taken over by Prime, the leader of the Shalka. Perhaps Joe should be grateful that in the final version he eventually got off lightly with a broken heart.

Shalka's innovation in the Doctor-companion relationship ends up being more subtle than adding a quarrelling couple. It's the first **Doctor Who** story to openly postulate that there is a reason for the Doctor to have a companion aside from the simple desire not to be alone[105]; that there is a mutual emotional need which means the companion is every bit as vital to the show as to the Doctor. To Alison the Doctor represents a chance of escape and recapturing dreams, but to **this** Doctor Alison offers the promise of emotional healing[106]. The backstory we have clearly indicates that the Doctor has lost a female companion in tragic circumstances at some point; allowing Alison to travel in the TARDIS is a sign that he is coming to terms with that tragedy. Given Shalka retains the 'no hanky panky in the TARDIS' rule this is a smart move which allows a deeper emotional attachment than friendship, but stops short of a relationship where the writer might have to ask awkward questions

---

[104] Cornell, *Scream of the Shalka* p213. This does, however, prefigure the scenario briefly played out in *Asylum of the Daleks* (2012) where the Ponds are on the verge of divorce. That they quickly resolve this suggests Steven Moffat also considers it problematic for an ongoing series.

[105] For instance, this reasoning is suggested when Steven considers leaving the Doctor in 'Bell of Doom', in Jo's departure in *The Green Death* and in Mel's final scene in *Dragonfire* episode 3.

[106] Although unlike the Doctor and Rose this relationship has no physical expression; Cornell's initial notes explicitly say that he is 'asexual, unattracted to humans'.

about what a centuries-old alien might see in a human of a mere couple of decades old[107]. It makes the companion more than a simple feed for the Doctor to explain the plot, and a device to get into peril if the story is flagging.

Shalka's progressive nature is also evident is in its casting of the first non-white companion in broadcast **Doctor Who**[108]. As written, there is no need for Alison to deviate from the default model of a white-skinned companion; indeed it might have been easier if a white actress had been cast – aside from Alison, Lannet has a noticeably pale-skinned population and yet her ethnicity never becomes an issue. In real life someone who stands out not only for their skin colour but their London accent would probably have this remarked upon at some point[109], but it's to *Shalka*'s credit that it attempts to portray a world where this does not matter.

Where *Shalka* perhaps falls down in relation to Davies' version of the show is in not quite making the companion as central to the drama as the Doctor. While Alison is a more fully realised character than 20th-century companions, with a detailed life including a

---

[107] The 21st-century version of the show has seemed content to allow the Doctor's appearance as a slightly older man to conceal dubious questions of interspecies relationships and age differences. As with much visual storytelling, the image helps awkward questions bypass the viewer; only fans will think deeply about them.

[108] DWM had featured a companion of colour as early as 1980; the **New Adventures** introduced Roz Forrester in 1995 and the **Eighth Doctor Adventures** Anji Kapoor in 2001.

[109] Cornell includes an explanation of how London girl with parents in Sheffield ends up in Lancashire in the novelisation (p 109).

home, job and motivations, there is never quite the sense that she is as vital to this version of the show as Rose is to hers. Whilst this may be put down to its being an introductory story, *Shalka* clearly prioritises reintroducing the Doctor; unlike in *Rose*, we aren't initially introduced to the Doctor through Alison's eyes. Both Alison and Rose demonstrate singular courage in the face of an alien threat – Alison as the sole resident of Lannet willing to join the Doctor in resisting the Shalka; Rose in pursuing the Doctor. Even when leading the mob controlled by the Shalka in episodes 4 and 5, and not in control of her own body, she attempts to resist their control and also encourages others to do so. However, while both Alison and Rose meet the Doctor almost purely by living at the epicentre of a place aliens choose to invade, Alison's continued involvement in the story has more of a contrivance to it; the only reason she plays any sort of role in the climax of the story is the Shalka's decision to implant a conduit in her head, something that could have happened to any random human. And, whilst this means her role is crucial, it is essentially an involuntary one with little agency to it; she is involved not out of choice but because a mechanical component in the resolution of the story demands it.

Without doubt, Alison's helping the Doctor in the face of the Shalka is a selfless act, but it lacks the voluntary bravery of Rose using her limited gymnastic skills to defeat the Nestenes. The crucial act which defeats the Nestenes is Rose's; she is the one who causes the anti-plastic to spill into the pool of plastic which represents the Nestene Consciousness. The act which defeats the Shalka – the counter scream – is the Doctor's. The Doctor also denies Alison the use of the network of Shalka slaves to clean up the Earth and repair the environmental damage done by humanity. Whilst this is painted as humanity having to face up to the consequences of its long term actions, rather than finding a miraculous deus ex machina solution, it again denies her the chance to make her own decision. Whilst Alison contributes to defeating the invasion, the implication is that the Doctor is very much the dominant character here; although this is unlikely to be a conscious choice on Cornell's part it looks very much like an inadvertent expression of the fan viewpoint that this series is essentially about the Doctor; that those watching are watching for the main character. It's frustratingly close to the model of companion integral to the success of the show from 2005 onwards, but is perhaps hemmed in by not being willing to push the show beyond a traditional model[110]. Like so much else about *Scream of the Shalka*, the role of the companion ends up as a curious halfway house between the 20th and 21st-century models of producing **Doctor Who.**

---

[110] Whilst not wasting the talents of Sophie Okenedo, it's certainly underusing them; just over a month after the final episode of *Shalka* was broadcast, she would become the sole **Doctor Who** companion to be nominated for an Academy Award, as 'Best Supporting Actress' in *Hotel Rwanda* (2004).

CHAPTER 3: 'I AM THE MASTER AND YOU WILL... COME TO LIKE ME WHEN YOU GET TO KNOW ME.'

Scream of the Shalka was deliberately intended to be light on references to the show's past; on the DVD commentary for episode 3, James Goss recounts how their request to Paul Cornell was: 'please don't mention old monsters, please don't mention [...] the Time Lords, don't mention Gallifrey, don't mention all the baggage.' This would extend to the military presence in the story very deliberately not being UNIT, and even small references which might have been used as kisses to the past, such as the alien currencies the Doctor carries in episode 1, are very deliberately not in-jokes[111]. Instead, what we get is a Doctor with hints of a traumatic past and a Master transformed from the character familiar from the 1970s and 1980s.

The role played by the Master was originally intended to be played by a holographic representation of a former Doctor. Cornell suggested that this should be the fifth Doctor, as 'his kind and open personality would provide a nice contrast with our rather more harsh and edgy Doctor.'[112] This was a contrast he'd used before, in his **New Adventures** novel *Timewyrm: Revelation* (1991), where the fifth Doctor was portrayed as an almost saintly presence in contrast

---

[111] However, it's worth noting that along with Zornic groats, the Doctor has some Atraxian semble seeds. It may be a coincidence, but it's worth noting the name Steven Moffat picked for his alien police in *The Eleventh Hour*.

[112] Cornell, *Scream of the Shalka*, p202.

to the seventh Doctor, who carried the weight of the universe on his shoulders. This would have given *Shalka* a very different flavour; the fifth Doctor was established as an unambiguously heroic figure, and whilst he often demonstrated a dry sense of humour, any edge to the relationship would have had to come from Grant's Doctor, rendering him even less sympathetic than he initially appears to be. Cornell changed this setup for two reasons: firstly because he felt that holograms had been overdone in telefantasy shows[113], and secondly so that this assistant could have a 'complicated, somewhat dangerous relationship' with the Doctor and be 'programmed to do the nastier things that our emotionally wounded and defensive Doctor couldn't bring himself to do'[114]. Essentially then, this version of the Master would retain the amoral methodology he had often demonstrated in his prior television appearances but, with apparently less selfish aims, he was now redefined as a hero.

---

[113] The obvious telefantasy antecedents Cornell is referring to which feature holograms able to assist but not interfere would have included **Quantum Leap** (1989-93), whose main character Sam was assisted by Al, a hologram of a person from Sam's original time; the Emergency Medical Hologram called 'the Doctor' in **Star Trek: Voyager** (1995-2001); and possibly even the command hologram from **Mighty Morphin Power Rangers** (1993-95). He may have also been referring to **Red Dwarf** (1988-99 and since revived) and **Stargate SG:1** (1997-2007); however, the holographic characters in these series serve very different roles. Holography was relatively uncommon in the series to this point, only appearing under that name in *The Talons of Weng-Chiang* (1977), *The Leisure Hive* (1980), *Time and the Rani* (1987) and *Dragonfire* (1987). The series' use of holograms has become more common since 2005.
[114] Cornell, *Scream of the Shalka*, p202.

The clear model for this version of the Master is the Roger Delgado incarnation, in keeping with Cornell reaching back to the Pertwee and Tom Baker eras of his childhood for inspiration. Whilst the Master's role in this version of **Doctor Who** is very different to his previous appearances, it's clearly modelled on what Philip Purser-Hallard has termed the 'mutual respect visible in Pertwee's and Delgado's performances'[115]. Whilst the Master is unambiguously coded as a villain in each of this incarnation's appearances, there are moments which suggest that, despite the character's stated aims, he is not irredeemable – he eventually turns on both Autons and Axons to foil their invasions (admittedly motivated by self-preservation)[116]. His greatest fear (exposed by a mind parasite as the Doctor's mockery of him) is an all too human one[117]. This suggests that his motivations during this period are to impress the Doctor, or at least to outshine him, rather than the apparently simple desire for world or universal domination. Add to this the reference in *The Sea Devils* (1972) to his once having been the Doctor's friend, and it's possible to see that, rather than the charm Delgado injects into his performance masking a form of psychopathy[118], there is the suggestion that some form of

---

[115] Purser-Hallard, Philip, *The Black Archive #4: Dark Water / Death In Heaven* (2016), pp117-8.

[116] *Terror of the Autons*, *The Claws of Axos* (both 1971).

[117] *The Mind of Evil* (1971).

[118] For instance, he repeatedly refers to Jo as 'Miss Grant' rather than insulting her as an inferior life form. There is an famous anecdote from the filming of *The Dæmons* (1971) where children asked to boo the Master wanted to cheer him on, and Delgado's obituary in *The Times* reflected that 'he was a villain whom it was hard to hate' (Haining Peter, *Doctor Who: A Celebration* (1983),

redemption may be possible for him. Indeed, the planned final story of **Doctor Who**'s 11th season, 'The Final Game', would have seen the Master sacrifice himself to save the Doctor, and the two characters revealed to be different aspects of the same person.[119]

Subsequent versions of the character – the 'decayed vampire'[120] of *The Deadly Assassin* (1976) and the apparently unhinged actions of the Anthony Ainley reincarnation[121] – are less nuanced than much of what we see from the Delgado incarnation, but there is a suggestion that the Doctor believes the Master to have been driven insane by the injuries he displays in *The Deadly Assassin* and *The Keeper of Traken* (1981), and his renewal in the latter story. This suggests that the Doctor does not hold the Master responsible for his actions during this period, and therefore perhaps still considers redemption a possibility.[122] Eric Roberts's performance in *Doctor*

---

p132. However, as Jon Ronson's *The Psychopath Test: A Journey Through the Madness Industry* (2011) points out numerous times, psychopaths are often charming if they perceive it as beneficial to their own ends.

[119] Sullivan, Shannon Patrick, 'Doctor Who: The Lost Stories'. This was ultimately abandoned due to Delgado's death in a taxi accident in June 1973.

[120] Purser-Hallard, *The Black Archive #4*, p116

[121] His actions include causing a large portion of the universe to be wiped out in *Logopolis* (1981); if any action puts a character beyond redemption in **Doctor Who**'s history it's this mass slaughter which wipes out at least the entire Traken Union and therefore numbers in at least billions.

[122] '[F]rom *The Deadly Assassin* onwards, the Master is repeatedly referred to as "mad" or "insane"' (Purser-Hallard, *The Black Archive #4*, p123); 'The Doctor seems to honestly believe that the Master's mad' (Miles, Lawrence, and Tat Wood, *About Time: The*

Who (1996) also suggests someone not in control of their faculties[123].

Cornell's version of the Master is therefore a logical extrapolation of this prior relationship; the Master has finally accepted the offer of redemption from the Doctor. It is a glimpse of how the character might have progressed if circumstances had meant that 'The Final Game' had been made and the character revived afterwards. This opportunity of redemption was due to the Master being 'of aid to the Doctor' – the offer may have been influenced by their past relationship, but it is one that the Master has earned. However, it's made clear that this was not necessarily a choice made of his own free will; the alternative was a 'slow painful death' and this 'last chance for salvation' was one he was 'foolish enough to accept.'[124] This suggests that the Master may regard his reduced status as a form of punishment or the Doctor inflicting control over him and, to a certain degree, reducing him to a subservient role. Given he has regarded himself as superior to the Doctor since his first appearance, this may even suggest that he sees himself as Jeeves to this Doctor's Wooster.

This choice between salvation and death being motivated purely by survival is entirely in line with the Master's actions; his overriding

---

Unauthorized Guide to Doctor Who #5 – 1980-1984: Seasons 18 to 21 (2005), p82).
[123] Whilst *The Curse of Fatal Death* was not intended as, nor is generally considered, part of the official continuity of the series, it's notable that the ending also suggests the Doctor can forgive the Master for his actions.
[124] Episode 6.

motivation has always been self-interest and survival at all costs[125]. The climax of *Terror of the Autons* turns on his likely death at the tentacles of the Nestenes; he only assists the Axons because they've captured him, and each of *The Deadly Assassin, The Keeper of Traken* and *Doctor Who* (1996) are driven by his need for a new body to replace a dying or dead form. This lends a certain ambiguity to his actions, which is further complicated by his apparent attempt to hypnotise Alison upon their first meeting. His only significant involvement with the plot is to defend the TARDIS from the Shalka when they gain access, firstly by their own technology and then with the Doctor. These actions can, of course, be read as an altruistic attempt to aid the Doctor against the monsters by preventing them controlling the TARDIS, but they can equally be read as self-preservation; the need to protect the only environment he can exist in.

Aside from Alison and the Shalka, the only interaction the Master has is with the Doctor. As performed it's reminiscent of the Pertwee-Delgado dynamic; the performances of both Derek Jacobi and Grant, and the animation of the characters, accentuate the aristocratic nature of the Time Lords; in class terms this is a partnership of equals. However, the Master's reduced physical status as an android who can be turned on and off means that, in terms of the power dynamic between the two, the Doctor clearly has the upper hand. The Master is unable to leave the TARDIS, which renders it both home and prison; to a certain degree, even

---

[125] This would be entirely in line with Barry Letts's intention in 'The Final Game' to have the Master mirror the 'id' of Freudian psychology to the Doctor's 'ego' (Sullivan, 'The Lost Stories').

though he has offered him redemption, the Doctor has imposed a penal sentence upon him. Added to this, the Doctor can deactivate the Master with a remote control – something repeated in the follow-up short story 'The Feast of the Stone' – and therefore to a degree this Master is more akin to a pet, though as is demonstrated when the TARDIS is invaded he's more of an attack dog than a housetrained puppy.

Despite this being '**Doctor Who** for beginners'[126] the clear intention is that this is a recognisable character to anyone watching *Shalka* – he has the combination of goatee beard and dark suit that characterise the TV incarnations portrayed by Roger Delgado and Anthony Ainley. His initial appearance in the TARDIS certainly seems intended as a shock to the viewer, and to provoke the question in their mind of what he's doing there.[127] However, in line with the intention of minimising continuity references, the viewer is not expected to know anything of the Master's history with the Doctor; what's important, and where the tension in the relationship between Master and Doctor is located, is in what he represents.

The Master is often cited as the Moriarty to the Doctor's Sherlock Holmes[128], and Cornell's script is clearly looking to subvert this

---

[126] James Goss, episode 3 DVD commentary.

[127] Though anyone who'd flicked through the 40th anniversary book *Doctor Who: The Legend* before watching would have been able to discover this.

[128] Though he's far more persistent than Moriarty ever was in the Holmes stories; Moriarty directly appears only once, but his status as Holmes's apparent nemesis means he's assumed a degree of prominence greater than his actual appearance justifies.

iconic status of the two as archenemies rather than indulging in the details of what's happened between them previously. Indeed, the only background we're supplied with for this Master relates to the backstory Cornell came up with for this incarnation of the Doctor. We simply know that the Master aided the Doctor in an episode which ended badly for the Doctor, but that this meant the Doctor offered the Master a chance of survival; the aim here is simply to provide an interesting relationship with ongoing dramatic potential, rather than parade the Master for a dramatically redundant fanboy thrill[129]. It's this, combined with the seemingly effortless urbane charm of Derek Jacobi's performance, that makes this use of the Master the most fascinating element of Shalka, and the area we should perhaps most regret not seeing explored further[130].

---

[129] As in, for example, *The Mark of the Rani* (1985), where his presence adds very little to a story which could easily have played out in a similar fashion without him, or a story such as *Time-Flight* (1982) which simply requires a generic villain rather than specifically the Master.

[130] There is the possibility that this did inspire an element of *Last of the Time Lords* (2007), where the Doctor offers the Master the chance to travel the universe with him but the Master chooses apparent death instead. In Cornell's DVD commentary for episode 4 he says that Russell T Davies emailed him to say he was thinking of Cornell when that scene was written; notably this scene plays out in entirely the opposite way to *Shalka*'s backstory, with the Master rejecting redemption. In an ongoing series in which an equal and opposite rival who's already explicitly a villain is of obvious dramatic potential, it's a wise choice.

CHAPTER 4: 'THE JOHN THE BAPTIST OF DOCTOR WHO'

At heart, *Shalka* is a regeneration story; doing 'the things a regeneration story is for, rather than doing a regeneration.'[131] It's intended to reintroduce **Doctor Who** to a 21st-century audience (though an audience mostly of fans rather than on the scale of the televised revival). This was a necessity: **Doctor Who** had been a fitful presence on television for 14 years prior to the making of *Shalka*; it lived on mainly through repeats. It had become a programme that you had to go out of your way to watch, rather than accruing fans by being a part of the television furniture. A generation did not have a Doctor to call their own[132].

In the first five years of the 21st century there were three serious attempts to revive **Doctor Who** as a broadcast drama: one in 2001 by Mark Gatiss, Gareth Roberts and Clayton Hickman that was pitched but never commissioned; *Shalka*; and Russell T Davies's revival for BBC Wales. Each of these proposals neatly demonstrates different approaches to reviving the series. The uncommissioned version went for a very traditional aesthetic; a Saturday teatime series which would have essentially replicated the feel of 1970s **Doctor Who** right down to episode length, multi-episode format and the probability of a Bernard Lodge title sequence[133]. It's

---

[131] Cornell, *Scream of the Shalka*, p210

[132] And no, a one-off appearance doesn't make you the Doctor for a generation.

[133] 'Oh Bernard Lodge, definitely... I don't think his work has ever been bettered.' Hickman, quoted in Kibble-White, 'Doctor Who 2001' p68. In the same feature Gatiss refers to *The Deadly Assassin*

essentially trying to replicate what worked in that decade, but in a different era of television – for instance, aside from soap opera, the half-hour drama was obsolete by 2000. Russell T Davies took the opposite approach; instead of trying to recreate what **Doctor Who** had done well in the past, he imagined the series as it might be if the concept had been invented in 2005. To reintroduce the series to a mass audience he pared the show down to its essential elements, ensuring it worked as a modern TV drama[134].

And halfway between these approaches fell *Scream of the Shalka*; looking to modernise the series but still, to a large degree, thinking in terms of how **Doctor Who** had done things in the past.

Much of the creative work we now think of as done by a 'showrunner' was by *Scream of the Shalka*'s writer Paul Cornell. Cornell was arguably the most influential **Doctor Who** writer of the 'wilderness years', yet by his own account he came to write *Scream of the Shalka* without this being a factor – this was down to working with Martha Hillier, the BBCi producer who had been asked to find a writer for the project. Cornell's first **Doctor Who** book, *Timewyrm: Revelation*, is the key text of post-*Survival* (1989), pre-*Rose* **Doctor Who** fiction. The three books which preceded it in the Virgin **New Adventures** range did little to live up to the bold back-cover claim of being 'too broad and too deep for the small screen', being more straightforward **Doctor Who** adventures with

---

as an example of good **Doctor Who** (p66), and *The Seeds of Doom* (1976) as an example of how the Doctor might act (p68), and Roberts describes 1970s **Doctor Who** as 'proper Doctor Who' (p70). [134] For a more in-depth discussion of this see Chapter 4 of Arnold, Jon, *The Black Archive #1: Rose* (2016).

an unlimited budget. Their broadness was limited to the inclusion of bare breasts (*Timewyrm: Genesys* (1991)) and, for the first time in the show's history, dealing directly with the historical figures of Nazi Germany (*Timewyrm: Exodus* (1991)). They were at heart extended versions of the Target novelisations: straightforward adventure stories which would have been familiar to anyone who had read one of the **Doctor Who** books.

Revelation was a clear break from this. Cornell was the first New Adventures author to come from a fan background with no previous professional Doctor Who credits[135] – although it's important to note he already had other professional credits to his name, most notably the play *Kingdom Come* in the **Debut on Two** series (1990). Developed from a story Cornell had written for the fanzine *Queen Bat*, the novel took place in the Doctor's psyche and employed the show's past as allegory and metaphor rather than using it as a cheap thrill or to prop up an otherwise thin story. Prior to this the Doctor had rarely been seen to deal with the emotional consequences of his actions; with the show's nature as essentially an anthology series of adventure serials, it would have interfered with the stories the writers wanted to tell, and with the production team's ability to move stories around in the broadcast schedule if necessity dictated. It was rare indeed that even departures of long-serving companions had consequences beyond the following

---

[135] Given that Davies, Steven Moffat and Chris Chibnall all self-identify as fans it's arguable that this was the point fans took creative control of the series, and they've never relinquished it since. Marx would no doubt be delighted at the way the fans ended up seizing the means of production.

story[136]; the show was about the current adventure. The most notorious demonstration of this came in *Time-Flight* (1982) episode 1, where Adric's death in the previous episode (*Earthshock* episode 4 (1982)) was abruptly dismissed in one scene.

Only towards the end of the 20th-century run, with the character of Ace, was there any attempt at character development, and even then the switching around of stories between production and broadcast order in season 26 demonstrates that developments are not really sustained from story to story, but perhaps aim for a more nebulous cumulative effect. Ace is demonstrably a calmer, more mature personality in *Survival*, but it's not the recognisable, structured development of character demonstrated by (for instance) both Rose and the Doctor during the 2005 season of **Doctor Who**[137]. Essentially, in dealing with the Doctor's guilt over all the deaths he feels responsible for, Cornell's novel turned the character from a figurehead who linked stories into one who could sustain an ongoing series of books which aspired to be more than simple tie-ins. The novels acquired a reputation for being angst-ridden, but there was often a sense of the events of previous adventures affecting characters and their actions in later stories, most clearly in what happened to Ace during her **New Adventures'** appearances. Davies might well have made the same decisions regarding the Doctor's character in 2005 as he did if the **New Adventures** had not existed, but the efforts of the **New Adventures** (and later the **Eighth Doctor Adventures**) meant that it was less of

---

[136] A notable exception to this is the Doctor's speech in 'Bell of Doom' where he reflects upon departed companions.
[137] For greater depth see Arnold, *The Black Archive #1*.

a culture shock to long-term fans than it might otherwise have been[138].

Twenty five years on, *Revelation* appears a relatively tame affair and clearly the work of an inexperienced author – it quotes, amongst others, Shakespeare, Oscar Wilde and Aldous Huxley; liberally sprinkles in the author's own pop-cultural interests; and, with the imagery of the crucified fifth Doctor, not-so-subtly equates the Doctor with Jesus[139]. Whilst an experienced author might dismiss such ideas out of hand, this gave the book an energy and vitality beyond the more straightforward adventures of the first three books. The success of *Revelation* meant that Virgin was more willing to take a chance on the 'huge, untapped and rather frustrated pool of talent amongst **Doctor Who** fandom'[140] that produced the first published **Doctor Who** work of writers such as Gatiss, Roberts, Davies and Moffat[141]. It also meant Cornell's books

---

[138] There is also a case to be made for *Doctor Who* (1996) showing a more emotional side to the Doctor; however its nature as a one-off story limits the scope of character development the Doctor undergoes during it.

[139] Given the often cult-like nature of fandom this may not be entirely inappropriate. Cornell would go further on the Doctor/Christ parallels by having this powerful being take on human form in *Human Nature* (1995, adapted for TV as *Human Nature / The Family of Blood* (2007)). It also prefigures the 10th Doctor as 'lonely god' and such imagery as him ascending with angels in *Voyage of the Damned*.

[140] Guerrier, Simon, *Bernice Summerfield: The Inside Story* (2009), p11.

[141] Clearly, for at least two of these writers, it wasn't a career break but more a chance to indulge a passion.

would be regarded as significant: *Love and War* (1992) introducing a new companion, *No Future* (1994) wrapping up a five-book arc and resolving long-running character conflicts; *Goth Opera* (1994) launching the **Missing Adventures** range; *Human Nature* (1995) putting the Doctor in human form, and *Happy Endings* (1996) celebrating the range reaching 50 books.

Cornell's career as a TV writer and novelist meant he was a less significant figure in **Doctor Who** terms than he had been during the 1990s; however the combination of his TV experience (at this point including **Coronation Street** (1960-), **Doctors** (2000-) and **Casualty** (1986-)) and status as a knowledgeable **Doctor Who** fan meant he was an ideal choice as the first writer in this potential ongoing series – knowing what was generally expected of a **Doctor Who** story, but not dogmatic that it should be done in the same way as in the past. This aim put it more in line with *Rose* than the more 'traditional' Gatiss-Roberts-Hickman proposal:

> 'What we were trying to do was something that was very much a reintroduction of **Doctor Who**, so it was kind of **Doctor Who** for beginners.'
>
> [James Goss][142]
>
> '[T]he thought in my head [...] was "new new new".'
>
> [Paul Cornell][143]

This shows the conflict at the heart of what *Shalka* was trying to achieve.

---

[142] Episode 3 DVD commentary.
[143] Episode 1 DVD commentary.

This would be a piece made for the BBC Cult website, something that would have to be hunted out rather than perhaps picking up channel-surfing viewers or anyone simply leaving the television on. The audience would be limited to pre-existing **Doctor Who** fans with a connection capable of streaming the broadcast[144]. The added aim of being a celebration of the show's 40th anniversary meant that, to a large extent, it would have been mildly inappropriate to attempt to be as radical as Davies would be.

Instead *Shalka* conceals its radical intentions inside a deliberately traditional story format: the base under siege[145]. Broadly speaking this is defined as a small group of humans trapped in a claustrophobic, defined location by an outside threat; a format modelled on such films as *The Thing From Another World* (1951). This began under Innes Lloyd and Gerry Davis as a means to maximise **Doctor Who**'s limited budget[146]. It became a much used

---

[144] The Office for National Statistics estimates that only 46% of UK households had internet access in 2003 ('Internet Access – Households and Individuals: 2013', PDF download), with the proportion of households with internet access not reaching 50% until 2005. With broadband not having an uptake of 50% of households until 2007, many connections would have been too slow to stream *Shalka* without repeated buffering.

[145] 'It's a very traditional story [...] told in a very traditional way.' Cornell, quoted in Cook, 'No One Can Hear You Scream', p14.

[146] 'I tried to get the writers to write economically, i.e. for sets, and then make sure the set was really used [...] So we get four episodes with one magnificent set, instead of half a dozen inferior sets.' Gerry Davis interviewed by Jan Vincent-Rudzki and Stephen Payne, *TARDIS* vol 3 #6, December 1978.

format in the Troughton era, particularly in season 5, and one the show has returned to as recently as *Under the Lake* (2015).

Given the self-selecting nature of the audience, the changes being made in other areas of the story (particularly to the character of the Doctor), and the need to set up the proposed new format, this is a wise move by Cornell[147]. It's as simple a model as **Doctor Who** stories get: the Doctor turns up, discovers an alien monster threatening the 'base' (in this case, the village of Lannet), defeats the invasion and moves on, leaving others to deal with the aftermath.

Where *Shalka* differs from other stories with this format is in its ability to extend the threat to a global one. Essentially, Cornell is writing for a series with no budgetary restrictions on sets, so whilst much of the action can be localised, he's able to demonstrate the threat on a global basis in a way the television series never really could until *Army of Ghosts / Doomsday* (2006). Previous base under siege stories such as *The Tenth Planet* (1966) or *The Seeds of Death* (1969) relied on inexpensive tricks such as communication via TV monitors or characters reporting on events being monitored in other areas of the planet. Cornell uses this ability to effectively up the stakes of the story; when the Shalka's plan to convert the Earth's atmosphere into one more conducive to them is enacted[148],

---

[147] It's a trick Davies uses in *Rose* too. For all that it plays games with the perspective from which the story is told, it also uses a relatively simple alien invasion format to introduce its innovations.
[148] This is also the Ice Warriors' scheme in *The Seeds of Death* and the Sontarans' in *The Sontaran Stratagem / The Poison Sky* (2008), although their methodology differs.

the effect is to render the planet as the base under siege. We get an opening scene set in New Zealand[149] and, when the invasion is underway, scenes representing India, the USA and Eastern Europe[150] to illustrate the scale of the threat.

Effectively, this is the first occasion on which **Doctor Who** has had the budget to match its ambition, and whilst the location in an English village might suggest it's not ambitious enough, the nature of the Shalka creatures, the vast caverns they inhabit and the eventual global scale of the invasion demonstrate that this is ultimately not the case. If anything, Cornell overreaches when the invasion is enacted, setting up a scenario in which it seems inevitable that millions will die from the radiation from the unfiltered sunlight, but reducing it to mere thousands with a few lines at the end. This is perhaps one of the things Cornell refers to in the DVD commentary when he refers to the story as having been written 'too big'[151].

Another way the story takes advantage of the lack of budgetary restriction is in the design of its main monster. The Shalka were

---

[149] Although this does beg the question of why, if the Shalka initially landed in New Zealand, they then chose Lancashire as their centre of operations. They may have burrowed directly through the planet, but that choice seems to reflect **Doctor Who**'s anglocentrism more than any merit to their centre of operations.

[150] Confirmed in the novelisation as Russia, specifically Siberia. *Doctor Who* (1996), of course, has scenes representing the planet being threatened by the opening of the Eye of Harmony, but these are generic location shots; an updated version of the cheats of the 1960s.

[151] Episode 1 DVD commentary.

deliberately designed as serpentine creatures, representing one of the two primal fears that every baby is born imprinted with[152]. Attempting to create an effective snake had been something the TV series had been noticeably ineffective at, including one of the most infamously poor effects in the show's history[153], and therefore an easier, quicker animated version was considered 'natural new ground to break'[154].

They're an intriguing society, though seem confused as to whether they're a confederacy or an empire (Prime uses both terms to describe them). They appear to have perfected specialisation (the novelisation indicates that Prime and the technicians have been genetically bred for their roles), including a smaller Shalka that can be implanted in the heads of other creatures, and at least one strain of Shalka which is able to form a giant colony creature. They're capable of liquefying rock with their scream; killing people by forcing them to bathe in lava (fortunately this happens offscreen) or making the ground beneath their feet molten. It's heavily implied that the individual creatures can survive an explosion; that Prime is their controlling intelligence (though the

---

[152] Cornell, *Scream of the Shalka*, p199.
[153] The Mara in *Kinda* (1982), later realised only slightly more effectively in *Snakedance* (1983). In *The Discontinuity Guide* (1995) Cornell, Martin Day and Keith Topping suggest ingeniously, and seemingly with tongue only partially in cheek, that with the Mara meant to be a creature of false fears, its real form as a poor origami monster may be apt. We fans can come up with justifications for almost anything if we squint hard enough. Improved special effects meant TV **Doctor Who** could realise snakes far more effectively in *The Magician's Apprentice / The Witch's Familiar* (2015).
[154] Cornell, *Scream of the Shalka*, p199.

technicians demonstrate individual awareness in the novelisation); and that their 'scream' forms a sonic web which is simultaneously Prime's instrument of control and a way of transmitting messages quickly. As Alison remarks, this scream means that the Shalka function a lot like a monstrous internet. Anyone with a dial-up connection could draw a further parallel, with the screaming sound a modem made when connecting them to the human hive-mind of the internet and transmitting their messages across the globe at high speed[155]. They apparently travel via meteor and by wormhole[156] and, as with so many other monsters, display a certain disdain for what they perceive as lesser creatures (which here includes Time Lords).

Furthering the deliberate parallels with 1970s **Doctor Who**, the threat of the Shalka is rendered topical, in this instance by relating their threat to global warming; a suggestion from original producer Jelena Djordjevic which Cornell eagerly took up as it reflected his own environmental concerns and had informed the **Doctor Who** he was drawing on for inspiration[157]. Cornell made this central to their motivation, originally suggesting that they feast on worlds in which the carbon cycle is out of control. He extended this further to make them the 'death principle of the universe'; the limiting factor which answers the scientific question of why civilisation doesn't spread

---

[155] You can be unkind and draw further parallels about social media such as Twitter and Facebook being a form of social control. Perhaps the Shalka were once individual creatures like us who ended up subsumed by the invention of their internet.

[156] Although the latter ability begs the question of why they needed to send a meteor to Earth; perhaps this requires a bridgehead.

[157] Most notably *The Green Death*.

everywhere[158]. They're the answer to the real-life question of why, given mathematical projections indicating that civilised alien life should have passed through Earth's stellar neighbourhood at least twice, they haven't[159]. They have an essentially parasitic methodology; they use the accelerated carbon cycle of industrial civilisations as a catalyst to make the world more suitable for them but inimical to native life forms; thereby bringing down a large number of civilisations which may have developed the capacity for interstellar travel.

Calling them the 'death principle' implies that they're almost a cosmic karma police, punishing the environmental crimes of civilisations, but this is very much not the impression given by the story. Cornell conceived the Shalka as monsters – usually a pejorative term in **Doctor Who** – and their motives do not appear to be altruistic or regretful. Instead their motive is the conquest of a planet, and the reference to an empire suggests their prime motive is territorial: to propagate their species across the universe. Whilst they appear to make other worlds uninhabitable they are in fact rendering them habitable to another form of life – Shalka life. Perhaps on that front the 'death principle' is somewhat misapplied.

---

[158] Cornell, *Scream of the Shalka*, p198-99. This was inspired by his reading Stephen Baxter's **Manifold** trilogy of novels (*Time* (1999), *Space* (2000) and *Origin* (2001), with a later volume of short stories, *Phase Space* (2003)). Baxter would submit a script as a potential follow-up to *Scream of the Shalka*; see Appendix 3.

[159] Cornell, *Scream of the Shalka*, p199. Obviously in the **Doctor Who** universe, with numerous aliens having visited or invaded the planet, this question doesn't actually arise. The question there would be more 'Why don't they leave us alone?'

They're not the galactic equivalent of pest controllers, but another form of life seeking to aggressively propagate their species; a predator on worlds rather than death incarnate.

With their empire extending to 'a billion worlds', and apparently covering 80% of the cosmos with billions of Shalka inhabiting each planet, it's remarkable that the Doctor has never encountered nor heard of them before; again perhaps this is Cornell trying too hard to impart a sense of scale[160]. That the Doctor is deliberately sent to Lannet, however, implies that whoever is controlling his journeys is familiar with the Shalka and their methodology.

This leads to the most tantalising element of *Scream of the Shalka* – the backstory. As presented onscreen and in the novelisation, we get a random selection of jigsaw pieces which don't quite link up: the Doctor railing at unseen superiors; the answering machine message that indicates a previous idyllic existence with a female companion; and the Master's mind having been placed in the body of an android as recompense for a favour during some traumatic event. Effectively this is a slightly less subtle writing trick than Davies would use during *Rose*. Both versions of the ninth Doctor are traumatised by nebulous events; what both Cornell and Davies are smart enough to realise is that the details of these events aren't particularly important. What's vital about them, particularly in an introductory story, is their role in driving the character to act as he does now.

---

[160] It should be noted that this is at the behest of Martin Trickey of BBCi, who wanted the threat to be 'universe-shattering' whereas Cornell was inclined to resist this as being 'a bit of a trap' (Cornell, *Scream of the Shalka*, p198).

The Eccleston Doctor has, we learn, been in a war, though details of this are drawn in only gradually[161]. Similarly there are enough pieces presented on screen for us to sketch the details of a story here without knowing precisely what happened; a female companion died in an incident where the Master helped the Doctor against the threat that killed her. Dramatic economy suggests that the Doctor effectively having a wandering exile is a punishment linked to this. From here we could do what fans do best and extemporise the details, as happened with the Time War; however, this was not Cornell's original intention – he wanted to return to fill in the details of the Doctor's recent past that he had hinted at[162]. The detail of the backstory was retold in the information text subtitles for episode 3 of the *Scream of the Shalka* DVD release (which is based on notes given to Paul Scoones[163], who wrote the info text, by Paul Cornell). It reads as follows:

---

[161] Davies never fully explains what happened; he unfolds occasional detail right up until his last story, *The End of Time* (2009-2010). It took until *The Day of the Doctor* for the detail of the Doctor's actions during the Time War to be explained; even then we only get details of his final actions, rather than his conduct over the course of the war.

[162] Cook, 'No One Can Hear You Scream', p15.

[163] In the first draft of the story the two speleologists we meet at the beginning were named after Scoones and fellow New Zealand fan Jon Preddle, as a thank you for the assistance they provided when Cornell was working on *Shalka* while in New Zealand (Scoones, Paul, 'Scream of the Shalka DVD Production Subtitles').

'The Doctor had retired home to Gallifrey[164] and fallen in love with the daughter of the President of the Time Lords. Gallifrey was invaded by aliens, and the Time Lords retreated into the Matrix. The Doctor bargained with the life of the woman he loved, and she was killed. The Master helped defeat the aliens but his physical body was destroyed. In return for his help, the Doctor stored the Master's mind in a robot body made of TARDIS materials. The Time Lords, now trapped inside the Matrix, punished the Doctor for the death of the President's daughter by sending him into exile, using him to solve dangerous problems in the universe.'

The detail involved in this backstory suggests it's perhaps better left unstated; it's a convoluted collision of soap opera tragedy with the show's mythology, and is filled with the sort of references that are deliberately kept out of *Shalka*. The intention is solid; this provides the Doctor with a tragic backstory, with a reason to be chaste, to have no interest in forming relationships in case those he cares about are hurt, and to travel the universe looking for danger. It turns the Doctor into the brooding, morally compromised figure who leads many successful genre shows and films: a Bruce Wayne, an Angel, a Jack Harkness[165]. It's trying to turn the Doctor into a

---

[164] This could be seen to tie in with Lance Parkin's novel *The Infinity Doctors* (1998), which features a Doctor retired to Gallifrey but is deliberately vague as to which Doctor it features and when it is set.

[165] Respectively in **Batman** (particularly the films of Christopher Nolan), **Angel** (1999-2004) and **Torchwood** (2006-11). Jack undergoes a significant character shift from his **Doctor Who** persona to become the lead in the latter.

tragic hero – a valid take on the character, but one which perhaps needs a Doctor with more warmth and charm; one who you'd actually want to accompany on his travels.

Ultimately the flaws in *Shalka*'s script comes down to the limits in Cornell's thinking about what can be done with a **Doctor Who** story. He doesn't quite write it as the near-pastiche of Gatiss, Roberts and Hickman's proposed version, but nor is he capable of the radical revamp Davies performed on the show. Davies allowed his deep and abiding love of popular television rather than his deep and abiding love of **Doctor Who** to be the chief influence on his version of the show[166], but Cornell's influences tend to be drawn from the narrower pool of science-fiction and fantasy TV, literature and comics[167]; the references he uses are consequently not quite as wide as Davies's. Davies's genuine love of popular TV gives him a wider range of influence, and a better instinctive understanding of what works for a large scale audience. Cornell has a profound affinity with genre and fandom and, to a large extent, this limits the range of stories he's able to tell. Davies is interested in using the SF of **Doctor Who** as a vehicle to tell stories about people: Cornell is

---

[166] Consider this one last plug for *The Black Archive #1*, specifically Chapter 4.

[167] That this genre material is his passion reflects in that much of his career has been spent writing it: aside from his **Who** work he has written comics for *2000 AD*, Marvel, DC, Vertigo and Dark Horse; written two standalone science-fiction novels and an ongoing urban fantasy series, **The Shadow Police**; co-authored five guides to cult TV series with Martin Day and Keith Topping; launched his own podcast series about various genre topics; and hosted the Hugo Awards.

interested in **Doctor Who** because it's **Doctor Who**. Hence, at heart, each season of Russell T Davies's **Doctor Who** is about the relationship between two people whilst *Scream of the Shalka* is a template for a series purely about the adventures of the Doctor and his friends. It's perhaps the ultimate achievement of the 'Wilderness Years' of **Doctor Who**; a broadcast story written by a professional writer and fan with its own version of the Doctor. Ultimately though, that fan mindset is its limiting factor.

CONCLUSION

Like any grand folly, *Scream of the Shalka* contained the seeds of its own downfall. Its biggest legacy lay not in any stories, characters or concepts it brought to **Doctor Who**, but as a peripheral foray to prove the series was viable.

Part of the reason there was a degree of inertia around **Doctor Who** returning to television in the late 1990s and early 2000s was that no one was quite sure of the rights situation surrounding the show, following the failure of *Doctor Who* (1996) to lead to a series. Not only was no one quite sure but there seemed to be little inclination to look into it. Anecdotal stories from around the BBC suggest it was thought of as an idea whose time had passed – Mark Gatiss recalled Jon Plowman initially being enthusiastic about reviving their proposed version of the show, but this falling apart with the lack of clarity regarding the rights, and which other parts of the BBC were doing with it[168]. James Goss, for instance, recalls his head of department at BBCi saying that **Doctor Who** only had a year left in it as late as 2003[169]. The rights situation to which the Gatiss-Roberts-Hickman proposal fell foul had become a complicated excuse not to contemplate bringing the show back; with no official will for the show to return, performing the investigative work required was too much effort.

However, when checking that there were no right issues with BBCi producing *Scream of the Shalka*, Jelena Djordjevic and researcher Daniel Judd found fewer issues than anticipated. Djordjevic has

---

[168] Recalled in Kibble-White, 'Doctor Who 2001', p71.
[169] Episode 3 DVD commentary.

recounted how the main problem she kept running into was people mentioning the rights to the Daleks[170]. In response to fan concerns, their findings were made public on the **Doctor Who** section of the Cult website on 21 August 2003[171]. This resulted in a meeting with Lorraine Heggessey, Jane Tranter and some lawyers; a fortnight after their statement about the rights was published, they were told that **Doctor Who** would be coming back. This meant that *Scream of the Shalka*, already the six-part remnant of an originally planned season of three four-part stories[172], became an orphaned version of the show before it had been broadcast. It had its thunder stolen before it had even been aired; what reason was there to care too much about an animated version of the series being shown online, when the show was coming back to television inside the next 18 months?

Shalka's reception was complicated not only by the announcement of the show's return to television, but by the lukewarm reception of the fan press. The issue of *Doctor Who Magazine* which should have launched it with a loud fanfare instead was most notable for the stop-press announcement of the new series[173]. Grant's Doctor was not accorded the traditional front cover announcement of a new lead actor, with his name in big letters followed by 'is the Doctor'[174]. This was partly down to a feeling on the part of editor

---

[170] 'Carry On Screaming', DVD extra.

[171] This page apparently no longer exists.

[172] The cut from 12 to six episodes and from three stories to one was purely for budgetary reasons, and came quite early in production ('Carry On Screaming').

[173] 'Gallifrey Guardian: He's Back!'. DWM #336, p5.

[174] In retrospect, a fortunate decision.

Clayton Hickman that he 'didn't feel that [Grant] warranted it'; he confessed that 'trouble' in their coverage of Shalka gave the magazine a 'sour disposition' towards it[175]. Much of this trouble is detailed at length in the main feature the magazine ran on Scream of the Shalka[176], some of which involves DWM reporter Benjamin Cook being kept waiting, sometimes while having to wait in a stationery cupboard. Whilst there's no question that the announcement of the new series would essentially always have overshadowed Shalka, the alienation of the main publication covering the show unquestionably soured the reception it did get; failing to court the media would not be a mistake made by Davies.

This combination of circumstance and a failure in media relations meant that Shalka would essentially became a neglected outcrop of **Doctor Who**. Whilst the new series continued to be a successful part of Saturday night programming for the BBC, stage plays from the 1960s, 70s and 80s were remade by Big Finish, and even the Peter Cushing Dalek movies aired on satellite TV channels from time to time, Shalka would languish on a corner of the **Doctor Who** website – a situation that barely changed when it was released on DVD as one of the last few releases in the line.

And yet this is unfair in many ways. Without Shalka, **Doctor Who** would almost certainly have taken a little longer to return[177], and it

---

[175] DWM, 'The Second Coming', Souvenir Special: 500 DWM Issues, p 58.
[176] Cook, 'No One Can Hear You Scream', pp12-18.
[177] Lorraine Heggessey, in a speech at the 2003 Edinburgh Festival made a few days after BBCi had posted up their discoveries about rights, had expressed a desire to bring **Doctor Who** back but spoke

showed that **Doctor Who** could be made in animated form and for an online audience[178]. The 2006 series was preceded by the 'TARDISodes'[179], short online dramas to whet the audience's appetite for that week's episode. 2007 would bring a second animated **Doctor Who** story, *The Infinite Quest*[180], and 2009 a third, *Dreamland*. Later, Cosgrove Hall would animate missing episodes of several incomplete stories for DVD release; if *Shalka* did not directly influence these productions, then it certainly made it easier for the producers of these programmes to argue for them.

This neglect of *Shalka* is a shame; while it's not a perfect attempt at reviving the series for the 21st century, it certainly provides a viable template; a second story had been commissioned[181], and several of its episodes written, by the time the TV revival meant the project was cancelled. The flash animation, while it might appear somewhat primitive given subsequent advances in technology, was innovative for the time: it even won an industry prize, the Big Chip

---

of the rights situation being too complicated. This suggests that the will to sort out the situation would have reached a critical mass sooner or later.

[178] Interestingly, in late 2001 the BBC were still saying there could never be an animated series of **Doctor Who** ('Does **Doctor Who** have a future as an animated series?').

[179] Something possible with the increasing number of households with internet access and improvement in internet speeds.

[180] Initially shown as part of **Totally Doctor Who.**

[181] 'Blood of the Robots' by Simon Clark. See Appendix 3 for further details.

Award[182] for Best Digital Animation. It has an interesting take on the Doctor and while it perhaps does not have the courage to raise the role of companion to joint lead, it does a lot of sterling work trying to modernise the role. Its treatment of the Master[183] is perhaps more interesting than John Simm's 'I'm mad, me' take, and nothing as interesting would be done with the role until Michelle Gomez took over the role for the 2014 season. And whilst it could not be quite as radical, it was the first **Doctor Who** production to think of how the series could work for a 21st-century audience. It's a brave, flawed attempt to find a future for **Doctor Who** when no-one thought it had one.

---

[182] These are awards for digital excellence: up to 2011 this was restricted to the North West of England but after that was extended to cover the entire North of England.

[183] *Scream of the Shalka*, of course, beat *Utopia* (2007) to the punch by casting Sir Derek Jacobi as the Master.

APPENDIX 1: COULD IT FIT?

The question of whether a **Doctor Who** story is canonical and therefore 'counts' is a particularly dull one that's been debated to death on mailing lists, message boards and podcasts over the years. Do the Virgin and BBC novels count? Do the Big Finish stories count? Do the stories in the annuals count? What about 'Masterplan Q'?[184] And frankly, who cares?[185] In the spirit of Oscar Wilde, I'll avoid the tedium of canon wars[186]. What I'm going to look at here is whether *Scream of the Shalka* could fit if you wanted it to.

The announcement of a new televised version of **Doctor Who** meant that *Scream of the Shalka* was essentially a dead end before

---

[184] 'Doctor Who Fights Masterplan Q' was a promotional short story serialised on Nestlé chocolate bars in 1971, and included as a PDF on the *Terror of the Autons* DVD release. It's not widely considered canonical. The author takes the position that anything you want to counts. The only official pronouncements on canonicity from BBC sources came when Steve Cole, then in charge of the BBC Books line, declared the Big Finish audio plays as canonical; and when the BBC declared the online game series **The Adventure Games** to count in a press release (BBC, 'BBC Unveils Doctor Who – The Adventure Games'). The closest anyone working on the TV show has come to this is Paul McGann reciting a list of companions from Big Finish plays in 'The Night of the Doctor'. But then if you're an ungenerous purist you can discount webcasts.

[185] And really, if you're enjoying a story, why should a notion of whether it counts or not worry you?

[186] If you're **really** desperate to scratch an itch I recommend the hardcore nerdery of the rec.arts.drwho and Jade Pagoda mailing list archives, or signing up for Gallifrey Base.

it was broadcast. It's difficult to imagine that the BBC would have countenanced a different branch of the organisation making a competing version claiming to be the ongoing version of the show, particularly when the BBC One version would be a flagship Saturday night drama. Whilst the BBC has never made any definitive declaration as to which versions or stories of **Doctor Who** count as official, *Shalka* has been reduced to a curio. It has, however, been released as part of the official DVD range and, like all bar two stories preceding the 2005 revival, novelised[187].

In discounting *Shalka* from the third edition of *Ahistory: An Unauthorised History of the Doctor Who Universe*[188], Lance Parkin and Lars Pearson declared that this was on the grounds that 'the sheer preponderance of material establishing the Eccleston version as the ninth Doctor means that almost nobody at the time of writing (not even the *Scream of the Shalka*'s creators) accepts the Grant Doctor as canon'[189]. Given that this is a book which seeks to reconcile the show explicitly having two versions of *Human Nature* and *Shada*, and that Parkin has posited a theory regarding the faces in *The Brain of Morbius* which relies on ignoring a preponderance of material, this seems a tad dismissive. This edition of *Ahistory* was published in late 2012, a few months before it became clear, via some ingenious sophistry on Steven Moffat's part, that Eccleston's Doctor was not, in fact, the Doctor's ninth incarnation but his 10th.

---

[187] The last two unnovelised stories being *Resurrection of the Daleks* (1984) and *Revelation of the Daleks* (1985).

[188] It had previously been included in both the first and second editions.

[189] Parkin, Lance and Pearson, Lars, *Ahistory* (3rd edition) (2012).

This lack of clarity in the numbering of incarnations was further complicated in *The Time of the Doctor* (2013) where it was revealed that the incarnation played by Matt Smith, generally thought to be the 11th Doctor, was actually the final body in the Doctor's cycle of 13 regenerations[190]. The conclusion to that story provided the Doctor with a new regenerative cycle of uncertain duration. This, along with the final scene from *The Day of the Doctor* (2013)[191], would seem to indicate fairly conclusively that the Doctors whose adventures we have witnessed as part of the ongoing story are the only incarnations the Doctor has had and that *Scream of the Shalka* counts, at best, as an 'Unbound' story.

This, however, goes against the contrarian soul of fandom. This book has no such space considerations as *Ahistory* and, indeed, has far more of an investment in suggesting that there are multiple methods by which *Shalka* could be fitted into continuity.

There are two indications in the episode itself that the *Shalka* Doctor is the ninth Doctor[192]: in the conversation with Mathilda in

---

[190] In addition to the John Hurt incarnation known as either the 'Other Doctor' or the 'War Doctor', the regeneration which formed the cliffhanger to *The Stolen Earth* (2008) and which resulted in a duplicate human version of the Doctor was revealed to count as a full regeneration.

[191] This featured all televised incarnations of the Doctor. To have included an animated character in an attempt to be inclusive would have been ludicrous. Even including Grant as a nod would have caused the larger non-fan section of the audience to wonder why the Great Intelligence was in the line-up after Clara's actions had defeated him in *The Name of the Doctor*.

[192] It's baldly stated in the novelisation that this is the Doctor's ninth incarnation (Cornell, *Scream of the Shalka*, p13). But then

episode 1 he make a reference to her cat having used up its nine lives 'rather like me', and episode 6 has a reference to Andy Warhol wanting to paint 'all nine of me'. The former can be taken as a joke (he's on his ninth life, he hasn't actually used nine lives up yet) and the second is a typically Doctorish piece of name-dropping[193]. It's unclear as to how seriously any of it can be taken – after all, as River Song has said on multiple occasions[194], the Doctor lies. If we are to take it at face value, it would indicate that Grant plays the incarnation immediately following McGann, something the mini-episode 'The Night of the Doctor' would appear explicitly to rule out.

However, Russell T Davies's generosity in not wishing to explicitly write the BBC and Virgin novels and Big Finish audios out of any canon means this isn't quite true. Although the events of the Time War portrayed on screen have been fairly straightforward war scenes with no real temporal element[195], the indications are that the war has ranged across time and altered or amended timelines. This raises the possibility that the Doctor himself may have amended his own timeline – in 'The Night of the Doctor' he faces a choice between healer and warrior and we see him choose to become a warrior, 'Doctor no more'. This is an extreme decision for the character, with the implication being that he has been driven to

---

novelisations have been contradicting the TV show since 1964, so they're unreliable sources at best.

[193] There's also nothing to indicate that this encounter with Warhol didn't occur in a previous incarnation.

[194] Starting with *The Big Bang* (2010).

[195] See primarily 'The Night of the Doctor', 'The Last Day' (2013) and *The Day of the Doctor*.

this by the events of the Time War which, according to the Sisterhood, 'threatens all reality'. Given the desperate nature of the Doctor's actions and the relative ease with which he is persuaded, despite this being the early days of the war, what if this is actually a correction of his original choice? Perhaps the *Shalka* Doctor was the result of his choosing to remain a 'healer' rather than a 'warrior' and this resulted in terrible eventual consequences (such as the Daleks winning the Time War)[196]. The *Shalka* Doctor represents a dead timeline where the Doctor is eventually able to correct a bad decision and reverse time to ensure that on this occasion he makes the harder decision. The *Shalka* Doctor would remain the 'original' ninth Doctor but not be an actual incarnation.

The second, simpler option is that the Doctor we see in *Shalka* is one of the Doctor's future regenerations[197] that we have yet to see.

---

[196] For all the Doctor's morality about not revising his own timeline, there is precedent; the key moment of *The Day of the Doctor* involves the Doctor revising a decision he made.

[197] This, incidentally, also validates the existence of the Doctor's evil (pseudo-)incarnation, the Valeyard. He is described in 'The Ultimate Foe' (*The Trial of a Time Lord* episodes 13-14 (1986)) as 'an amalgamation of darker sides of your nature, somewhere between your 12th and final incarnation'. Given the new regenerative cycle granted in *The Time of the Doctor* all this means is that he comes into existence between the Doctor's 12th incarnation (so after the events of *The Stolen Earth* with the David Tennant incarnation regenerating into himself) and his final body. Both *Kill the Moon* (2014) and *Hell Bent* indicate that the number of regenerations granted to the Doctor in his new lifecycle is uncertain, possibly indefinite, so this merely indicates that the Valeyard is a Doctor we have yet to see.

The production team may have originally intended him to be the ninth Doctor, but there is only that single line as confirmation of this intention. That we automatically place him as the ninth Doctor is merely a factor of timing of production; we think of him as the ninth Doctor due to publicity material and because his sole broadcast appearance comes between the eighth and ninth televised incarnations. In reality he could be easily be placed in a future timeline – each Doctor with multiple stories has experienced what, from our perspective, is Earth's history, on multiple occasions. Why not a future incarnation dipping backwards in such a way? Perhaps Alison can be a historical companion in the same way as Katarina, Jamie or Victoria. In pure story terms, even the sole reference to nine Doctors can be explained away with a little imagination; perhaps the Doctor suffers a form of amnesia at some point and forgets some past lives, or this version of the Doctor has, for some reason, been cloned multiple times.

This could be even more interesting with the revelation that the Doctor can choose his faces. This was suggested in *The War Games* (1969) where the Time Lords offer him a choice of faces for his forced regeneration, and by Romana's regeneration in *Destiny of the Daleks* (1979); however, it's strongly implied that the Doctor is not in control of his regenerative process (for example 'That's the trouble with regeneration. You never quite know what you're going to get'[198] and 'I hope the ears are a bit less conspicuous this time'[199]). Perhaps this is a freshly discovered ability to select a face, bestowed by his new regenerative cycle. In *The Girl Who Died*

---

[198] *Castrovalva* episode 1 (1982).
[199] The War Doctor, *The Day of the Doctor*.

(2015) he realises that he chose his face to remind him that his purpose as the Doctor was to save people, no matter how impossible or wrong it might seem. If you like, it's a restatement of his principles following the 11th Doctor's sacrifice of centuries of his own life simply to save a small town on what would be an obscure planet without the Doctor's involvement[200]. It's of a piece with the character re-establishing his ideals in *The Day of the Doctor* by changing his own actions during the Time War. So what if, at some undetermined future point he takes on the face of Dr Simeon (played by Richard E Grant in *The Snowmen* (2012), *The Bells of Saint John* (2013) and *The Name of the Doctor* (2013)), perhaps as a penance of some kind? Or perhaps a strand of Simeon's DNA survived in the Doctor's timeline following the events of *The Name of the Doctor*, and this incarnation could be gradually being corrupted...

---

[200] *The Time of the Doctor.*

APPENDIX 2: 'THE FEAST OF THE STONE'

The only further story featuring Richard E Grant's version of the Doctor appeared on the BBC's Cult website. It didn't even appear in the **Doctor Who** section but one dedicated to vampires. It kept company with Dracula and Sherlock Holmes[201] rather than Haemovores and ancient Time Lord enemies skulking in E-Space. 'The Feast of the Stone' came as part of a series of six stories, four by authors known mostly or entirely for their horror fiction (Michael Marshall Smith, Kim Newman, Graham Masterton; SF author Brian Stableford also contributed) and two based on animated series for the BBC site (*Shalka* and *The Ghosts of Albion*). There's a certain pleasing strategy to that; it provided a coherence to the cult site and a cross-promotion for what might otherwise be an obscure subsection which wouldn't have an obvious TV link to attract visitors.

The temptation to link this Doctor to vampires is perhaps irresistible – as animated by Cosgrove Hall, his appearance is reasonably similar to that of Christopher Lee's Dracula[202]. The image accompanying the short story plays up to this, with the Doctor's hair flattened and swept back and his skin bleached vampire-white by the one bright light source in the picture (the TARDIS lantern). You could be forgiven for taking the Doctor as a

---

[201] Apt given the influences on this Doctor's character.
[202] Notably, Cornell describes him as 'vampiric' in the episode 1 DVD commentary.

potential vampiric protagonist for this story from this image alone[203].

According to the interview which accompanies the story on the site, Cavan Scott and Mark Wright were asked to write the story as they'd written a **Doctor Who** vampire story for Big Finish (*Project: Twilight* (2001), which blended vampires with government conspiracies[204]). To their credit they decided against a straightforward vampire story, and instead used a psychic vampire to allow them to explore the dynamic between the Doctor and the Master. Whilst the Doctor is essentially at the same point in his character arc as he is at the end of *Scream of the Shalka*, what's really interesting is the revelation of the Master's character. Despite his role as a member of the TARDIS crew rendering him essentially benevolent, he's still seen to have taken a certain pleasure in a death of a fairly graphic nature in the past. This maintains a certain ambivalence to the Doctor-Master relationship that's only briefly played up in *Scream of the Shalka*.

Alison's role in this story is fairly traditional for companions: to get into trouble and need to be rescued. We get flashbacks to her Nana's death and the night she got together with Joe – from the concept of the story these would appear to be her most important memories. Otherwise we learn very little about her that we didn't know from *Scream of the Shalka*.

---

[203] It's also the only official image of this incarnation that isn't derived from Cosgrove Hall's animation.

[204] This proved fertile territory for Scott and Wright; there have since been two audio sequels, a non-**Doctor Who** novel and web comic and even an **Iris Wildthyme** short story.

There's also a possibility that the imaginary scene the Doctor finds himself in during the story feeds into the backstory; although the line 'Where was she?' refers to his separation from Alison, this scenario has a similar tone to the Doctor's answerphone message and can be read as a further reference to the backstory hinted at in *Shalka*.

Ultimately, whilst constraints of space mean that there wasn't room to explore the characters in any great depth, the story at least indicates how the series may have continued; whilst the Doctor-companion relationship is straightforward, it's the potential dark undercurrents of the relationship with the Master which intrigue. It's very much following up on *Shalka*'s hint of his interrupted hypnosis of Alison to indicate that his redemption is a continuing struggle, so he may not be entirely reliable. Similarly he's quite happy to prevent the Doctor going to rescue Alison, as per the TARDIS scene in episode 4 of *Shalka*. Despite his being trapped, this story offers a potential way of the Master being involved in the drama without the need for much of the story to take place within the TARDIS.

APPENDIX 3: 'LAST WORDS FOR THE UNIVERSE'

Work on the sequel to *Scream of the Shalka* was relatively far advanced by the time the series was cancelled. There were four potential scripts for the second story: one from Paul Cornell, one from Jonathan Clements, one from Stephen Baxter, and Simon Clark's 'Blood of the Robots'[205].

Paul Cornell's submission was reworked for the other ninth Doctor as 'The Masks of Makassar' in *The Doctor Who Annual 2006* (2005). This story, like *Scream of the Shalka*, drew inspiration from the medium it would have been broadcast in as it featured an 'internet of brains'[206]. In the published version, Christopher Eccleston's Doctor and Rose face a villain, Makassar, who hijacks a planet's mask-based telepathic technology to take control of a summit of galactic leaders. Though it has been adapted to fit the format Russell T Davies brought to **Doctor Who** (it begins with a teaser sequence), it's remarkable how easy it is to substitute Grant's Doctor into the story.

Baxter's submission would have been a 'magical version of "The Dead Planet"' (*The Daleks* episode 1, 1963), according to James Goss. Clements's proposal was entitled 'The Kingmaker' and the

---

[205] Also known as 'Rise of the Robots' according to Richard Dinnick ('The Forgotten Doctor', *Doctor Who Insider* #9). In personal correspondence, Paul Scoones states he believes this to be an error.

[206] Cornell, Paul, 'The Masks of Makassar'. Hickman, Clayton, ed, *The Doctor Who Annual 2006*, p22.

storyline was subsequently used as the basis for the Big Finish **Doctor Who** audio drama *Immortal Beloved* (2007)[207]. His proposal ran as follows:

> The TARDIS arrives on Kaleva, a world settled in the distant past by human colonists who arrived on the vessel *Catherine's Wheel*. The descendants of the Crew live a life of luxury, making full use of advanced technology for the prolonging of life, and the augmenting of physical and mental powers. The descendants of the Colonists are kept in a state of ignorance and deprivation, convinced that they are ruled over by capricious gods.
>
> The 'gods,' however, are divided, between those who favour gene manipulation (The Flesh) and those who prefer more artificial, digitally-based means of achieving immortality (The Metal).
>
> Alison is scandalised by the 'gods'' attitude towards the majority of the populace, she assumes this is the situation the Doctor has been sent to correct. But he thinks the inequalities are something that the people need to work out themselves, and that his mission is to negotiate some sort of pact between the divine opponents, lest millions of their followers die in the war that may follow.
>
> The Master, for his part, supports the Doctor's diplomatic mission – because if he unifies the opposing factions, he realises that he may be able to create an organic clone of his

---

[207] Clements, Jonathan, personal correspondence with the author, 27 November 2016.

old self (using Flesh techniques), and download his brain from his robotic body (using Metal technique). And while he's at it, he might even manage to make a few clones of himself.

However, all three of the travellers from the TARDIS are in for a shock, when they discover that both Flesh and Metal place very little value in the lives of their followers, and in fact, need a form of human sacrifice to maintain their quality of divine life. The realisation causes both the Doctor, and... with some reluctance, the Master, to come round to Alison's way of thinking, and proclaim that it is time to admit that it is the twilight of the gods.

The Doctor must somehow bring down the gods themselves, or risk unleashing an apocalypse that will engulf the entire planet. His one ally is Kalkin, a younger clone of the aging God-King, who is unwilling to have his brain wiped when his 'father' inevitably decides its time for a new body.[208]

The story which was eventually commissioned was Clark's 'Blood of the Robots', the initial proposal for which has been mislaid. This would have followed the same format as *Shalka*, of six episodes of between 10 and 15 minutes. Unlike *Shalka*, the voice work for the story would have been produced by Big Finish, possibly as they were regarded as experienced and therefore a safe pair of hands for the production[209].

---

[208] Clements, personal correspondence.
[209] Scoones, personal correspondence with the author, 20 November 2016.

Whilst the majority of Clark's work has been in the horror genre (particularly the **Vampyrrhic** series of novels[210]) he had also written science fiction before, most notably *The Night of the Triffids* (2001), an approved sequel to John Wyndham's *The Day of the Triffids* (1951). Clark was also a long-term **Doctor Who** fan; family legend has it that he never missed an episode[211] and in an interview with Ian Berriman for *SFX* he described it as the 'video track of his life'. In 2003 he had also written the last of the **Doctor Who** novellas published by Telos Publishing, *The Dalek Factor* (2004), and suspects that this led to BBCi inviting him to pitch a story[212]. In correspondence with the present author he described the commissioning of his pitch as a 'dream come true', and said that 'dreaming up new adventures for the Doctor and his companions gifted me some of the happiest days of my professional life.'

Although Clark was an experienced writer, 'Blood of the Robots' would be his first attempt at writing a script as opposed to prose and this was very much a case of learning the discipline as he went along:

> 'I was completely new to writing scripts when I was commissioned to write "Blood of the Robots". At first, the technical aspects of simply rendering the story into script form were immensely daunting. Ultimately, I just dived in and started writing the episodes as the story flowed through my head and decided to worry about adding such directions

---

[210] Beginning with *Vampyrrhic* (1998).
[211] Clark, Simon, personal correspondence with the author, 25 October 2016.
[212] Berriman, Ian, 'The Simon Clark Story That Never Was'.

as "close up", "long shot", "unassigned camera", and so on after the first draft. I'm a firm believer in the "catching the tiger by the tail" approach to writing anyway. That is to say, once the story begins running through my head like a movie I just keep writing down what my mind's eye sees and tidy up the prose later. [...]

'Writing any kind of TV script was a challenge to me as I was new to it. I suspect writing for an animated show would be even more of a challenge, but ignorance is bliss, so I just wrote down what I wanted to see on screen.'[213]

The story was to be set in a junkyard, something that could be seen as harking back to *An Unearthly Child* (1963). However, this would be a futuristic junkyard rather than the more conventional one we first met the Doctor in[214]:

'What inspired the story was the simple idea of a planet that is a dumping-ground for old, worn-out robots. Some still function and build a new life for themselves, of sorts, in the junkyard.' [215]

The story would have seen a conflict between humans and robots, with the humans who abandoned them now seeking to move them on, even from the world they've been forced to make their own.

---

[213] Clark, personal correspondence.

[214] It's notable that the initial structure of the proposed series mirrors that eventually adopted by Russell T Davies in 2005. After beginning with a relatively straightforward Earth invasion story which introduces us to the new Doctor and companion, the next step is to show the new companion a futuristic SF environment.

[215] Clark, personal correspondence.

The almost survivalist nature of the environment would have naturally led to a slightly downbeat atmosphere to the story[216], albeit tempered by the **Doctor Who** adventure format:

'Growing up watching **Doctor Who** from the very first episode governed my approach to how I believed the story should feel and what the viewer would experience. For me, **Doctor Who** is about excitement, a sense of wonder, mystery, some frightening scenes, and a sprinkle of humour. One dominating element would have been a certain sense of melancholy, deriving from the abandonment of intelligent robots on what is a graveyard of a world, with gigantic androids buried up to their shoulders in shifting dunes. However, amid all the junked robots and skeletons of machines a new life is stirring that can feel, and hope, and yearns for survival.' [217]

The atmosphere being aimed for is demonstrated in the following script extract from episode 2:

4.   EXT. VORADA - DAY

DOCTOR AND ALISON CONTINUE WALKING BY LIFELESS ROBO-JUNK TOWARD THE SOURCE OF THE HAUNTING MUSIC. THEY APPROACH A TALL, EERIE ROBOT LOOKING LIKE A PHANTOM ARMOURED KNIGHT STANDING ERECT ON AN OUTCROP OF ROCK THAT FORMS A NATURAL PLINTH. A PHANTOM SENTINEL. IT APPEARS DEAD, ITS METALWORK

---

[216] Something very much in keeping with the tone of *Scream of the Shalka*.

[217] Clark, personal correspondence.

ENCRUSTED WITH CORROSION. BEHIND IT HANGS THE
GHOSTLY RINGED WORLD. THE ROBOT DOESN'T SO MUCH
LOOK TOWARD THE MOUNTAINS BUT GAZES INTO THE FACE
OF ETERNITY.[218]

An element of the story which must undoubtedly have endeared
the script to the animators was the opportunity to create a variety
of robots for the story, some of which would have been used to
bring a streak of black humour to the story:

> 'An interesting, and downright fun, part of writing the story
> was dreaming up different kinds of robots. I must admit I
> had **Robot Wars**[219] in mind for some of the robots. I was
> particularly proud of Funeralbot. "His" job was to be a
> pallbearer at human funerals and respectfully and delicately
> carry the coffin into the cemetery and place it in the grave.
> However, a malfunction in his pneumatics resulted in the
> steel arm, which carried the coffin, acting as a powerful
> flipper. Consequently, he would, during the most solemn of
> graveside moments, hurl the coffin over the treetops toward
> the distant horizon. This flaw led to him being consigned to
> the scrapheap. My horror roots were coming out there to
> pen some very dark, macabre humour.'

Although the scripts were written prior to the broadcast of *Scream
of the Shalka*, Clark's approach to writing this version of the Doctor

---

[218] Clark, Simon, 'Blood of the Robots', quoted in personal
correspondence with author.
[219] A game show based on combat between home-made robots
which ran from 1998 to 2004 on the BBC and elsewhere.

was similar to Cornell's. It would seem to be very much in keeping with the character as portrayed in his sole onscreen appearance:

> 'If, say, the Doctor was played by Colin Baker I'd know the character from all the TV episodes I'd watched, and could have studied his turns of phrase, mannerisms and so on. In this case, the Doctor was going to be played by Richard E Grant, so it meant looking at his earlier roles in the likes of *Withnail and I*, and doing some guessing. I imagined Richard E Grant's portrayal of the Doctor would be aristocratic, even imperious at times, with overtones of Sherlock Holmes.'

Whilst he was given more of a free hand to decide how Alison and the Master would act[220], the opportunity to write for Jacobi was something Clark found inspiring:

> 'I've been in awe of Jacobi since I saw him in **I, Claudius** [1976] [...] He has such a wonderful melodic voice. Right from the start, I thought of having the Master talking about his favourite tipples, just so I could have the great actor voicing the words Merlot, Amontillado and so on in such a resonant way.'[221]

Clark also put some thought into how the medium of a streamed broadcast could be used to enhance the story; using the smaller size of PC screens in much the same way that stories such as *The Sensorites* (1964) had used the size of 1960s screens to their advantage:

---

[220] Clark, personal correspondence.
[221] Clark, Simon, quoted in Berriman, 'The Simon Clark Story That Never Was'.

'It occurred to me that because this series would be broadcast on the internet in the days before smart TVs people would watch in a slightly different way. Instead of sitting watching a TV some distance away, they would be sat close up before a PC screen. With that kind of proximity I realised there might be ways to deliver shocks to the viewer (in an enjoyable way!) by having faces suddenly appearing in close up. For example, a character looks out of a window and a scary face crashes forward to fill the screen, with an accompanying roar. Seeing this description in cold print looks anything but scary but I'm sure the animator's skill would make it work perfectly!'

The story itself would remain only partially written. Clark completed a detailed storyline (reproduced here) and drafts of the first four episodes before the cancellation of further episodes was announced; the first draft of episode 4 was completed only minutes before the news broke[222]. The final scene provides a tantalising glimpse of what might have been: a traditional **Doctor Who** cliffhanger which offers the intriguing possibility of the Master returning to a slightly more sinister interpretation and would have been a practice run for Derek Jacobi's portrayal of the Master in *Utopia* (2007). It remains the final scene written for this version of **Doctor Who**:

19.   INT. TARDIS – DAY

THE MASTER BATTLES AGAINST THE PROGRAMMING. A ROBOT CAN'T PERSPIRE BUT THE MASTER COMES CLOSE.

---

[222] Clark, personal correspondence.

HUSPIDOR

I'm no longer chained to past habits. Try it, Master. Try and do the thing you are NOT programmed to do.

MASTER (VOICE BOOMS OUT TO THE COSMOS)

Enough! You fools! (A BEAT) I am the Master! I decide what I do! Where I go. For I am the Master of my destiny... And I am the Master of your fate.

LAUGHS EVILLY. THE MASTER OPERATES THE CONTROLS WITH PANACHE. THE TARDIS BEGINS TO DEMATERIALIZE WITH CHARACTERISTIC WHEEZING SOUND. THE MASTER LAUGHS AND LAUGHS...

DOCTOR WHO THEME MUSIC.

END OF EPISODE FOUR[223]

Although the final episodes of 'Blood of the Robots' were never written, the detailed episode breakdown for the story still exists. What follows is the full storyline for what would have been the second fully animated **Doctor Who** story[224].

---

[223] Clark, 'Blood of the Robots', quoted in personal correspondence.
[224] While some of the formatting has been changed for ease of reading, the wording has been preserved exactly as in Clark's typescript.

'BLOOD OF THE ROBOTS': DETAILED EPISODE BREAKDOWN

DOCTOR WHO

THE ANIMATED SERIES

BBCi 2003

BLOOD OF THE ROBOTS

Simon Clark

6 x 10' Episodes

Setting:

The robot scrapyards located on the barren moon of Vorada.

Theme:

What makes a human a human?

Story in a sentence:

A blend of adventure, drama and humour: the Doctor arrives to find a world full of intelligent, sensitive robots being hunted by ruthless salvage squads in order to make room for human settlers forced to migrate from their over-crowded home planet.

Episode One

EXT. VORADA. Desolate. No vegetation. Purple rocked beneath a sky of fiery reds, where a green-blue Earth-like world hangs. A little robot, cute as a puppy, limps through the desert. We see it being pursued. Our POV is that of its pursuer. Remorselessly, the little robot is chased over rocks, down gullies, across craters. It weakens, dragging its damaged leg Repeatedly, it glances back at its pursuer. Even though it has a robotic face its expression is the epitome of terror. Closer. Closer. Its eyes grow wider, its flight even more desperate. We know the chase is near its grim conclusion. Now we hear an ominous rumble swell over the robot's whimper. Then it reaches a rock face. It can run no further. Still from the pursuer's POV we close in on the terror-stricken robot as first it tries to climb the cliff, fails, then turns to face its destroyer. A pair of long limbs armed with pincers appear in vision as the pursuer reaches out to grasp its quarry. In the grip of the claws the robot squirms helpless as the limbs retract, drawing the robot to where we assume the pursuer's unseen mouth would be. The doomed robot fills the screen then vanishes. Crunching metal, the robot screams and screams and...

...And the scream transmutes into **Doctor Who** theme music.

INT. TARDIS. A wine cellar of staggering proportions. Stone vaulted ceilings run away into infinity. There's a suggestion of the lofty, gothic interior of Paris's Notre Dame. Gorgeous shafts of light from incredible windows. A real soda fountain effervesces nearby, fizzing liquid cascades over statues.

The Doctor, the Master and Alison gaze at this Grand Canyon of wine racks.

Aiming to impress, the Doctor proclaims, *Behold! My wine cellar.*

Alison is astonished, *This is your wine cellar? In the TARDIS?*

The Master sniffs disdainfully. *Adequate. Ah, but I see you have a perfectly charming Amontillado... although one would prefer it stored in a cask rather than a bottle. It's as much the piquancy of the wooden barrel as the quality of the palomino grape that yields such a unique flavour.*

The Doctor cannot resist showing off his impressive collection of wine to Alison. They are choosing wine for a meal. The Master helps, knowing the importance of the growing bond between companion and The Doctor, and conscious that the emotional scars of his old adversary are healing. Genuinely, he cares. He's sweet but cannot prevent himself indulging in gentle verbal sparring over the Doctor's choice of wine, especially when the Doctor becomes a little snobbish over an amphora of wine presented to him by Psellus of Byzantium. *Of course, there's an absolute devil of a problem getting wine to age in the TARDIS...*

Then, unexpectedly, the bottles begin to vibrate in there thousands – an astonishing sound. Unexpectedly the TARDIS is landing.

EXT. VORADA. As before from the POV of a merciless hunter. This time a thesp-bot stands defiant. It is rusty but luminously noble. Clawed limbs extend towards it. Through a decaying voice generator it sighs. *Go on, angel of death... Break me rib and thigh. But you will never destroy our heart.*

Now we see the claws belong to a scrapyard Crusher that glides above the ground catching robots in its claws, depositing them in something like a champing mouth that crushes, grinds, pulverizes, before dropping a small compressed cube of metal into its hold. Many more Crushers in the background do likewise. The pilot of the Crusher locates the next corroded robot in this global scrapyard. As he does so his boss radios him. Work faster. The contract must be completed in thirty days or the bonus will not be paid. What's more, the first settlers have arrived. Living space on the home planet – the green world we see in the sky – is so restricted that the terraforming of Vorada has been brought forward. Junked robots must be recycled into terraforming machinery. Time is of the essence. Faster. Faster.

INT. TARDIS. From the TARDIS the three see Vorada's surface on the monitor. A bleak vista of arid mountains, rusting junk. Robot skeletons. In this view, nothing moves.

The Master is appalled. *For once, my dear Doctor, I am profoundly grateful that I am unable to leave the TARDIS. For that is an unforgiving and desolate place in extremis.* Alison: *Huh, so you've never seen Stockport on a wet Sunday in March then?*

The Doctor is troubled. He knows that those who have exiled him have brought him here for a purpose. Leaving the TARDIS, he stands alone on a mountaintop to call out: *Why have you brought me to this place? There's nothing here. Tell me! What do you expect from me?*

Doctor! Look out! Alison throws herself at him as a Crusher darts toward them, mistaking them for robots. Together they tumble down the steep slope in a shower of debris. The Doctor is angry that she saved him. She shouldn't have endangered herself. Still dazed they pick themselves up to the sound of astonishing music in the distance. Harmonious electronic notes. A poignant melody suggesting loss. Alison thinks she's merely imagining the music after her fall. Now the Doctor begins to understand why he is here. This is a world of ineffable sadness. A tragedy unfolding. They head toward the source of the ghostly music, although he would have preferred it if Alison had returned to the protection of the TARDIS. On the way they pass an area where soft rock has crumbled away to reveal buried artifacts. A metal arm protrudes from the vertical rock face. Embedded beside that, a beautiful silver face. Alison is curious – too curious the protruding arm snaps into life, grabs her. The Doctor tries to pull her away; when he's almost face-to-face with the silver visage its eyes open and looks into his with soulful electronic eyes. With a heartfelt sigh, it whispers: *Ahhh… you are the one who has come… to bring us salvation…* The arm drops limp. The eyes close. Easily now the Doctor frees Alison, telling her these are discarded robots, but shrewdly she asks what the golden robot meant. The Doctor doesn't have the answer – yet.

They continue, encountering mystifying glimpses of machines that scuttle away before they can get near. The Master contacts the Doctor on his mobile to say that he has a mysterious visitor of his own, But then, before they can discuss it further...

CLIFFHANGER

What appeared to be a rock face lumbers forward. A huge robot, as high as an eight-story building, with limbs that serve as drills, bulldozers, backhoes. Though they don't know it yet they have encountered the abandoned quarry-robot, Gobble. It attacks.

Doctor Who theme music.

Episode Two

EXT. VORADA. Reprise cliffhanger from previous episode. Drills scream. Backhoes stab at the pair as they duck away. They escape, but after an exciting chase are captured by a gang of desperate robots. First robot: *They are here to steal our land. Kill them.* Second robot: *No.* The Doctor and Alison are massively relieved. But... Second robot: *We will disfigure them then return them to their camp. We will prove that we are not meek.* In the nick of time Pip intervenes, a handy-bot who is quirky, intelligent, optimistic, yet spectacularly unrealistic in his plans. They return to Gobble, the quarry-bot and enter the belly of the beast. Now the Doctor ponders their fate as Gobble crunches forward across the desert. Along with Gobble hundreds of other robots of this Diaspora of robotica move north.

Meanwhile back at the TARDIS. Meet Huspidor, in a previous life a window cleaner bot. He's taken a keen interest in the TARDIS. The Master invites him to clear off. After arguing, they strike up a conversation. Huspidor, now a philosopher of sorts, has interesting observations, and some tantalizing suggestions. How far can he tempt the Master? Will it lead to the Master rebelling against the Doctor's programming that prevents him from leaving the ship — or worse leaving WITH the ship when the Doctor isn't there?

Pip is dismissive of the robots that captured the Doctor and Alison. He knows they're not settlers. Pip: *These two are from out of town. Waaa-aay out of town.* In a Q&A the Doctor learns from Pip. Vorada is a huge scrapyard, that the 'humans' on the nearby planet have invaded to destroy the peace-loving robots. During this it is established that the mighty Gobble (before decommission, a rock-gobbling quarry-bot) and tiny, monkey-like Pip are a double-act. Deep emotional ties bind them. The indefatigable Pip refuels and repairs robots. Cares for those that are so decrepit that they have to ride in Gobble's labyrinthine interior. These are the Abandoned. Still proud, yet puzzled why they are on the scrap heap. This episode will introduce their day-to-day life as they migrate from the killing fields in their mistaken hope of finding a new Eden. We hear the thousand robotic floor polishers sing 'The Lament of the Obsolete'. Alison is touched when she sees the Doctor repair a decrepit robot that was hitherto considered *too far-gone*.

Pip is optimistic: *See Doctor, there is hope for the future. All we need is to be left in peace.*

INT. DEFLOE'S OFFICE. Defloe is administrator for the Regenerator Project. Well-mannered, well-educated, his is a controversial task. He is meeting the brusque B'rakk, the woman in charge of the Salvage Squads. The kind of gal that make men nervously cross their legs when they enter a room. She gives Defloe a progress report. He reminds her for the necessity for speed. The first settlers have arrived at their outposts. She's confident of ridding the world of junk robots soon. Defloe stresses: *I don't have to remind you how important it is that the public sees how humanely we deal with the robots. That brain loops and sensory inputs are deactivated before the robots are sent for processing.* B'rakk lies easily: *But of course. Every single robot is handled with complete sensitivity.*

EXT. VORADA. Cut away to scenes of robot slaughter. Mash 'em, chop 'em, squish 'em. You will believe a robot can bleed. Salvage Squads have a deadline: no time for the pain-free dismantling of fleeing robots.

INT. DEFLOE'S OFFICE. B'rakk reassures Defloe that the robots will be treated with mercy. He says *They better be.* Back on home planet there are massive demonstrations against terraforming Vorada. The population is under the delusion that their hardworking robots are retired here for a well-earned rest. Even B'rakk is surprised: *You mean they don't know this place is nothing more than a scrapyard?*

INT. TARDIS. Huspidor, still on the outside, discusses free will and housework with the Master. *Just how do you keep this vessel so clean? And any chance of a peep inside?* Huspidor will also speak wistfully of leaving this barren world for somewhere better. Escape is his passion.

INT. GOBBLE. The Doctor and Alison explore the interior of Gobble as it grinds across the landscape crushing rocks beneath its massive rollers. Pip explains as he does his rounds of the other robots that here in the northern region of Vorada they are relatively safe. Mainly, there are only advance Salvage scouts. Meanwhile he has unrealistic plans for Gobble to construct a vast underground city for the robots where they can live in peace. *Not in pieces*. Unlike the poor wretches being pulverized in the Southlands. But then everything changes. Gobble has seen a settlement. The other robots chant that it must be destroyed. The Doctor begs them not to attack. Innocent people might live there. They must consider the repercussions.

CLIFFHANGER

The mighty Gobble approaches the settlement buildings. The Doctor cries: *No! Stop this. People will die.* Gobble crunches through perimeter fences. Settlers flee.

Doctor Who theme music.

Episode Three

EXT. VORADA. Reprise cliffhanger from previous episode. Gobble ignores Doctor's cries and smashes buildings with its 'quarry limbs'. People flee in panic from collapsing shanty houses. Gobble corners fleeing men and women. He rolls forward to crush them, but the Doctor leaps from one of Gobble's hatches to stand there defiantly, hand raised: *STOP!* Pip orders Gobble to halt. The settlers are safe. The Doctor to Pip and Gobble: *You've just made a lot of people very angry. You must get away from here – and don't spare the horses!*

Once more the robots flee into the desert led by the huge Gobble. Pip says they should combat the invaders. Although they cannot fight them, despite all the robots' aggressive posturing suggesting otherwise. This is a salient point; robots are programmed to make them *absolutely* incapable of harming humans. Gobble could smash settlement buildings but he couldn't knowingly kill. But then there are legends of rogue robots who have attained free will and then harmed humans. So will these 'leopards' change their spots? The Doctor doesn't believe the people in the shanty camp were an invading army – merely frightened civilians. He needs more information. He talks to the Master by phone. But the Master sounds odd for some reason; nevertheless the Master agrees what is asked of him. Scan the world's broadcasts. Find out what's happening here.

INT. DEFLOE'S OFFICE. Defloe learns about the damage to the settlement outpost. B'rakk plays it down. An accident. B'rakk, however, is furious; she orders that the band of rebel robots be tracked down and destroyed. Why not tell Defloe the truth? Because the Salvage Squads are using illegal methods to destroy the robots before recycling. B'rakk: *Not only will we lose the contract, the government will sue the living daylights out of us.*

EXT. VORADA. The Master contacts the Doctor. This is no invasion. Rather a land reclamation scheme. The Doctor says there must be some way to talk to those in charge. With a superior tone the Master points out there is. *Doctor? Might I suggest your phone?* Patched through the Doctor speaks to Defloe: *You don't know me.* To which Alison pointedly responds under her breath: *Who does?* Mistaking the Doctor for some journalist from home planet, Defloe patiently repeats the official line. Home planet is over-crowded... Vital that there is room for expansion... Vorada must be terraformed... Every care is taken that the robots are closed down mercifully (oh how those debates have raged down through the centuries, even finding their way onto student exam papers: A ROBOT FEELS NO PAIN. DISCUSS). Rare metals in the robot bodies will be recycled into terraform machinery as there aren't enough reserves on Home Planet. The Doctor says he has vital information about the reclamation work. It's too important to discuss on the phone. They arrange to meet.

B'rakk prides herself knowing about what's important to her profession; she's listening in on the conversation. She must ensure this stranger and Defloe never meet.

CLIFFHANGER

The Doctor and Alison wait at the rendezvous point. A vessel approaches across the mountains. It is B'rakk. She will reach the Doctor before Defloe's ship. She watches the Doctor on her monitor, activates a system and suddenly the crosshairs of a weapon's sight appears on the Doctor's face. She breathes, *On my order, fire. Fire.* A blast of silver. The Doctor falls.

Doctor Who theme music.

Episode Four

EXT. VORADA. Reprise cliffhanger from previous episode. The Doctor lies unconscious on the ground. Alison examines the Doctor. He's still alive. And very wet. Pip tells her the weapon is merely a high-pressure water hose that the enemy uses to flush robots out of hiding places. Alison calls to waiting robots that accompanied her to help move the Doctor to safety. B'rakk's ship swoops down. Two arms that terminate in something like steel lobster claws extend from the ship. Bravely the robots fend them off, although one robot is snipped nearly in two. During the struggle Pip and a robot carry the Doctor to safety. B'rakk's monitor centres on Alison: *A human!* B'rakk exclaims. Not gently, but without injuring her B'rakk's pincer grabs her and brings her on board the ship.

INT. TARDIS. The Master is back in the wine cellar musing over wine. Robots can't lick their lips but he comes close. *Cotes Du Rhone. Humble but honest. Oh for tastebuds. Oh! For just one single tastebud.* Huspidor and the Master are still able to converse even though Huspidor is outside the TARDIS. They have talked about robotic duty and free will. The Master confesses he isn't free to do what he wishes. The Doctor has hard-wired inhibitions that prevent him from leaving the TARDIS. Even more powerful than that is a prohibition that will stop the Master from piloting the ship without the Doctor's consent. Huspidor postulates that it is possible to reprogram oneself, if only one is prepared to expend sufficient willpower. And if The Master could win his freedom, what would he do? Might he adopt Huspidor as a travelling companion? They could leave this planet for new worlds. The Master ogles bottles of champagne. Does he have the power to reconfigure the robotic brain that contains his mind? Moreover, add a sense of taste? In the Master's electronic brain the internal struggle has begun. Can the Master of old break free?

EXT. VORADA. Waves of salvage ships sweep down on robots. Alison, captive on the deck of the vessel pleads with B'rakk. The robots are sentient. They suffer. Have pity. B'rakk: *Have pity, my dear? I have a deadline. That's far more important.* She'll add that the 'fact' that robots don't feel pain.

INT. A CAVE. The Doctor is conscious; he's aghast that Alison has been taken. Alone, he now engages in a one way conversation with those who have exiled him. He senses they are there somehow listening. Maybe seeing. He talks about how he never intended to let people he cares about become endangered on his behalf. He asks what the exilers want from him. This is where the Doctor asks not only questions of THEM, but himself, a self-analysis. Did he do the right thing? Has he failed Alison? What is his purpose? A moving glimpse into the mysterious inner-landscape of the Doctor. We exit this scene perhaps none the wiser about the backstory but with a deeper emotional bond with the Timelord.

INT. B'RAKK'S CRAFT. Alison examines her situation, then step-by-step develops a plan. B'rakk hasn't reached the point of murder yet; instead she deliberates on some way of preventing Alison from revealing the Salvage Squads inhumane treatment of the robots. If news leaks out she will lose the contract, probably face litigation, too.

INT. TARDIS. The Master fiddles with the controls. Hesitates. Dare he take a trip on his own? Just a little one? We see an inner battle rage within the Master. His loyalty to the Doctor versus the old wicked impulses that the Doctor blocked when housing the Master's mind in android form. Meanwhile, Huspidor, the voice of temptation continues to sweet talk the Master. *Open the door. Go on, just a little bit. I just want a tincy wincey glimpse inside.*

EXT. VORADA. The Doctor trudges back to Gobble. *What now?* asks Pip. The Doctor tries his phone. The water has disabled it. He's alone.

INT. TARDIS. Huspidor pours honeyed words into the Master's ear via the intercom, while the Master wrestles with conscience and the Doctor's programming. *Why not try it? Try and do the thing you are programmed NOT to do.*

INT. B'RAKK'S CRAFT. Alison plays for time while she works on her plan. *Where are you taking me?* B'RAKK: *We have rescued you from the robots. Clearly the ordeal has left you confused. You need treatment at one of our field hospitals.* B'rakk will make sure that Alison talks to no one.

EXT. VORADA. The Doctor is gripped with indecision. What now? He can't contact the TARDIS or Defloe. The Salvage Squads are bearing down on the robots; soon there will be the final slaughter. On a crest he stands looking down at Gobble and the caravan of forlorn robots. Then at his lowest ebb he stiffens, an expression of revelation flares in his eyes. The Doctor breathes: *Of course.* Then: *Pip. Can you gather your robots together? There is something I have to ask of them.* A beat: *This is the time to stop running away.*

INT. TARDIS: On monitor Huspidor is cleaning the lens as he speaks. *You can take me for a little ride on your ship... if you really, really wanted to...* The Master continues his internal battle of wills. A robot can't perspire but we sense the fraught Master is close, then... Enough! Suddenly the 'old Master's' voice breaks out, booming. *I am the Master! I decide what I do. Where I go. For I am the Master of my destiny...* Laughs evilly in the Masterly way, then to camera. *And I am the Master of YOUR fate.* Touches a control. The TARDIS begins to dematerialise.

Doctor Who theme music.

Episode Five

INT. TARDIS. Reprise cliffhanger from previous episode. Then Master realizes the error of his ways. Crash stops dematerialization sequence. *No, This is not my nature. Not any more! I am a loyal friend of the Doctor.* Huspidor, disconcerted, points out that he thought he would be going for the ride too, thus escaping Vorada. The Master says he can no longer contact his friend, The Doctor. Huspidor's sulky now. *Not my problem.* The Master: *You need my help.* Huspidor disagrees, stressing he has free will, he has overcome his programming. The Master: *Just why is it then, you are cleaning the TARDIS's windows?*

EXT. GOBBLE. The Doctor, looking magnificent with hair streaming in the breeze; he stands four square on the huge robot, like a ship's captain standing on its prow. The machine surges across the desert. Gobble approaches a sea of robots then stops. The Doctor on his 'stage' declaims: *If you keep running you will be hunted to extinction. You must stand up to bullies. But that doesn't mean you attack them. War is for... losers. Go to Central Command. Talk to them. Prove that though you have bodies of steel you have the heart of a humane being!* Robots cheer. The long march begins.

INT. FIELD HOSPITAL. Alison is isolated in a room. But she's not beaten yet.

INT. TARDIS. The Master hacks into B'rakk's encoded communications. Quickly he assesses what's happening. B'rakk needs to move fast now she knows that the stranger intends to reveal her illegal methods regarding the robot cull. B'rakk plans to trigger an electron-bomb at noon tomorrow; it will wipe out the robot minds en-masse. It is illegal, and will damage government-owned infrastructure, but she realizes she can blame the robots in the light of their attack on the settlement. They foolishly triggered it, she will claim, not realizing the consequences. Then the robot problem on Vorada will be solved. The Master tells Huspidor that he needs the robots help. *I must get a message to my friend the Doctor.* Huspidor responds: *Leave it to me.*

EXT. VORADA. The spectacular march of the Abandoned. On the way they call to others to join them. Robots of all types stop what they're doing to emerge from hiding places to join the crusade.

Meanwhile Huspidor goes to the edge of the cliff to call out: *Message for the Doctor. Danger. Return to the TARDIS.* A robot in the valley hears the message, passes it on to the nest. We see the silver-faced robot again, embedded in the rock face. It opens its eyes, hearing the message. Then it calls out, passes the message on to an immobile vending machine covered in cobwebs, then on to an abandoned industrial pump... and so on...

Then night. Robots rest, refuel; squeaky joints are lubed. Compassionately, robots repair faulty comrades. The Doctor stands on Gobble's mighty back to survey this robot-scape, the mountains and a magnificent aurora borealis above them. From the distance comes a spine tingling sound. Akin to whale song, a call to lost souls. *What is that sound?* he asks Pip. Pip replies: *Those are the ancient ones – robots from before the dawn of time.* Doctor: *What is it they are saying?* Pip: *No-one knows. Nobody even sees them. But it is said that when lives are in danger we will hear their song.*

Meanwhile the robots pass on the refrain: *Message for the Doctor...*

INT. FIELD HOSPITAL. Alison makes contact with settlers forced to shelter here after Gobble trashed their buildings. They give her the other side of the story. Home world is desperately over-crowded. Famine looms. Couples aren't permitted to have children, unless they become settlers on Vorada. The junkyards must be cleared; what's more, the rare metals in the robots bodies are vital. They will be recycled into terraforming machines to green this arid world. Alison realises the magnitude of the dilemma.

Salvage squaddies ready the e-bomb. The countdown to detonation has begun.

The Doctor receives the Master's message. Return to the TARDIS. *How can I get back?* he asks. There is a way... but it's risky.

INT. FIELD HOSPITAL. The e-bomb is also there and Alison sees it being loaded onto B'rakk's ship. She escapes to stow away on board.

EXT. VORADA. We see the Doctor surfing on the back of an antiquated hover-bot that dashes crazily across the landscape. *Hurry, please hurry,* the Doctor urges. A Salvage Crusher lunges at him but the hover-bot evades it. Just. When the Doctor reaches the TARDIS the Master tells the Doctor of B'rakk's plans to detonate the e-bomb. The Doctor should be able use the TARDIS's own system to communicate with Defloe but B'rakk's anticipated this and is jamming the global communications, blaming rebel robots. There's no alternative. The Doctor must dash back to Pip and Gobble on the hover-bot. But is there time?

CLIFFHANGER

Racing back on the hover-bot, a wild surf across a cratered plain, near misses aplenty: the Doctor hears the call of the Ancients; mysterious lights shine in the mountains. The

Doctor makes a Holmes-like deduction. *Of course! Take me to the lights!* Then disaster. The hover-bot crashes.

Doctor Who theme music.

Episode Six

EXT. VORADA. Reprise cliffhanger from previous episode. The hover-bot is badly damaged. The Doctor lies dazed as the mysterious lights in the hills swoop down. They dance, then coalesce. A fabulous golden-eyed robot appears like a god, complete with a sunburst radiating from its head.

INT. TARDIS. Via the monitor the Master hears the eerie song of the Ancients. He asks Huspidor what the sound means. Huspidor: *Momentous events are at hand. Lives hang in the balance...*

EXT. VORADA. Formations of B'rakk's Salvage Squad in their formidable Crushers tear across the desert toward the robots.

Meanwhile the Doctor climbs to his feet. The golden-eyed robot shimmers. The Doctor eyes it shrewdly, then: *You, I believe, are one of the Ancients. I think it's time we had a little talk.*

INT. DEFLOE'S SHIP. He's heading for a humdrum meeting. Suddenly his ship is hijacked by an invisible force. It changes course, heading for the robots massed in the desert.

EXT. VORADA. The Doctor thanks the Ancients for diverting Defloe's ship. Their powers, when they choose to exercise them, are formidable. This meeting with Defloe is long overdue. He must speak face-to-face, as planet-wide communications are jammed.

INT. B'RAKK'S SHIP. She is exultant. All the robots are gathered together. The e-bomb can kill them all. She urges her squadrons ever faster. She must also deal with this intruder known as the Doctor.

EXT. VORADA. Pip knows that Salvage Squads are on their way. He sends out messages to delay the approach of the enemy to give the Doctor chance to return. As gymnasts can form a human pyramid the Abandoned on the plains create robotic pyramids in a bravely futile attempt to act as barriers to the Crushers. Most Crushers sweep through them, using their massive circular cutting discs, pincers and chainsaw limbs. But one heroic tower of robots hurl themselves onto a Crusher and take it down with them to smash on the desert floor. And...

The Ancients help the Doctor. Their powers restore the hover-bot; the Doctor surfs back to Pip and Gobble and the rest of the robots at lightning speed. He arrives before Defloe and B'rakk. Bemused, Defloe arrives in his hijacked craft. He sees a sea of seated robots in front of him. Defloe: *Why have you brought me here?* A rusting laundry-bot sighs, *To meet the Doctor.* Defloe calls out *Which one of you is the Doctor.* Protective of their guest one robot answers *I am the Doctor.* Yet another on a mound stands up, *No I am the Doctor.* Then another, *I am the Doctor.* And another in the background, *Don't listen to him, I am the Doctor.* Clanking, hundreds of robots stand, while calling out: *I am the Doctor.* The Doctor is touched but reveals himself.

INT. B'RAKK'S SHIP. Alison has managed to frustrate attempts to detonate the e-bomb. With the passion of the hunt upon her B'rakk hardly cares. She has her massed Crushers. When she sees the robots with Gobble rising up like an office block in the center, she yells out to her Squads to smash all the robots.

EXT. VORADA. The Doctor is explaining to Defloe that this salvage operation is the epitome of cruelty. Defloe will reply that living space is desperately needed by human beings. The bodies of the robots must be recycled to build terraforming machines.

Meanwhile, the Crushers swoop down. The Doctor leaps to stand in their way, his arms raised. They must go through him to reach the robots. Defloe joins him, hand held high. *Halt.* B'rakk knows she must pause. Briefly there's debate. What makes a human a human? Do sentient robots have rights? The need for living space v humane traits.

B'rakk tells Defloe to run from the robots before they harm him. But the Doctor says that's impossible, isn't it? Aren't all robots programmed with the one over-riding law that they can never harm a human? Defloe agrees. The Doctor leaps from one of Gobble's mighty limbs onto the back of one Crusher then another, using them as stepping stones to reach B'rakk's ship and so confront her.

Desperate now, B'rakk threatens to harm Alison. More argument where B'rakk will declaim that though she concedes robots can be *humane* they can never be *human*. The Doctor replies: *And does that apply to you?* The Doctor has made a significant deduction. He calls out, *B'rakk. Unmask!* Then repeats: *Unmask, unmask!* The assembled robots take up the chant. B'rakk once more threatens to kill Alison. Surprisingly, the Doctor invites her to do just that. We see Alison flinch as B'rakk looks as if she is about to pounce then she freezes. *Unmask! Unmask!* The chorus robotica continues. Alison understands. She seizes B'rakk's face, pulls. The human face breaks away to reveal a robot visage. Woe struck, B'rakk wails. *I am not a robot! I am human!* Defloe admits that their new line in robots that don't know they are robots has been a mistake. B'rakk can't over-ride her programming. She freezes.

But what of the dilemma? Defloe's people need Vorada. They need the rare metals in the robot bodies to build the machines that will turn this desolate place into a green world with rivers and oceans.

The Doctor calls out to the Ancients. The golden-eyed robot manifests itself in a sunburst of dazzling rays. The Doctor explains: The Ancients are indeed ancient robots. They abandoned their corroded bodies when they learnt to reformat this moon's natural magnetic field. Long ago they downloaded their minds into its complex magnetosphere to become incorporeal beings. The golden-eyed one adds that they have been studying the Abandoned robots for some time. They know of their humanity, their kindness to one another. How they have evolved into beings with human feelings and emotions. To feel pain. To suffer. Yet hope. The

Ancients have agreed among themselves it is time to invite the Abandoned to join them. Robotic minds will be downloaded into the magnetic field – Robo Heaven – where they will live in peace. No longer will their worn out bodies afflict them. Transmigration commences. One by one the robots droop. They are lifeless shells now.

Cut to Huspidor. Something is happening, he tells the Master, something wonderful. He is escaping from the planet at last. To the Master's dismay Huspidor appears to 'die'.

Meanwhile Alison is distraught, too, seeing this mass of dead metal. Cruel B'rakk hasn't been 'taken up'. An apologetic Defloe switches her off. The Doctor tells Defloe that now he has his raw materials for the terraforming machines, and new territories for his people.

The Doctor and Alison return to the TARDIS. They find the Master going out from the TARDIS. He is sad at the loss of Huspidor. The Doctor tells the Master and Alison not to mourn. They should rejoice that the robots are in a better place. *But where are they exactly?* Alison asks. The Doctor gazes up at the beautiful aurora that shines in the sky. *Up there.* Together they look up, and whether they hear or imagine it we don't know. But just for a moment we hear the voices of Huspidor, Pip and Gobble for one last time. They're delighted with their new improved incorporeal state. Huspidor is now truly free for the first time. *My friends, I do believe I'm happy... truly happy...*

The Doctor: *Something tells me they like their new home. Come on! Time and tide and all that...*

Satisfied by the outcome of this chapter in their lives they enter the TARDIS. It dematerializes. Once more talk turns to wine. *Have you ever tried a Martian Merlot?*

INT. RECYCLING UNIT. Cut to a close up of B'rakk, complete with unhinged face hanging askew. She groans weakly: *I am not a robot. I am not a robot.* Pull out. We see she lies on a conveyor belt that moves slowly, remorselessly, to a recycling hopper. Slowly the 'camera' rises directly above her, so B'rakk recedes and we see that hundreds of other lifeless robots lie end-to-end on the conveyor. She is the only one not to be elevated to Robo Heaven. The conveyor moves remorselessly. *Please, I'm not a robot.* B'rakk is bound for Robo Hell.

Doctor Who theme music.

THE END

BIBLIOGRAPHY

Books

Arnold, Jon, *Rose*. **The Black Archive** #1. Edinburgh, Obverse Books, 2016. ISBN 9781909031371.

Bucher-Jones, Simon, *Image of the Fendahl*. **The Black Archive** #5. Edinburgh, Obverse Books, 2016. ISBN 9781909031418.

Chapman, James, *Inside the TARDIS: The Worlds of Doctor Who – A Cultural History*. London, I B Tauris, 2006. ISBN 9781845111632.

Clapham, Mark, Eddie Robson and Jim Smith, *Who's Next: An Unofficial and Unauthorised Guide to Doctor Who*. London, Virgin Publishing, 2005. ISBN 9780753509487.

Colgan, Jenny T, *In the Blood*. **Doctor Who**. London, BBC Books, 2016. ISBN 9781785941108.

Cornell, Paul, *Timewyrm: Revelation*. **Doctor Who: The New Adventures**. London, Virgin Publishing Ltd, 1991. ISBN 9780426203605.

Cornell, Paul, *Scream of the Shalka*. London, BBC Books, 2004. ISBN 9780563486190.

Cornell, Paul, *A Better Way To Die*. NewCon Press, 2015, ISBN 9781907069840.

Cornell, Paul, *Who Killed Sherlock Holmes?* Tor Books UK, 2016, ISBN 9781447273264.

Cornell, Paul, Martin Day and Keith Topping, *Doctor Who: The Discontinuity Guide*. London, Virgin Publishing, 1995. ISBN 9780426204428.

Dicks, Terrance, *Timewyrm: Exodus*. **Doctor Who: The New Adventures**. London, Virgin Publishing Ltd, 1991. ISBN 9780426203575.

Dicks, Terrance, and Barry Letts, *Deadly Reunion*. **Doctor Who: The Eighth Doctor Adventures**. BBC Books, 2003. ISBN 9780563486107.

Guerrier, Simon, *Bernice Summerfield: The Inside Story*. Maidenhead, Big Finish Productions, 2009. ISBN 9781844352807.

Hickman, Clayton, ed, *The Doctor Who Annual 2006*. Tunbridge Wells, Panini, 2005. ISBN 9781904419730.

Hughes, William, *Historical Dictionary of Gothic Literature*. Lanham MD, Scarecrow Press, 2012. ISBN 9780810872288.

Lewis, CS, *The Lion, the Witch and the Wardrobe*. **The Chronicles of Narnia** #2. 1950. London, Fontana Lions, 1980. ISBN 9780006716631.

Millsted, Ian, *Black Orchid*. **The Black Archive** #8. Edinburgh, Obverse Books, 2016. ISBN 9781909031463

Miles, Lawrence, and Tat Wood, *1980-1984: Seasons 18 to 21*. **About Time: The Unauthorized Guide to Doctor Who** #5. Des Moines, Mad Norwegian Press, 2005. ISBN 9780975944646.

Parkin, Lance, and Lars Pearson, *Ahistory: An Unauthorised History of the Doctor Who Universe*. Third edition. Mad Norwegian Press, Des Moines, 2012. ISBN 9781935234111.

Peel, John, *Timewyrm: Genesys*. **Doctor Who: The New Adventures**. London, Virgin Publishing Ltd, 1991. ISBN 9780426203551.

Platt, Marc, *Lungbarrow*. **Doctor Who: The New Adventures**. London, Virgin Publishing Ltd, 1997. ISBN 9780426205029.

Purser-Hallard, Philip, *Dark Water / Death in Heaven*. **The Black Archive #4**. Edinburgh, Obverse Books, 2016. ISBN 9781909031401.

Rees, Dylan, *Downtime: The Lost Years of Doctor Who*. Edinburgh, Obverse Books, 2017. ISBN 9781909031425.

Ronson, Jon, *The Psychopath Test*. London, Picador, 2012. ISBN 9780330492270.

Periodicals

Doctor Who Magazine (DWM). Marvel UK, Panini, BBC, 1979-.

'Gallifrey Guardian: He's Back!'. DWM #336, cover date November 2003.

Cook, Benjamin, 'The DWM Interview: Steven Moffat', DWM #502, cover date September 2016.

Cook, Benjamin, 'No One Can Hear You Scream'. DWM #336, cover date November 2003.

Cook, Benjamin, 'Tooth and Claw'. DWM #360, cover date September 2005.

DWM, 'The Second Coming'. *Souvenir Special: 500 DWM Issues*. Issued with DWM #500, cover date July 2016.

Gray, Scott, Martin Geraghty and Robin Smith, *Wormwood*. DWM #266-71, cover dates July to November 1998.

Kibble-White, Graham, 'Doctor Who 2001'. DWM #500, cover date July 2016.

Roberts, Gareth, 'Guess Who?' DWM Special Edition, *The Doctor Who Companion Series One*, cover date August 2005.

Dinnick, Richard, 'The Forgotten Doctor'. *Doctor Who Insider* #9, January 2012.

'The Wilderness Years'. *In-Vision* #107, May 2003.

The Strand Magazine. George Newnes Ltd 1891-1950.

Television

Doctor Who. BBC, 1963-.

Scream of the Shalka. DVD release, 2013.

'Carry on Screaming'. DVD extra, 2013.

'Interweb of Fear'. DVD extra, 2013.

Elementary. CBS Television Studios, Timberman/Beverly Productions, Hill of Beans Productions, 2012-.

Encounters. BBC, 1992.

The Other Side, 1992.

Mighty Morphin Power Rangers. MMPR Productions Inc et al, 1993-95.

Quantum Leap. Belisarius Productions, Universal Television, 1989-93.

Red Dwarf. Grant Naylor, Baby Cow Productions, 1988-99, 2009, 2012-.

The Scarlet Pimpernel. BBC, 1999-2000.

Sherlock, Box TV, Castel Films Romania, Pueblo AG, 2002

Star Trek: Voyager. Paramount Network Television, 1995-2001.

Stargate SG:1. Double Secret Productions et al, 1997-2007.

Film

Coppola, Francis Ford, dir, *Bram Stoker's Dracula*. American Zoetrope, Columbia Pictures, Corporation, Osiris Films, 1992.

Fisher, Terence, dir. *Dracula*. Hammer Films, 1958.

Nyby, Christian, dir, *The Thing from Another World*. RKO Radio Pictures, Winchester Pictures Corporation,1951.

Audio CD

Clement, Jonathan, *Immortal Beloved*. Big Finish Productions, 2007.

Meek, Colin, *Doctor Who: Death Comes to Time*. BBC Radio Collection, 2002.

Scott, Cavan, and Mark Wright, *Project: Twilight*. Big Finish Productions, 2001.

Web

BBC **Doctor Who** website. http://www.bbc.co.uk/doctorwho/. Accessed 23 October 2016.

'Does Doctor Who have a future as an animated series?' 21 December 2001. Preserved at the Internet Archive. http://web.archive.org/web/20011222134643/http://www.bbc.co.uk/cult/doctorwho/features/animation.shtml. Accessed 15 January 2017.

Real Time. Webcast. BBC, 2002.
http://www.bbc.co.uk/doctorwho/classic/webcasts/realtim
e/. Accessed 23 October 2016.

Shada. Webcast. BBC, 2003.
http://www.bbc.co.uk/doctorwho/classic/webcasts/shada/.
Accessed 23 October 2016.

Scream of the Shalka. Webcast. BBC, 2003.
http://www.bbc.co.uk/doctorwho/classic/webcasts/shalka/.
Accessed v.

'BBC Unveils Doctor Who – The Adventure Games'. BBC Press
Office, 8 April 2010.
http://www.bbc.co.uk/pressoffice/pressreleases/stories/2010/04_
april/08/doctor_who.shtml. Accessed 29 October 2016.

'Grant takes on Doctor Who role'. BBC News, 10 July 2003
http://news.bbc.co.uk/1/hi/entertainment/3054539.stm. Accessed
29 October 2016.

Cult Presents... Sherlock Homes. BBC, 2005.
http://www.bbc.co.uk/cult/sherlock/index.shtml. Accessed 5
December 2016.

Cornell, Paul, 'The Deer Stalker'. BBC, 2005.
http://www.bbc.co.uk/cult/sherlock/deerstalker1.shtml.
Accessed 5 December 2016.

Cult Vampire Magazine. BBC, 2004.
www.bbc.co.uk/cult/vampires/index.shtml. Accessed 23 October
2016.

Scott, Cavan, and Mark Wright, 'Doctor Who: The Feast of the Stone'. BBC, 2004. http://www.bbc.co.uk/cult/vampires/newstory/scottwright.shtml. Accessed 23 October 2016.

Bahn, Christopher, 'Doctor Who (Classic): *Scream of the Shalka*'. AV Club, 21 December 2013. www.avclub.com/tvclub/scream-of-the-shalka-106395. Accessed 23 October 2016.

Berriman, Ian, 'The Simon Clark Story That Never Was'. Games Radar, 9 September 2013. http://www.gamesradar.com/doctor-who-the-simon-clark-story-that-never-was/. Accessed 12 November 2016.

Fitch, Alex, 'Book List: Novelising **Doctor Who**'. Resonance FM Podcast, 12 December 2013. http://podcasts.resonancefm.com/archives/11660. Accessed 23 October 2016.

Harris, Lee, 'Back to School with Paul Cornell's *Chalk*'. http://www.tor.com/2015/11/11/back-to-school-with-paul-cornells-chalk/. Accessed 28 October 2016.

Office for National Statistics, 'Internet Access – Households and Individuals: 2013'. http://www.ons.gov.uk/peoplepopulationandcommunity/household characteristics/homeinternetandsocialmediausage/bulletins/inter netaccesshouseholdsandindividuals/2013-08-08. Accessed 23 October 2016.

Ortiz, Julio Angel, 'Throwback Interview: Paul Cornell, 2002. https://jaowriter.com/2014/08/28/throwback-interview-paul-cornell-2002/. Accessed 29 October 2016.

Sandifer, Philip, 'You Were Expecting Someone Else 19 (Scream of the Shalka)'. Eruditorum Press, 2013. http://www.eruditorumpress.com/blog/you-were-expecting-someone-else-19-scream-of-the-shalka/. Accessed 23 October 2016.

Scoones, Paul, 'Scream of the Shalka DVD Production Subtitles. http://paulscoones.blogspot.co.uk/2013/09/scream-of-shalka-dvd-production.html. Accessed 29 October 2016.

Sullivan, Shannon Patrick, 'Doctor Who: The Lost Stories'. http://www.shannonsullivan.com/drwho/lost.html. Accessed 23 October 2016.

BIOGRAPHY

Jon Arnold is the author of *The Black Archive #1: Rose* and the co-editor of *Shooty Dog Thing: 2th and Claw* and *Me and the Starman*. He has contributed to 11 essay collections including *Hating to Love* and *Outside In*, and to innumerable fanzines and websites such as *The Two Unfortunates* and *We Are Cult*. His fiction has appeared in *Shelf Life, Seasons of War, Terrors of the Theatre Diabolique, Secret Invasion: Tales of Eldritch Horrors from the West Country* and *A Time Lord for Change*. He's also an occasional contributor to the Reality Bomb podcast. He lives in Belfast with his wife and son.

THE REUNION

M. A. HUNTER

Boldwood

For Parashar and Anthony: friends for over 30 years.

First published in Great Britain in 2024 by Boldwood Books Ltd.

Copyright © M. A. Hunter, 2024

Cover Design by 12 Orchards Ltd

Cover Photography: Shutterstock

The moral right of M. A. Hunter to be identified as the author of this work has been asserted in accordance with the Copyright, Designs and Patents Act 1988.

A CIP catalogue record for this book is available from the British Library.

Paperback ISBN 978-1-83561-722-9

Large Print ISBN 978-1-83561-721-2

Hardback ISBN 978-1-83561-720-5

Ebook ISBN 978-1-83561-723-6

Kindle ISBN 978-1-83561-724-3

Audio CD ISBN 978-1-83561-715-1

MP3 CD ISBN 978-1-83561-716-8

Digital audio download ISBN 978-1-83561-719-9

This book is printed on certified sustainable paper. Boldwood Books is dedicated to putting sustainability at the heart of our business. For more information please visit https://www.boldwoodbooks.com/about-us/sustainability/

Boldwood Books Ltd, 23 Bowerdean Street, London, SW6 3TN

www.boldwoodbooks.com

PROLOGUE

Oh, God, what have I done? He literally came out of nowhere. It all happened so quickly, and yet as if in slow motion as well. I didn't mean to hit him, but there wasn't time to swerve. No time to think. I didn't even apply the brake until after the collision but by then it was already too late.

This can't be happening. It must be a bad dream; just a seriously fucked up nightmare. I'm not really here. No, I'm fast asleep at home where I'm safe and not behind the wheel of this fucking deathmobile.

I slowly open my eyes, hoping I'll see the familiarity of the curtains and picture frames on my bedroom wall, but all I see is the dark night sky, and the mist beyond the bumper that the headlights can't penetrate and are being slowly swallowed by.

I don't need to get out of the car to know he's dead. In fact, if I don't get out then it's almost like it hasn't happened. There's no sight of him beyond the end of the bonnet, thankfully, but I can feel his presence on the road beneath the ever-growing blanket of fog. I lift myself slightly higher in the seat but can't see his body.

What was he doing out here in the pitch black anyway? He

wasn't wearing anything reflective, just that dark overcoat, so how was I supposed to know he was there? It wasn't my fault if I couldn't see him. He shouldn't have been out here, at this ungodly hour, so I shouldn't be the one to take the blame. But then, I shouldn't be out here either.

Oh, God, what is everyone going to say when they realise what I've done? Will they think I did it deliberately? Because that definitely isn't true. I didn't mean to hit him.

I didn't mean to hit him.

If I say it often enough, maybe it will feel truer.

I didn't mean to hit him.

I repeat the phrase over and over, ignoring the tiny voice at the back of my mind that asks if I'm sure.

And what will the police think? Will they question my motivation as well? Will they think it was an act of revenge? Will they drag up my history and use it against me? Will they call me unstable like so many others have before?

This will be the end for me. Arrested, charged, sentenced. A life flushed down the toilet, and for what? I don't gain from him being dead. It's not like I went out and stole money to benefit myself financially. It's not like I cheated on my taxes. Yes, I've killed him, but I didn't mean to. That has to count for something.

But that voice in the back of my head is getting louder. It's saying that I do benefit from his death; that it wasn't simply an accident.

And that is what everybody else is going to think too.

Oh, God, if I could turn back time then I would. I wouldn't get behind the wheel. I wouldn't have driven to this particular spot on this dark and uneven road. I would do it *all* again differently, if you'd just give me the chance to start over. To turn to a fresh page, one that isn't covered in the blood of an innocent man.

My eyes widen as my mind focuses in on that point.

He *wasn't* an innocent man.

So, it would be wrong for me to be penalised for his death. Maybe this is what God or fate or some other unknown force wanted. Maybe they set our paths on a collision course and there was nothing I could have done to avoid being in this seat, in this car, on this road, at this time. So if this accident was inevitable, it wasn't my fault. I am nothing but a pawn in someone else's twisted game.

So, I shouldn't have to suffer. I shouldn't take the blame for something beyond my control.

I shouldn't phone the police. What I need to do is get out of here. There are no witnesses who will place me behind the wheel of the car, and if I act quickly and keep my mouth shut there is no reason anyone should ever find out what really happened here.

I just need to keep quiet. And run.

1

ZOË

They say the bonds made between friends during university are the ones that stay strongest for the longest, and yet none of the people I've met and befriended since school know me as well as Lily, Dan and Rod. We were virtually inseparable from that first summer break when the air was hot and dry, and the holidays seemed to last forever.

Everything was so much simpler back then.

We were equals.

But, of course, nothing ever stands still; life happens and it's how each of us adapt that determines who we'll be, and what we'll stand for. And if a friendship can withstand the shit that puberty drags with it, well, then you could almost argue that that's a relationship forged in blood.

In our case, it really is.

My stomach turns with fluttering butterflies, as I stand on the corner studying each windscreen as cars pass by left and right. It's been more than two years since I last met up with Lily at my surprise fortieth birthday party. I have been so busy with work, and the regular daily commute between Winchester and London is taking a toll; on my mental health as well as my marriage. And although Lily and I have been messaging for weeks about this gathering, I can't escape the feeling that she's probably also changed in that time; I know I certainly have. My face definitely isn't as smooth as it once was and I'm now paying to have the emerging greys hidden like all the other secrets I don't want anyone else to know.

I can't just blame my job and marriage counselling for why I haven't made more of an effort to come and visit Lily up here. Seeing her at my birthday brought all the memories of that night flooding back, and all the barriers I have spent years building fell in an instant. I almost messaged last night to feign illness and back out of the weekend, but with everything going on at home, this seemed the lesser of two evils. I need space from Evan *and* Tim. I almost pull out my phone to check for further messages, but will myself not to. The point of heading north was to give myself a break from all of that, and although my mountain of problems will still be there when I get home, I have three days to develop a strategy to deal with it.

I chase thoughts of Evan's last message from my mind's eye, and turn back to the free-flowing traffic. Lily said she would be driving her dad's old 4x4, but neglected to share the make, model, colour, or registration number. I could have asked, but I wanted to test our intuitive bond; if I can guess which car is hers before she actually pulls over, then maybe there's still a chance for us.

A road trip to the Scottish Highlands in early October sounded absurd when Rod suggested it, but it isn't every day one of your oldest friends is set to get married in the large manor he inherited from his recently deceased mother. The last time I spoke to him, he said that money and title are more of a burden than most realise, and I told him to pull his head out of his arse.

Why is it the most privileged don't even realise how easy they have it?

The Yorkshire wind whips at the hair I spent hours washing, conditioning, and straightening this morning. I dread to think what it looks like now; definitely not the chic and professional solicitor image I was hoping to convey. I guess my appearance won't be as deceptive as I'd hoped.

I pull the long red overcoat around my middle and fasten the large black button. There is rain in the air, as the dark clouds gather overhead, and given I didn't pack an umbrella, or my regular waterproof ski jacket, I really hope Lily arrives before I have to go searching for shelter. I think through the four new outfits packed in the cabin case, one for each day we're due to be away, including a spare just in case. I tried on each outfit, removed the tags, and then had them drycleaned so it won't appear like I've gone to any great lengths for this trip. It's the first time we're all meeting up as a group in more than a decade, and I want them to see that I've finally put the past behind me and have moved on with my life. Hopefully, they'll buy the lie.

I have stuck to the pact we swore that night beneath the canopy of trees, despite how painful and difficult it was. I stuck to the story, and eventually the police stopped asking awkward questions and I left Wakefield, escaping to Southampton for the safety of a fresh start at university. I do wonder whether they all obsess over what happened when the night is darkest and they're alone. Do the ghosts visit them too?

I start at the honking of a horn, and as I look up, trying to determine where the sound emanated from, I see a dark Land Rover caked in mud indicating. The windscreen is misted up, so it's difficult to see who's behind the wheel, but as the vehicle pulls to a stop at the kerb, and the window lowers, I can't help smiling at the brown eyes of Lily beaming back at me. They're not quite as bright as I remember, and there's something else about her appearance that is different, but I really can't place exactly what it is. She's wearing a strappy vest, despite the cold climate, and as I open the passenger door and pull myself in, the hot air pumping out of the dashboard fan has me quickly tearing off my overcoat. I've barely sat down when Lily is pulling me into her arms.

'Fuck me, it's good to see you, Zo,' she says, dropping the last letter of my name as she always has.

'It's so good to see you too,' I whisper back as our cheeks collide, and she squeezes just a little too tight.

'I can't believe you're really here, and still looking as stunning as you ever did.'

She slowly releases her grip and we just stare at each other for a moment. Her face is free of make-up, but she looks so young and fresh that I wouldn't have guessed she was the one with the stressful career that she mentioned in her last message.

She's about to speak again, when another car horn blares as a driver narrowly avoids careering with the front wing. Lily slams her hand down on the central console of the tired-looking steering wheel.

'Fuck you too, pal,' she shouts back, though I doubt the other driver will have heard.

I don't mention that she's illegally parked on a main carriageway, and instead pull my seat belt around me and lock it in place to show I'm ready for the road trip to commence; even though I'm struggling to shake off the feeling of dread about this whole weekend.

I glance into the back, and although the cabin seems spacious, there is little by way of boot space, so Dan is going to have to squeeze in with the cases. I hoist mine into the well behind my chair as Lily pulls back into the flow of traffic.

'Do you remember this car?' she asks me after a few seconds.

'Should I?'

'Do you not remember? Oh my God, I was sure you would. When I asked my dad if I could borrow the old wagon for our trip, he told me I should make sure I pack a sick bag for you.'

In a flash I see the two of us in tight mini dresses stumbling out of the formal prom when I was sixteen and seeing Lily's dad waiting in a layby for us in this car. We'd been drinking the vodka Dan had smuggled into the event, and we were both wasted. But it was so warm and bouncy in the car that I ended up vomiting over the mat between my legs.

My cheeks burn with embarrassment.

'Oh, Jeez, I'd forgotten about that. Is he still angry after all this time?'

Lily bursts out laughing. 'Of course not. He was only teasing. I remember it took months before the smell finally faded, but I reckon if you put your nose down by the carpet you'd still be able to smell it.'

I gag at the memory.

'That was the night you and Dan formally declared your love for one another,' Lily continues, oblivious to my own discomfort. 'Do you remember we ducked out of the prom early and walked around the woods until the two of you found that tree stump and carved your names into it?' She pauses at the memory, her face glazing over in reminiscence. 'I thought you two would be together forever.'

So did I, I think, but don't say.

'We were just a couple of dumb kids,' I say instead.

'True, but what the two of you had seemed pretty special, especially from the outside. Have you spoken to him much recently?'

I shake my head.

'It's been a while, actually. He's been busy with work, and we're on very different career paths now.'

'Still, I bet Dan hasn't given up hope of the two of you rekindling what you had.'

'I'm sure he's moved on,' I say firmly, and I really hope he has. 'Besides, I'm married, as he might also be.'

I'm not in a place where I want a permanent reminder of what happened before I left for university; though at least things were simpler with Dan than they are with Tim. And Evan. I inwardly cringe at the mess I now find myself in. I tried to justify Evan based on my suspicions that Tim was having an affair, but was it more than that? It was exciting being coveted by someone younger, and although I knew it didn't have a future, I wanted to remember what it was to be lusted after. I have yet to reply to his last message, and am in no hurry to do so. He can stew this whole weekend as far as I'm concerned. In fact, maybe I should post a picture of me and Dan on my socials, so Evan finally gets the message.

'Too much water has passed under that bridge,' I add.

'Good for you! It's going to be so weird seeing the old gang all back together though, isn't it? Did you read *Lord* Rod's invitation?' She chuckles. 'Like he wasn't already rich enough, now he's inheriting the family title as well as the country estate. How the other half live.'

It's moments like this that always remind me of the different upbringings we had. Whilst my teacher dad and nurse mam took early retirement and spend almost half their time holidaying overseas, Lily's dad and stepmam still run a pub in Wakefield. There's never been an obvious class divide between us, but I do sometimes forget that life was that bit tougher for Lily.

'Do you know much about the woman he's marrying?' I ask to lighten the mood.

'Only that her name is Bella and their romance has been a whirlwind. I didn't even know he was seeing anyone until she tagged him in a post on social media, declaring the engagement.'

'Yeah, I saw that too,' I say, unable to hide my concern. 'Several years younger than him too.'

'Surely that doesn't surprise you, though? Rod was never the most mature of the group.'

It's a fair point.

'We can ask him all about her, as we're due to collect him from Leeds Bradford Airport next.'

'He's coming with us?'

She nods with excitement.

'I assumed he'd be meeting us at his new manor,' I continue.

'He said it's not easy to get to, and GPS signal can be a bit intermittent. He suggested we all travel together so we all arrive safely in one piece. It's going to be just like the old days, apart from the fact that I'll be driving instead of one of our parents.'

I'd been looking forward to spending time with Lily, and it was shock enough when she messaged this morning to ask if it was okay if Dan tagged along with us, but now Rod too? Any hope I'd had of trying not to think about those final days in sixth form are about to be crushed once and for all.

2

ZOË

It takes forty-five miles of tail-to-tail traffic and stilted conversation until we make it to Leeds Bradford Airport. My hope that Lily and I would just fall back into the old routine was clearly misplaced. And maybe that's the real reason we haven't caught up in person since my birthday. I'm not the same doe-eyed girl that left Yorkshire twenty-three years ago. I've had to become more cutthroat to survive in my professional and personal life, and that means we've naturally drifted apart.

Lily remained living at her parents' pub while she completed her course in creative writing at Sheffield Hallam University, commuting the thirty-mile distance each day via train in order to keep the costs down. But that isn't to say that her experience of student life was massively different to my own, so if I've grown up then so has she, so it was naïve of me to expect things to be as they always were. And if they're this stilted with my best friend, how bad are they going to be with Rod? And worse still Dan, who has spent the last two decades running the family business after his dad's stroke and eventually passing. Can we really spend the next three days just reliving old memories? I'm worried that will soon get boring.

'My dad said we need to follow the signs to the short-stay car park,' Lily narrates, as she pulls into the corresponding lane. 'He said they have cameras everywhere and fine drivers for stopping too long.'

It's a typical example of how the dialogue has played out, with Lily regularly quoting her dad and stepmam as we've battled the traffic. I'd never realised just how much of an influence they have on her. I want to grab her by the shoulders and demand to know what her opinion is on matters, rather than listening to her regurgitate their words. But maybe she was always like that. Or maybe I am just being overly judgemental because I'm projecting my own inadequacies.

My phone buzzes in my hand, and as I stare down at another message from Evan, my skin crawls. Here's me judging my friend when my own life is far from well-structured and flying. I knew it was the right call ending things with Dan before I left for university, because the distance would be too great and too big a demand on both of us, but I didn't rush out for a slew of one-night stands. Lectures in Property Law, Contracts, and Constitutional Law were a huge step up from what I was used to in sixth form, and for those first four months I could barely keep my head above water. It seemed so much easier for everyone else, as if they'd been given a handbook of how much time to spend in the library, and how to provide the professors with the answers they sought. And trying to cram an education in with being sociable took a toll.

There were plenty of offers in that first year, but I didn't hook up with anyone until the final term. Paolo grew up in Rome, had floppy jet-black hair, and his accent used to make the hairs on the back of my neck stand on end. He wooed me for weeks until I finally caved, and invited him back to mine, but caught him sneaking out just after two, and then he refused to return any of my calls. I later learned he'd only chased me as part of a bet with another girl in my halls who thought I 'had a stick up my arse'.

I remember thinking a lot about Dan in the weeks that followed, wondering whether I'd been foolhardy in ending things with him. He'd always treated me well, practically worshipped the ground on which I walked, and had never made any demands of me. It was only after I'd let him go that I realised not all boys and men are quite so attentive and well mannered. I came so close to phoning and begging for another chance, but I resisted, and ploughed myself into my studies instead.

And then eventually I met Tim, a blind date set up by a mutual acquaintance. He couldn't do enough for me, and I hate to say I settled, but I definitely refocused my priorities. As a teacher, his salary was never going to be great, but I could see myself growing old with him, even though he is more like my dad than either of us care to admit. Our inability to conceive has been laid firmly at his door – the various GP tests confirmed it – and things grew cold as he blamed himself. We considered adoption, but we haven't progressed past a few snatched conversations.

And so when Evan started paying me extra attention, I allowed myself to get carried away with the notion that I am still young enough to pull. If I'd known what a conniving bastard he really was, I wouldn't have looked twice. And now he's sent me a still taken from the security camera in the boardroom at work. If the senior partners see this, I'll be kicked out of the door and my reputation will be in ruins. This latest message is another reminder of how bad I am at judging character.

'Is that Rod checking where we are?' Lily asks, glancing over at my phone.

I quickly lock the screen.

'No, just a work thing. I'm not sure I have Rod's number any more.'

She takes a ticket at the barrier and pulls into a parking space near the lift, and ten minutes later we are standing at the arrivals gate, trying to work out whether Rod's flight from Amsterdam has landed yet. There's certainly no sign of him in either of the cafés, which is where Lily tells me she told him to wait. I head to the information desk and learn that the plane has landed and the luggage has been loaded onto the conveyor, so presumably he should be through the doors in the next few minutes. I head back to where Lily is standing by the barrier near the arrivals doors, but stop when I see she is on the phone.

'You know how much I miss you, darling,' I hear her say into the phone.

She didn't mention that she's been seeing anyone, so I'm surprised, but pleased for her.

'I told you: I'll be away until Monday night... Yes, I promise I will wake you the moment I'm back and show you just how much I've missed you.'

I shouldn't be surprised that Lily has fallen in love, because she is gorgeous and a kind soul, and deserves every happiness. I guess I'm still seeing her as that geeky teenage sidekick who had no interest in boys when we were in school and sixth form. Given how much I can see that I've changed, I shouldn't be surprised that she's blossomed as well.

'Listen, I'd better go,' she says when she catches me hovering. 'I'll try and call you again tomorrow. I love you.'

I smile awkwardly, as heat rises to her cheeks.

'That was...' she begins, but I wave both my hands in front of my face.

'None of my business,' I say, cutting her off. 'I'm pleased for you.'

The truth is I'm more than a little envious that she's found someone who makes her smile as she is right now. It was never like that with Evan, and I never fell in love with him, much to my relief now. Anyone who sends threatening messages is not worthy of my time, nor my love. I need to put him out of my mind for the next three days, and then I can worry about how I extract him from my life once and for all when I get back to Winchester.

'Oh, hey, I meant to show you this when I collected you,' she says, reaching inside her denim jacket and sliding out an A5 photograph, handing it to me. 'I found it when going through some of my old bits and pieces.'

It's a picture of the *five* of us. We are sitting beside a roaring fire, tinsel hanging from the ceiling, and the edge of a Christmas tree behind Rod. I remember it was taken at Saul's house, and there he is front and centre, full of life as he always was.

I am sitting on Dan's lap in an armchair, Rod is gurning at the camera and Lily is toasting the lens with a flute of bubbly. It may even have been the last picture of us all together. We all look so happy. *I* look so happy, with Dan's arms around my waist. I attempt to pass it back to Lily, but she tells me to keep it, saying she made a copy.

I can't take my eyes off Dan's face, feeling a surge of emotions that I haven't felt in a long time. It's going to be weird seeing him in person again, and I've no idea how much he will have changed. I follow his socials, but he doesn't post much, aside from the occasional advert for the plumbing business, but he hasn't posted a picture of himself in several years. Will the skin around his nose still bunch up when he laughs? Will the dimple in his cheek still be there when he smiles?

I need to stop thinking about him in this way. I need to

remember that the distance between our addresses wasn't the only reason we broke up. The gulf between us started forming after that night with Saul, and I don't need a permanent reminder of what happened, which is exactly what Dan will be.

No, the best thing for me will be to learn that Dan is spoken for. He could be married and settled with children by now for all I know. He threw himself into the family business after his dad's stroke, more through necessity than desire. He was all that stood between the business failing and his parents losing their home. As I understand it from Lily, he's the sole breadwinner in the household, as his mam now needs 24/7 care herself. So, even if he still has a spark for me after all this time, the distance between us will still be an insurmountable hurdle.

We have been watching the doors for several minutes, as people have emerged in flurries, but when they next open, we hear Rod before we see him.

'Ladies and gentlemen, please welcome back to the UK, Lord Roderick of Astor,' his voice bellows, and a moment later I see him advance through the doors, arms astride, a large pair of sunglasses covering much of his face.

He is dressed in a full tartan kilt, sporran, Prince Charlie jacket, and brogues. For someone who previously ignored his family heritage, he seems to have embraced it since learning the trust protecting the estate of Tarbert was set to end following his mother's passing.

'Och aye, and all that jazz,' he calls out when he spots us behind the barrier, in one of the worst attempted Scottish accents I've ever heard.

He hurries over and puts his large arms around the pair of us.

'As always I am the rose between two thorns,' he teases, stepping back and taking in our appearance. 'What, no welcome sign for the new lord? No brass band to serenade my return?'

'I'm very sorry, your lordship,' I play along, curtsying. 'Welcome home.'

He kisses our cheeks, and ducks beneath the barrier so he can hug us both properly.

'You're late,' Lily points out.

'Aye, there was a wee problem at Customs. Long story short, let's just say it's lucky they only checked my case, and didn't insist on a full-body search, if you catch my drift,' he adds with a wink.

'We should get going,' I say, even though I'm dreading spending any longer in the car than is necessary.

'Before we do,' Rod cautions, holding up a finger, 'may I introduce the future Mrs Astor?'

He half-turns and behind him is standing a young blonde woman dressed in a designer suit with matching handbag and enormous sunglasses. She's about average height, pretty, but not the catwalk-model looks I imagined would catch Rod's eye.

She proffers a hand that Lily and I take it in turns to shake, while Rod introduces us.

'It's so wonderful to meet you both,' she says, her accent difficult to place.

'You're American?' I ask, hoping I haven't just offended a native of Canada.

'That's right. From Manhattan originally but I've lived all over. Army brat.'

'I hadn't realised Bella would be joining us on this trip,' Lily says now. 'It's going to be a tight squeeze in the back.'

Rod waves away her concern.

'We'll be fine, won't we, darling?'

He leans in to kiss her, and I can't help feeling like she's not expecting it but isn't fast enough to move out of the way. Maybe I'm just imagining it, but something doesn't quite feel right about them.

I offer to pull one of the cases as we head out through the automatic doors in the direction of the car. I thought it would be a tight enough squeeze for Dan and the suitcases, but now with Rod and Bella joining too, it's going to be even more crammed. I'm glad I bagged the front seat.

3

ZOË

I pay for the parking ticket when Rod and Bella don't offer to, as it isn't fair for Lily to be lumbered with the cost on top of driving. Rod certainly has more money than the rest of us, but he's never been one to dip his hand into his own pocket voluntarily. I know it isn't that he's tight, he just never thinks about the challenges that come with not having money. He's always had it, and never had to worry about making ends meet, so it isn't in his nature to think of it that way. We'll have to come up with a plan for diesel when we next need to fill up, and I'll have a quiet word, so he knows we all need to contribute.

'Oh my God, it even looks like that shit-heap your dad used to drive,' Rod marvels when we make it back to the Land Rover. 'I don't know where you got it from, but you've hit nostalgia on the head. Bravo!'

'That's because it really is my dad's old car,' Lily says, with more than a hint of pride. 'He said I could borrow it for the weekend.'

'No fucking way! Well, then it's the perfect chariot for us to ride in as we descend on Tarbert.'

'You could have had it washed first,' I hear Bella mutter under her breath, as she examines the dried mud clinging to the tyres and bodywork.

Thankfully it doesn't appear that Lily heard.

'This is exactly what we're going to need,' Rod continues. 'Some of the hills we're going to encounter need the oomph of four-wheel drive. It's perfect, Lily.'

I open the front passenger door and begin to climb in when I hear Bella audibly tut.

'Who says you get to sit in the front?' she scowls in her American accent. 'Shouldn't we draw straws or something?'

'Oh, my stuff's already in the front,' I reply, trying desperately to maintain an even tone, 'and given you only know Rod, I figured you'd want to sit nearest to him.'

I roll my eyes in Lily's direction to release some of the tension in my shoulders.

'Quite right too,' Rod echoes, slapping the top of the car. 'Bella, get in and stop making a fuss. You can travel in the back with me.'

I can feel her stare burning a hole in the back of my head, but I ignore it as I climb in and pull the door closed. I think I'm starting to understand why Rod didn't mention earlier that his fiancée would be joining us on the trip.

The echo of three other doors closing, and then we're off. I open my window as the windscreen begins to steam up. I can see Bella silently mouthing her disgust at Rod from the mirror in the sun visor, and once again I find myself questioning why I agreed to make this trip. I should be back home in Winchester sorting out the mess of my marriage with Tim. Nobody has asked me yet why I haven't brought him as my plus one. The official line is that he couldn't get today off work, but I don't want the others to see just how frosty things have become between us.

'So, what's the craic with the two of you then?' Rod says, sitting forward so his face is between the gap in the front seats.

'Rod, you need to be belted in,' Lily warns.

'Pish! My old man would have told you they didn't have seat belts in the early cars, and they don't really provide much safety in the event of a pile-up anyway. Relax!'

'Actually, Lily could be prosecuted for driving while one of her passengers isn't wearing a seat belt,' I chime in, knowing it won't make any difference, but wanting to lend my support.

'Yeah, yeah, well, I promise I'll put my belt on, as soon as you tell me who you've been shagging, and whether any of them will live up – or down, as the case may be – to our good friend Daniel. I notice you haven't brought hubby with you, Zoë. Is this a hint that you might be looking to relive old times with Dan?'

My cheeks burn in an instant, but I don't turn to face Rod, hoping he won't notice. So much for me believing Rod's inheriting the family title and estate would lead to greater maturity.

'My husband had to work,' I say firmly, hoping that will be the end of it.

'And you, sweet Lily, have you found *the one* yet?'

'Too busy with work,' she fires back in a heartbeat, and I can't blame her for wanting to keep the topic of her love life off the table.

'What, nobody since you and—'

'No!' she screams, the car swerving as she momentarily loses concentration, before straightening.

I look over to Lily to check if she's okay, but her eyes remain firmly glued to the road ahead.

'Why don't you tell us how the two of you met?' I say, turning the focus on him, his favourite subject.

He sits back, and fastens his seat belt as promised, though he is occupying the middle seat beside Bella, so it does little to restrain him.

'Do you want to tell them, or should I?' he says to her.

'We met at a party last Christmas,' she begins, clearly not trusting him not to elaborate. 'And it was love at first sight, or something like that.'

'Lust at first sight, more likely,' he guffaws, squeezing her closer to him. 'Isn't that right, babe?'

She shifts uncomfortably in her chair, and although she agrees, her expression tells a different story. I can't say why, but there is something familiar about her face, but I can't place what it is. I'm pretty sure I'd remember if we'd met before, but maybe I've seen her picture in a glossy magazine or somewhere.

'He swept me off my feet,' she continues, 'and we've been inseparable ever since.'

'Well, none of us ever thought anyone would get Rod down the aisle,' Lily adds, 'so kudos to you.'

'All it takes is finding the right person, and everything else slots into place,' she fires back. 'Wouldn't you agree, Zoë?'

I look up at the mirror again and see her staring back at me, so quickly close the visor. What is that supposed to mean? I don't know her from Adam, so there's no way she can know about my marriage troubles and my mistake with Evan. I'm just reading too much into her words, I tell myself; paranoia driven by the fact that at least one of the people in this car knows my deepest, darkest secret.

The silence suggests they're all waiting for me to respond.

'Absolutely,' I eventually say. 'What is it you do, Bella? Have I seen you in something?'

'My betrothed will be heading up a new foundation I'm setting up,' Rod interjects. 'I thought it was about time I gave back to those in society who are struggling. But I want to do more than just spaff a few notes at local charities.'

'We're going to focus on supporting families who've lost a child, or whose children are facing terminal illnesses,' Bella adds.

'See, I told you she was passionate!' Rod declares, smitten.

I'm not one to criticise Rod's newfound benevolence, and clearly Bella has had an influence on him, but I do worry that she seems to be more in love with his family fortune than with the man himself, but maybe I'm just being unkind. It's not like I can be held aloft on a pedestal when it comes to picking the right partner for marriage.

'Is that what the two of you were doing in Amsterdam?' Lily asks.

'Amongst other things...' Rod confirms. 'The truth is: I needed a break, and where better to really get a grip on your identity than cycling along the great canals?'

Lily snorts with laughter at this.

'I'm sorry but I'm having a hard time imagining you on a bicycle.'

Rod joins in the laughter.

'Well, it's the thought that counts, right? No, my trip to the Netherlands was purely for medicinal purposes. And I wasn't joking when I said it was lucky the woman at Customs didn't insist on a rectal examination. Which reminds me, we'll have to stop at a services or something along the way, so I can get this shit out of me.'

I don't tell him that I have absolutely no intention of getting high this weekend, especially on drugs that have been riding around inside of him for God knows how long.

'We'll be stopping in ten minutes or so when we collect Dan from the train station,' Lily tells him. 'They should have toilets there you can use.'

'Wait, we're picking up someone else?' Bella groans. 'And where the hell are they going to sit?'

Rod pats her leg.

'It'll be fine. There's plenty of room. This car used to carry five of us in the back alone. You remember that, Lily? Your dad used to belt three of us in while the other two lay across the rest. It'll be just like old times. You'll love Dan, he's a great guy. Are you looking forward to seeing him after all this time, Zoë?'

'Of course,' I say as casually as I can manage.

'I hear he's still single, and you know what they say: what happens on Jura stays on Jura.'

I ignore the comment as Rod howls with laughter, enjoying making me feel uneasy. The last thing that I need now is to be thinking about my history with Dan. And if he had any idea about what Saul told me the night of the accident, he'd more likely kill me than worry about sparing my feelings.

4

DAN

The rain clacks against the corrugated roof of the bus shelter as I huddle beneath, my rucksack already damp through. Who in their right mind decides to take a road trip this deep into autumn, with winter just around the corner?

Oh yeah, Rod, of course, and if there was ever an example of someone *not* in their right mind, it's Rod.

I chuckle at the thought, as memories of him goofing about in Mrs Dupont's French class fire to the front of my mind. How any of our secondary school teachers didn't have mental breakdowns trying to cope with his mischief and hijinks is beyond me. Rumour was one of the school governors had a soft spot for Rod, when in truth, it was more that he couldn't resist the lure of the Astor family wallet. During one particular incident, Rod set the chemistry lab on fire while sitting our GCSE mock exam, but rather than facing suspension, the school unveiled plans for an Olympic-sized swimming pool. Coincidence? I think not.

I'm looking forward to catching up with the old gang, and hearing all their war stories from university; I'm sure Rod will have enough tales to keep us entertained all weekend. And inevitably he'll dominate the conversation as always, but at least that should help cover any awkwardness that I might feel when I see Zoë. It's been years since I last saw her, while she's been hiding away down south. Lily told me she's married to a teacher, of all people. Funny, but I never saw her settling for someone. The Zoë I remember was ready to set the world alight with her passion and compassion for those who've suffered. It's only with the passage of time that I can see it was inevitable she'd leave me behind.

And, in fairness, it's not like I'm the same guy she left in Wakefield. I had to grow up quickly when Dad suffered his stroke, and I worked all hours to keep a roof over their heads when Mam became his full-time carer. And now that her health has deteriorated since his passing, the burden has yet to be eased. Not that I wouldn't work every day for the rest of my life to have them both back and in good health. I can't complain about my lot; there are others in far worse situations than me. I just need to figure a way out of this hole.

And as if on cue my phone bursts to life, and I'm not surprised when I see the contact name on the screen. I could ignore it for once, force the person on the other end to leave an answerphone message, but I know my conscience won't allow me to.

'Morning,' I say, answering the call.

'Hi, Dan, I wanted to let you know that I've just left your mam. She's had lunch and I've washed up. I'll be back to check on her in a couple of hours, and get her cleaned up before making her dinner.'

'That's great, thanks for letting me know, Jem. I appreciate it.'

'That's what we're here to do.' She pauses. 'The thing is,

Dan... the agency said they've been trying to get hold of you. Something about an unpaid bill?'

I swallow hard, feeling some of the rain's cooling spray against my burning cheeks.

'Oh yeah, I know. Sorry, I missed a few calls because I'm travelling up to Scotland today and the signal is a bit intermittent.'

I hate lying to someone I've grown quite close to because of the great devotion she shows to Mam, but I just need to buy myself some more time.

'And I will have the bill settled in a couple of days. All my assets are tied up at the moment, and... uh, I'm waiting for a client's cheque to clear. As soon as the bank release the funds, I'll immediately phone the agency and settle up.'

'Forgive me for speaking out of turn, but they asked me to remind you you're three months in arrears, and they can't sustain that.' She sighs audibly. 'They even told me I shouldn't call in on your mam today, but I said you are away and it isn't fair on her.'

I shouldn't have come away this weekend. I wrestled with the decision for weeks before I finally accepted Rod's invitation. I've tried getting a loan from the bank, but they won't even entertain the idea with my patchy credit history. But there was a time when Rod and I were close, and as much as it is eating me up inside, I'm hoping that my presence at the wedding might persuade him to lend me the money to get my head back above water.

'They're right to have concerns, of course they are, but I promise you I will make things right with them. I really appreciate you helping me out like this, Jem. Mam lives for your visits, and I don't know how...'

My words trail off as my voice cracks, the lump in my throat too vast to overcome.

'I will make sure she's okay today, but I really need you to phone the agency and tell them when they can expect the bill to be settled. Can you do that for me? It means they'll stop giving me shit about maintaining our schedule.'

'Absolutely,' I say, biting down to swallow the emotion. 'They'll be my next call.'

'Great. Okay, well, I'll let you get back to your holiday. Try not to worry about your mam this weekend. You deserve a break, and I'll make sure she doesn't realise you're not there.'

I end the call, and squeeze my eyes with my hand, reminding myself that I'm doing the right thing, and that this is the only option I have left.

I'm lost in this thought when a muddy Land Rover pulls into the bus stop layby, and it's only when the window lowers and I see Lily inside that I realise my lift has arrived. I've spent all week worrying about how I would react to seeing Zoë again that I hadn't even thought about what it could mean seeing them both at the same time. Does Zoë know?

I quickly rub my eyes with the sleeve of my coat, and step closer to the car, keen to see if Zoë is inside yet, a tiny part of me hoping she's bailed out of the weekend.

'Hey,' Lily says awkwardly, 'you're in the back with Rod and his fiancée.'

She leans back, and that's when my eyes meet Zoë's, and I swear my jaw practically hits the floor. She smiles back and holds her hand up to give a little wave, and I find myself involuntarily copying the action. She's certainly no longer the girl I remember collecting from her parents' place for prom over twenty years ago. I didn't think she could look any more beautiful than the face I see in my dreams most nights, but I clearly underestimated.

My tongue feels as though it's swollen to twice the size, and I'm unable to formulate words, so instead I offer a simple nod, and open the door behind Lily. Warm, musky air greets me, and I see Rod squashed in beside a woman with short blonde hair who looks as excited to be in the car as an inmate on death row.

I climb in as Rod bursts into a chorus of 'Danny Boy', and then we are on our way to whatever fate has planned for the five of us this weekend.

5

ZOË

Oh, God, I'd forgotten Rod's insistence on singing 'Danny Boy' whenever he sees Dan. I'm a little surprised he remembered, but I suppose Rod always was against any of us growing up. A classic Peter Pan complex, a therapist would probably say.

I keep my eyes focused on the road ahead of us, not daring to look up at the rearview mirror, even though I can see in my periphery that Dan is watching me. When I saw him standing beneath the bus shelter, I didn't know what to say, he looked as though he was about to cry, and I now regret the mute wave of my hand. At least he was kind enough to reciprocate. Why is it that this guy I've been intimate with suddenly has me lost for words and once again feeling like a pre-pubescent teenager?

I knew it would be weird seeing him again after all this time, but hadn't anticipated it being quite so awkward. I've not spoken to him properly since the day I left for university, figuring space was in both of our best interests, but the attraction I always felt for him is still there; more so in fact, it would appear. I was surprised when he came to my surprise fortieth party, but I avoided getting into an in-depth conversation with him, too terrified that he would bring up that night. But now that he's here, and I can smell his cologne... What is wrong with me? I was the one who broke his heart, and I have no right to be experiencing these old feelings.

It's just a rebound thing, I tell myself. The mess with Evan, and being back here with the old gang, and seeing Dan again after all this time was bound to stir up memories and feelings. It's nothing to panic about. Besides, I'm sure Dan has moved on anyway, so it wouldn't be right to start fantasising about what might have been had I stayed closer to home.

I continue to study the bumper of the car in front as Rod reaches the crescendo of his tone-deaf rendition, and promptly applauds himself.

'Dan, it's great to see you,' I hear him say loudly. 'You're looking well. How's life treating you?'

'You okay, Zo?' Lily whispers in my direction, and I miss Dan's response to Rod.

'Yeah, I'm fine,' I reply quickly, fiddling with the heating controls in the central console. 'Is it me or is it hot in here?'

'I need the fans on to keep the windscreen from fogging up,' she replies. 'Crack the window if you need.'

I fiddle with the switch and lower the window an inch or so, and push my forehead towards the cool air. The surface water on the road echoes as cars whizz through beside us, and between that and the heating, I can barely hear Rod and Dan's voices.

'I didn't ask how work is going,' Lily continues, as Rod and Dan's conversation drifts into background noise.

I nod encouragingly.

'Yeah, it's going well, I guess,' I say, not wanting to outright lie, but also not ready to share the mess my fling with Evan has landed me in.

I probably will chat to her about it – God knows, I could do with some honest advice – but once we're settled and away from the rest of the group. I don't want everyone knowing how bad things really are.

I ask what she's doing now, vaguely remembering seeing her post something about working in the publishing industry. She tells me it's an independent publisher and she's responsible for reading submitted works from agents and authors.

'That sounds like such a cool job!' I say. 'You get paid to read books. If you ever want to do a job swap for a couple of weeks, I'd bite your hand off.'

She begins to say something, but then stops herself.

'What is it?' I press, but she shakes her head.

'Forgive me again,' I say, 'but I'm sure I also read something about you writing a book of your own.'

'Yes, that's right. I have written two children's books, but need an agent if I'm going to get them published.'

'I love that you're following your dream of writing.'

I don't add that I was always envious of her vivid imagination, and that my mam would frequently say she wished I was more creative.

I feel pressure as my seat is pulled back slightly, and when I look over my shoulder I can see that Rod is using the corners of mine and Lily's seats for leverage to pull himself forward.

'Wait until you all hear about the accommodation I've got booked for us tonight,' he says, with a huge smile on his face. 'It's a huge farmhouse in a tiny village just west of Glasgow. It sleeps up to six, across three rooms, which means a couple of you might need to bunk in together.'

He waggles his eyebrows at my reflection as he says this, but I resist the urge to correct him. Is that because I don't want to appear prudish, or because I don't want to discourage Dan from making a move?

What is wrong with me? I'm like a bitch on heat!

'There's a huge hot tub and sauna on site as well.'

'What about broadband?' Lily asks. 'I need to get online later for a videocall.'

'It's the twenty-first century, of course there'll be broadband,' Rod fires back dismissively, but it wouldn't surprise me if he hadn't checked. He's never been a detail-oriented kind of person. 'When I say no expense has been spared, I mean it.'

'How long will it take to get to Glasgow?' I ask Lily, and she studies the satnav.

'We should be there in about three and a half hours, depending on traffic, but I'll probably have to stop for a break before we get there.'

'I don't mind driving for a bit if you're feeling tired. It's not fair that you should have to do the whole trip.'

'Thanks, yeah, I might take you up on that.'

'How come we're stopping over in Glasgow?' Bella asks, disappointment in her tone.

'Not in Glasgow, my dear, but just to the west of it,' Rod replies. 'The journey to Jura becomes decidedly more challenging after Dumbarton, and it's not something worth attempting in the dark. Even in daylight, it'll probably still take several hours depending on when we make it to the Kennacraig ferry terminal.'

'I'm aiming to stop between Penrith and Carlisle,' Lily advises, 'but if anyone needs to stop beforehand, can you give me plenty of warning?'

'The Airbnb host said she will leave a basket of goodies for us when we arrive,' Rod continues, 'but if that isn't sufficient there's supposed to be a lovely little pub in the village, which is walking distance.'

He sits back and suddenly my eyes are staring at Dan's in the mirror, and I feel the heat rise to my cheeks. This really won't do, and I'm going to have to speak to him at some point, even if it's just to make it clear that the history between us is better left in the past.

My phone vibrates in my hand, and I open the message without thinking, grateful for the distraction, until I realise it's from Evan, and he'll now know that I've seen and read it.

> You can't keep ignoring me, Zoë. I meant what I said. I will tell them everything and then your career will be finished.

'Is that work again?' Lily asks, nodding at my phone.

'Yeah,' I lie.

'Bloody hell, why won't they just leave you be? That must be the third or fourth time since you got in the car.'

'My boss is a tyrant,' I say, instantly racked with guilt, because Mae is anything but a tyrant, and was only too supportive when I asked for a couple of days' leave.

'I guess that's the pain that comes with such a high-powered job,' she says sympathetically. 'Do you need me to stop so you can phone them and answer whatever their query is?'

'No, no, it's fine. I'll phone when we get to the services.'

I switch my phone to airplane mode.

'Dan's looking well,' Lily leans over and whispers.

'Yep,' I whisper back.

'Are you still sure there's no chance the two of you might—'

'None whatsoever,' I repeat, though not sure which of us I'm trying hardest to convince. 'Anyway,' I say, louder now so it's clear I've changed the subject, 'I overheard you on the phone at the airport. A new man in your life, I take it?'

She sheepishly glances at the mirror, before signalling and

moving into the outside lane, accelerating to overtake the car ahead of us.

'You could say that.'

'I want details. Where did you meet? How long have you been seeing each other? What does he do for a living? Is he the one? Will there be wedding bells in the near future?'

'Fuck, that's a lot of questions. Is this what you're like in court? I feel like I'm being cross-examined or interrogated.'

I smile to show I mean no harm.

'I'm just curious to know more about the guy who's clearly putting a smile on my best friend's face.'

'Do you mean that? You still consider me your best friend?'

The question throws me at first, and I'm not sure how to respond. Can I really call Lily my best friend when we haven't met up in so long? If I was her best friend wouldn't I already know about the new man in her life? Wouldn't I already have confided in her about the mess with Evan?

'Of course I do,' I say, hoping she didn't notice the pause. 'We're BFFs, right?'

'It's so great to see you all,' Dan calls out. 'The old gang back together again.'

Lily cheers, but stops when Rod says, 'We're not all here though, are we?'

And there it is again: the elephant in the room. I knew it wouldn't be long before the topic of conversation turned to Saul. And in that moment, my feelings of irritation about Evan are replaced with overwhelming guilt.

6

DAN

Two hours into the journey, Lily tells us she needs caffeine and to stretch her legs, so we pull into Southwaite Services on the outskirts of Carlisle. The car park is rammed, so we're forced to park some distance from the building, but actually the fresh air and exercise couldn't have come at a better time. It's uncomfortably warm being squashed in next to Rod, and having his trouser-less, hairy leg pressed against mine is also irksome.

'There's a Greggs, KFC, and Pret on site,' Lily informs us, as if we can't all see the logos stuck to the side of the building. 'We've probably got another couple of hours in the car once we get started again, so I'm going to grab some food, and get a tea to take away. Shall we say, meet back at the car at half three? That gives us just over half an hour.'

She doesn't wait for a response, before marching onwards, arm linked through Zoë's. I had hoped to get Zoë alone for a few minutes just to clear the air and overcome the wall of awkwardness that feels like it's growing between us. But if she has any interest in catching up, she makes no sign of it. And with Rod and Bella deep in conversation as they deviate to the right, I find myself alone, and once again wondering whether I was being naïve to think that things would be like the old days.

I head inside the building as light rain starts to fall again, and spend five minutes flicking through the books and magazines in WH Smith's before joining the queue at Burger King. There's no sign of my travelling companions, so I collect my food and carry the tray to a vacant table and eat.

I've caught Zoë watching me in the mirror a couple of times, but I can't read the expression on her face. I noticed her avoiding eye contact when Rod brought up Saul, and I suppose I shouldn't be surprised that his name carries such weight amongst this group. He was one of us. No, he was more than that. He was the glue that held us together. It's hardly surprising that the group splintered after... what happened. I'd hoped time and distance would heal those wounds, but I guess that was naïve too.

Maybe I should just tell them I'm feeling ill and head back to Wakefield. As much as I need a break from Mam, the business, and my financial woes, what's the point in sitting in silence in the back of Lily's dad's car?

When I see Jem's name on my phone's screen again, I sense she's phoning to ask why I still haven't phoned the agency to give them an update on when I'm going to settle my bill. The thing is, I don't want to lie to them, so I'm hoping if I can get Rod alone and just pour my heart out to him, then he'll show me the mercy I'm pleading for.

When the pandemic hit, many local businesses like mine were impacted, and we almost folded when the country went into lockdown. I wasn't allowed to service my customers at first, and then when restrictions were gradually lifted, and I could start servicing boilers and repairing leaky taps again, I did, but a lot of my customers were on furlough or unemployed and unable to settle their bills. I did what I could for them, cutting prices and allowing them to settle bills over a longer timeframe, but that sucked what little capital I had dry. I had to cut corners too, and my biggest regret – the reason my financial affairs are in such dire straits – is I cancelled my public liability insurance. And then when there was an accident at a new build site, and it was decided that culpability had to be apportioned to all contractors, I was left up shit creek without a paddle. I have done what I can, taking cash-in-hand jobs where possible, but the grains of sand are disappearing beneath me and I'm clinging on by a thread.

If Rod refuses to help, I really will be at the end.

The answerphone cuts in, and I instantly regret not answering the phone. I shouldn't be putting Jem between me and the agency she works for. My phone buzzes with a voice message, but I force myself to finish my food before listening to it. When I do, I wish I hadn't.

'Hey, Dan, I guess your signal is still pretty bad. The thing is, when I returned to your mam's house there was this guy at the door, demanding entry. He said he was a bailiff and was within his rights to enter the property and seize valuables. I told him it wasn't my house and that the resident was in a vulnerable position. He was aggressive and it was only when I threatened to call the police that he said he would give us a day to sort our mess but that he'll return tomorrow.'

I close my eyes as she pauses, knowing that a visit from the bailiffs only shows just how bad things have become, and how long I've been lying to her.

'It's none of my business, Dan, but I don't know what would have happened had I not got there when I did. Your mam was in the process of opening the door, and if I'd been five minutes later... I don't think it's right that she should be on her own this weekend. Is there any family or friends that could stay with her while you're away? I would offer to stay the night, but... I don't think you can afford it. Please give me a call back when you get this and let's see if we can figure something out.'

I press a paper napkin to my eyes, as my vision blurs. I shouldn't have come away. I shouldn't have left Mam alone. I should find Rod now. Ask him for a few minutes alone, beg him for some money and then head home, but I don't want him to think I only came on this trip to ask for money. I genuinely want to see him get married and hang out like we used to do.

The irony is there's nothing of any real value left at home, as I pawned most of Mam's jewellery earlier this year just to tide us over until I could get things sorted. Even the television, which is Mam's only real connection to the world outside, is second hand and not worth anything on the black market. The walls are closing in on me.

* * *

I carry my rubbish to the bin, heading outside in search of Rod. But it isn't him that finds me.

'Have you got five minutes?' Lily asks.

I look around to see if Zoë is watching, but there's no sign of her in the vicinity. I take Lily's arm and quickly lead her around the side of the building where we won't be disturbed.

'What's wrong? Embarrassed to be seen with me?' she asks testily.

'No, but I don't want anyone getting the wrong idea.'

She scoffs.

'About you and me? Why would they? You're just some guy who fucked me at a birthday party, and then refused to acknowledge it ever happened.'

I was worried this was going to come up, and in fairness, I acted like a dick that night, and wish I could go back in time and correct things. Lily deserves better, but right now I have bigger things on my mind.

'I'm sorry,' I say sincerely. 'We were both drunk and lonely, and what we did met a need. I thought we were on the same page about it.'

'You didn't need to avoid me for the last two years since.'

'It's not been two years.'

'It was Zoë's fortieth birthday party. It's just over two years ago.'

'Okay, I'm sorry. I should have phoned and spoken to you about it afterwards, but I didn't get the impression that you were looking for any kind of relationship on the back of it. It was just sex, right?'

Her eyes are shining as she sighs.

'Yes, it was just sex, but I feel like I lost a friend because of it. I've seen you about town a couple of times, but it feels like you spot me and turn the other way. What did I do wrong?'

I pull her into an awkward embrace, knowing that an apology is long overdue.

'You didn't do anything wrong. I'm sorry. It's just difficult, what with you and Zoë being best friends, and her being my ex-girlfriend. You must see that, right?'

She pushes away from me, but I'm not sure if it's because she believes me, or is just upset by my honesty.

'Of course I do. Do you think I want her finding out that I went behind her back and shagged you? Of course I don't. But we need to figure this out or she's going to notice that something's up, and then we'll be forced to reveal the truth.'

'No, she can't find out.'

I don't go so far as to admit I'm still in love with Zoë, but she sees through me anyway.

'So, you do still care for her then?'

'Yes. No. Honestly, I don't know.'

It's my turn to sigh.

'Well, why don't we just pretend like it never happened,' Lily says. 'Can we do that?'

'Absolutely,' I say, holding out a hand, which she promptly shakes.

'Good. Then let me be the bearer of bad news: Zo's not inter-ested in hooking up with you this weekend. We spoke about it earlier.'

It's a cruel blow, but I'm not overly surprised. Of course she's moved on. And I need to as well. We slowly walk back towards the car, and when we get there I see it's like a game of musical chairs. Zoë is now behind the wheel, and Bella is pressed up to Rod in the middle seat. I need to speak to him, but I can't say what I need to in front of everyone else. I'm about to ask him for five minutes, when Zoë declares we need to get moving if we're to avoid the rush hour. And as I stare at the back of her head, I can't help but wonder how far the rest of them will go to keep our dirty little secret quiet.

7

ZOË

We bounce around as the car's lack of decent suspension becomes more and more apparent. It's been hours since we crossed the border into Scotland, and the condition of the roads, if that's a fair description, has been worsening the further north we travel. There's an almighty crash as the front bumper bounces off the ground as we hit another enormous pothole in the mud-covered track. I apologise to those in the back who are crashing into one another with every bend and divot.

Dan certainly doesn't seem to care; every time I catch sight of him in the rearview mirror, he looks distracted, like he has the weight of the world on his shoulders. Maybe he's also battling to keep the ghosts of the past from breaking free.

I've kept my phone on airplane mode so that I won't have to be startled every time it vibrates with a new notification, terrified of how quickly Evan's behaviour and messages have escalated. I know I shouldn't have encouraged his flirtation, and I know I shouldn't have deliberately stayed late that night in the office so I could seduce him in the boardroom. It was reckless and I hate myself even more for how much I enjoyed the physicality of us ripping through each other's clothes, knowing that what we were doing was illicit and unprofessional.

I thought he realised it was a one-off. That there could be no future with me being married, and him the nephew of a senior partner. But he kept hanging around my desk, making lewd innuendos to the point where I had to drag him into my office and tell him to cut it out. He mistook my intention, but I made it very clear that I wasn't interested in continuing. He said that was fine, and for a few days things returned to how they were before. But then he started bragging around the office about how he was getting laid every night – I think in some misplaced effort to make me jealous – but when I didn't rise to the bait, he then told people how he'd been seduced by a cougar who couldn't get enough of his young and virile body.

It felt like everyone around the office connected the dots and knew he was referring to me, and I again told him to stop and if he didn't I would report his behaviour. And he just smiled at me. A huge, satisfied grin that instantly revealed just how naïve I had been.

'If you tell on me, I'll tell my Aunt Mae how you lured me into the boardroom and seduced me after hours before tossing me aside once you'd had your wicked way.'

I told him I'd deny such an accusation, and then he played me the footage from the security cameras that night. I hadn't even realised there were cameras in the boardroom. He assured me he'd deleted the original from the mainframe so nobody would see it unless he wanted them to. He told me there was only one way I could keep him quiet.

I shudder at the memory of going back to his flat and how I had to repress my gag reflex to pleasure him. I hoped one last night together would be enough but then he continued making demands. And now that I've refused to cave any more, he's once again threatening to expose me. And the worst part is, I'm not even that bothered if Tim finds out, given our current stand-off, but if Mae sees what I did, what I allowed to happen, she'll fire me in an instant for gross misconduct. And my career as a solicitor will be over.

The car crashes into another pothole, and I realise how dangerous it is for me to be driving when I'm so distracted by Evan. The car shudders to a stop as I slam on the brakes.

'I'm done,' I declare, loud enough for everyone to hear. 'Between this shit road, and Rod's less than helpful instructions, I've had enough. Lily, I'm sorry, but we're going to need to switch places.'

'Probably best if I drive anyway,' she says kindly. 'This beast takes some handling, but I'm used to her.'

I squeeze her hand in gratitude.

'But it might be an idea if you and Rod swap places as well,' she continues unexpectedly. 'That way, he can point where I need to go, and won't have to shout over everybody else.'

I'm about to argue that I don't want to be squashed into the back beside Bella and Dan, but Rod is already out of the car, banging on the passenger window.

* * *

It's almost six when Lily brings the car to a stop at a horizontal farm gate above a cattle grid. The rain is splashing into the enormous puddles where the track meets the vast field to our right. Undoubtedly this is a farm, but it looks nothing like the idyll Rod described to us earlier.

'Is this it?' he exclaims now, more than a hint of doubt in his tone.

'These are the coordinates you gave me,' Lily replies defensively. 'This is where the satnav says we should be.'

'Maybe it's nicer on the inside,' I say with genuine sincerity.

Dan gets out and moves to the gate, figuring out how to open the latch and then swinging it open so Lily can drive us through. Massive divots are covered with green-brown rainwater. A tall wooden barn stands about thirty metres away at the end of the current road, but it's seen better days. There are huge holes where planks of wood are missing, and the paint is peeling in waves.

I hope that's not our accommodation.

On Rod's instruction, Lily parks up outside the barn, and we all climb out, battling over suitcases, as Rod advises us that we're supposed to walk around the barn to get to the property. The grass bordering the barn is reminiscent of a paddy field, but there doesn't seem to be any other way around, so each of us collects our baggage, and carries it as we attempt to walk through without losing our shoes.

The barn seems to stretch forever, and we make slow progress through the mud. I'm surprised Rod hasn't already called off this debacle. It will take more time, but surely we'd be better off getting on the main road and returning to Glasgow city centre and finding a hotel for the night? I'm about to suggest as much, when I reach the far edge of the barn structure and see the house that presumably will be our home for the night. It looks like a regular detached three-bed. Nothing special from the outside, and obvious damp around the frames of the single-pane windows visible from the front. There's part of me half-expecting Rod to now reveal his jape, and that this isn't really where we're staying, but he moves across to the small key safe by the front door and enters the code. The box opens and he extracts the key, before unlocking the front door.

This really isn't a joke.

I wipe my feet on the mat and follow Lily in through the door. The smell of dog fur and damp hits me immediately. The floor in the hallway is laminated wood, which creaks as each of us enters. There is a kitchen immediately to the right, small but efficient with two countertops either side of an electric stove and oven. There's no sign of a washing machine or dishwasher, so I guess we'll have to draw straws to see who does the washing up later.

I continue along the hallway until we reach a large room, lined with three sofas, all facing the fireplace and chimney. This room is noticeably colder than the kitchen, probably a result of the wall of floor-to-ceiling windows that lead to the sprawling, overgrown lawn out back.

Dan collapses into one of the sofas and a cloud of dust erupts from beneath him, which he swots away. Poor Rod doesn't know where to look first, his face a picture of exasperation.

'I swear this isn't what it looked like in the pictures,' he says, the closest we'll come to an apology.

'Listen, it's only for one night,' I say, remembering the first student digs I lived in, which was far worse. 'Why don't we find the bedrooms, and then figure out what to eat?'

Lily nods and heads back out of the room, leading me to the wooden staircase, which creaks with each step we take. Upstairs is divided into three evenly sized bedrooms and a smaller bathroom. Each bedroom has a double bed and flatpack wardrobe. We opt for the room with an electric radiator plugged in, at the front of the house.

We both start at a knock at the door. It opens a moment later and Dan pops his head around the corner.

'Sorry to disturb. Have either of you managed to get a decent phone signal in the house? I've got no bars anywhere so far.'

We both check our phones, but we might as well be in the twilight zone.

'Sorry,' I say. 'It might be worth venturing outside but maybe wait until it stops chucking it down.'

'Rod says the Airbnb host hasn't left any provisions, so he's suggested we head down to the village and find that local pub for dinner. You both happy with that?'

Lily looks exhausted by all the driving, but I don't like the idea of us all traipsing through the mud in the rain in search of the village centre.

'Sure. Give us five minutes, and we'll be down,' she says.

It's just as well we drove to the village centre as the track from the farm was flooded, and any smaller car wouldn't have made it through in one piece. I've never been more grateful that Lily brought her dad's Land Rover. Unfortunately, there's no car park at the tiny village inn, and so Lily abandons the car on a sideroad, and we hustle around.

The gentle rumble of conversation stops as soon as we enter, the ceiling so low that Rod is forced to stoop. There are maybe eight people already in the bar, the men all with thick, unkempt beards, and the three ladies glaring at Lily, Bella and me as if they think we've come to lure their partners like mythological sirens. All of them are looking at us with disdain.

'Why don't you find a table, and Lily and I will see if we can find some menus,' I say, nodding towards the sign on the door that says *dining*.

The three of them shuffle off, and Lily and I head to the bar. The girl behind it looks about seventeen, but I presume she's older. She's busy talking to one of the locals as we approach, and although we make eye contact and clear our throats several times, she seems oblivious to our overtures.

When she does come over, and I ask for menus, she informs us that the oven is broken, so she's only able to make sandwiches. She hands us a lunch menu, and I order a bottle of wine – the only options are red, white, or rosé, no grape varieties mentioned – as well as a jug of tap water, and five glasses. Lily helps me carry the haul out to the table the others have found in what is essentially a conservatory. They have had to push three of the four square tables together to make a space suitable for us, but there is nobody else in the room. I explain the kitchen's limited options, and although Rod complains, we agree that the pub is warmer than the accommodation.

I open the wine – described on the bottle as Australian white – and fill all of our glasses.

'I think we should have a toast to the happy couple,' I say, trying to lift the dour mood. 'It's been a long time since we've all been together like this, and it's because of Rod and Bella that we're all here now, so let's toast them.'

We all raise and clink glasses, before grimacing at the acidic taste of the wine. The menu choice is limited to cheese, ham, cheese and ham, or tuna, so we all reluctantly make our selections, with Bella stating that she'll ask if there is anything vegan the kitchen can rustle up.

'You'll have to vacate that room at eight,' the barmaid tells Rod and me when she comes to take our order. 'We've got a private function tonight.'

'We're only in the village for one night,' he says. 'Is there anywhere else where we can have a good time? Another pub perhaps? Or a club?'

She laughs at this.

'Nothing nearby, no. Not like you're hoping for, I imagine.'

'What about an off-licence?'

'There's a supermarket about three miles away, but it closes at eight, so you'll be lucky if you make it there now.'

'Could we buy some spirits from you? Some Scotch perhaps? Or vodka?' Rod asks.

'I'm not allowed to sell bottles.'

'What if I make it worth your while?' he says, removing his wallet. 'As I said, we're only here overnight, staying up at the McFadden farm. So, we won't tell anyone if you sell us a couple of bottles. I'm willing to pay more than cost price. It can be our little secret.'

'Sorry, no, but I tell you what... I'm aware of a party that's happening tonight, a couple of villages over. It's a private affair, but there'll be a couple of hundred people there, so nobody will notice five more of you.'

Rod's eyes light up.

'That sounds perfect. Do you reckon you can get us in?'

'I could take you with me, but it's gonna cost you... two hundred pounds.'

The way her eyes darted, I'm pretty sure she's just invented that number, but before I can tell Rod not to waste his money, he's already shaking her hand.

'It's a deal. I can give you the cash as soon as we find an ATM.'

'Listen, guys,' Dan says. 'I'm happy to be the designated driver tonight, so the rest of you can have a drink.'

'There's one other condition,' the woman continues. 'You'll have to give me a lift?'

'Sounds fine,' Rod says. 'What's the worst that can happen?'

8

DAN

My heart is racing as I wake with a start, but there is an almighty ache in my neck that I need to crack out. My eyelids feel stuck together as I try to prise them apart, only now realising I'm slumped forwards, and not stretched out on my back as I usually am. Something hard is pressed into my chin and chest, and as I squash my hands between my torso and the object, I feel the rough fibres of my woollen jumper scratch at the skin.

I'm wearing last night's clothes.

I rub at my eyes, and blink several times until my hazy vision clears. I'm behind the wheel of the Land Rover, and as I look over to my left, I see Bella in the passenger seat, her head back, pressed against the window. For a moment, I don't think she's breathing, but then her nose wrinkles, and she coughs.

What happened last night?

The last thing I remember is driving from the village inn with Rod beside me, the others squashed in the back. That's right, I remember now, Bella was moaning that the barmaid we'd collected was squashing her and so I had to pull over and the barmaid squashed in beside Rod on the front passenger seat.

What was her name? Why can't I remember?

She was giving me directions, but the roads were so dark, hardly any streetlights to guide us, so I was having to squint and trust the beams of the headlights.

My head is pounding, and my mouth is so dry, but I wasn't drinking alcohol last night. I had water at the pub and then stuck to juice. Wait, I remember someone giving me a can of energy drink at some point because I was flagging and starting to yawn.

A voice echoes in the back of my mind somewhere: *That'll pep you up.*

I can't place whose voice it was.

We were in a large barn, and people were sitting about on bales of hay. There must have been at least a hundred people milling about the place while several DJs were mixing music at the front, the lights of their equipment making the interior look more like a night out in Ibiza than a remote village on the outskirts of Glasgow.

Why can't I remember us leaving? I have no memory of getting in the car.

As I adjust the rearview mirror, I spot Zoë, Lily and Rod huddled together in the back, all sound asleep. Rod is gently snoring, but the others remain oblivious to it.

Was my drink spiked?

It seems a farfetched conclusion to jump to, but it's the only explanation for my pounding head, dehydration and lack of memory. Wouldn't it be just like Rod to slip us all something he'd brought back from his trip to Amsterdam? But surely he wouldn't be stupid enough to drug the designated driver as well?

I use the sleeve of my jumper to wipe some of the condensation from the windscreen, trying to work out how far back we got, or whether we're still at the barn. The sun is rising on the horizon, squashed between two large mounds, but as I stare out into the dimness, I don't recognise the drystone wall we're facing at an angle. I lower my window, not expecting the blast of freezing air that scratches at my face as I lean out and look around for any recognisable landmark. The drystone wall stretches back along the narrow road we appear to be parked on. We're in a layby of some kind.

Did we break down?

Zoë gasps for air as she suddenly wakes as if she's being chased in a nightmare.

'Morning,' I say delicately, nodding at her via the rearview mirror.

She wipes drool from the corner of her mouth, stifling a yawn as she stretches her arms out, the look of confusion on her face mirroring my own.

'Where are we?' she asks.

'Your guess is as good as mine. Do you remember leaving the party?'

'What party?' she asks, her brow creasing until the penny drops. 'Oh, yeah, the party. Um, no, not really. I remember Rod carrying over a tray of shot glasses and something in a bright green bottle, but not much after that.'

It's certainly more than I remember.

'What time was that?'

'Um, not long after we arrived, I think. He was trying to get you to have one, but you refused and went off in search of a soft drink.'

'What's the last thing you remember?' I ask, still unable to get past the blackhole in my memory.

She rolls her neck, inadvertently bumping her shoulder into the side of Lily's face, the impact waking Lily instantly.

'Shit, sorry, did I fall asleep?' she asks, her eyes slowly taking in the scene before her. 'Where the fuck are we?'

'No idea,' I admit, 'but at least we're all together. Not like that school trip to Hereford where we were two junctions away before the teachers realised Rod was still at the services.'

'Is anyone else's head really banging?' Lily says next.

'It's like an elephant is trampling over every nerve,' I say. 'We were just trying to piece together what happened last night. Do you remember getting into the car?'

'No, not really. I remember Rod stripping down to the waist and waving his jacket over his head, doing *Braveheart* impressions.'

'Oh, yeah, I remember that,' Zoë chimes in, snickering at the memory. 'He kept shouting for one of us to video him doing it.'

'Our phones,' I exclaim, as the thought smashes into the side of my head. 'Check your phones for any pictures, videos, or messages.'

I pull out mine and unlock the screen, only now remembering the issues I was having yesterday. My signal bar is greyed out, and the battery indicator is on 4 per cent. Did I manage to phone Jem back? I remember us arriving at the barn, and wandering about outside trying to get a signal, but I don't remember getting through. I headed inside to see if I could borrow someone else's phone, and then it all gets a bit hazy after that. Did we reach an arrangement where she'd stay and be with Mam overnight? That was what her voice message hinted at, but I can't remember whether I ever phoned her back.

One crisis at a time. There's nothing I can do until I can get my phone charged and a signal. For all I know, we spoke and the voice gnawing away at the back of my mind is nothing more than paranoia.

I search my phone for recent images, but there's nothing there for over a month, when I took a screenshot of a customer's invoice to send to them.

'Found anything?' I say over my shoulder.

A tinny sound plays from behind me, and I can just about make out the sound of Rod shouting, 'They may take our lives, but they'll never take our freedom!'

'What time did you record that?' I check.

'Um, it says 23:47,' Lily confirms. 'Rod was clearly wasted. He even grabbed some random bloke in a neck hold, before the guy's mates intervened.'

'That's right,' Zoë says. 'There was a fight. Well, handbags really, but yeah, didn't Rod get thrown out of the barn? I vaguely remember thinking that that was our cue to head home, but while I was looking for you, Dan, he snuck back in, and said it was still early and would order more drinks.'

'Drinks?' Rod suddenly pipes up, stirring from his slumber. 'I'll have a Scotch.'

'The way you were packing it away last night, I think what you need is coffee and a fry-up,' Zoë says. 'In fact, I think we'd all benefit from some sustenance. Do you reckon there's a restaurant or café open somewhere nearby?'

'Your guess is as good as mine. If you can tell me where the hell we are and can direct us to one, I'll drive us.'

My phone vibrates in my hand as the phone switches itself off.

'Have any of you got a USB cable so I can charge my phone?'

'Won't do you any good,' Lily replies. 'No USB ports in the car.'

Getting hold of Jem will have to wait until we get back to the Airbnb, I guess, although I'm not sure what I'm going to say to her. I can't remember whether I got Rod alone to ask for help, but even if I did, he probably won't remember either. Back to square one.

'Has anyone got any signal?' I ask next, peering into the mist rolling off the field beyond the drystone wall, still unable to make sense of exactly where we are.

There's no sign of the barn, so I can only assume we left the party with the intention of returning to our accommodation, but got waylaid on the way back. It really is a wonder nobody has come by and found us in this state.

'Mine says No Service,' Zoë says.

'Mine too,' Lily echoes.

'Wake up Bella and see if she has any signal,' Rod says. 'Her iPhone is newer than mine.'

I press my hand to her sleeveless arm, her skin as cold as ice, and gently nudge her.

'Bella? Time to wake up.'

Her eyes snap open and she stares back at me in terror until her mind engages and she realises where she is.

'Oh hey, shit, did I fall asleep? Are we back at the house now?'

'Not exactly. We all fell asleep in the car. Um, could you check your phone and see if you have any signal?'

She nods and yawns, fishing around in her clutch purse until she locates the phone, and then checks.

'No signal. Sorry. Maybe it'll be better outside.'

She opens the door and climbs out, the phone held high above her head. The cold air seeps into the car, and I shiver. Bella isn't wearing a coat, and I'm about to get out and offer her mine, when she turns back and looks at the car in horror. The hairs on the back of my neck stand as she lets out a bloodcurdling scream.

•

9

ZOË

The scream echoes through the car and chills my blood instantly. I see Bella fold into herself, as the scream fades into tears, and I know straight away that something is very wrong.

Dan is the first to step out of the car, and I watch as he moves closer to Bella, the blood draining from his face as soon as his gaze falls on whatever Bella discovered. He takes her in his arms, using the embrace as an excuse to hide his eyes from whatever offending article has terrified them both.

An animal of some sort, I presume; trapped in the bull bars beneath the bonnet. I hope it isn't a Highland cow. We saw several wandering the field near the barn last night, their ginger fur, cute faces, and the fringe that hangs down between their horns.

Rod is next to slide from his seat, the blast of frozen air breaching the car door a reminder of the severity of the elements out here. His eyes immediately search the space in front of the Land Rover and as soon as he spots it his face betrays his own horror.

Or maybe it's a sheep that took a wrong turn and ended up in a head-on collision. Whatever we've hit, it was clearly an accident, and my friends' reactions to the incident suggests it's messy.

Lily slides out through Rod's door before I have the chance to grab her and warn her not to bother. I watch as she slowly moves around to the front, her eyes on stalks as they survey the damage, before she turns and buries her face in Rod's chest. I stay where I am; resolute. I don't need to see a bloody corpse to imagine how horrific it must look. In an area like this, where cattle roam freely, it must be commonplace for accidents like this to happen. We just need to separate ourselves from whatever we've hit and be on our way.

But as I continue to watch my friends' horror, I realise now their shock has quickly transformed into anger, and whilst I can't hear exactly what is being said from in here, I can see the vitriolic glare that Bella is firing at Dan as she spits and snaps at him. His head is bowed, as if unable to meet her stare, but it's when I see Lily joining in that I realise I may have misjudged the situation. Dan turns his back on the three of them and takes several steps away, his head bowed, and his shoulders gently rocking. In all the years I've known Dan, I've only ever seen him cry once before.

They're blaming him for hitting the animal, and I'm not prepared to let him bear the brunt of their accusations. We've already established that we were all paralytic last night, so it's not like anyone would have been in a better state to take care of us.

I slowly open my door, ready to go to Dan's rescue. Having both doors open creates something of a wind tunnel, and I shiver as my breath escapes in thick clouds. I'm not wearing my coat, and I have no idea where it is, but I don't have time to search.

I take a deep breath, and force myself not to look at the car, as I approach Dan and put a sympathetic arm around his shoulders.

'Are you all right?'

He doesn't answer, his eyes scrunched closed, the tears on his cheeks practically freezing in the icy climate. But it's only when I dare to look back at the others that I truly understand the cause of their consternation.

The human-shaped bundle in the thick grey overcoat is not what I'm expecting to see. There's no bloody mess of fur, just the coat and mound beneath it. My hand races to my mouth as I realise what I'm looking at.

'Who's that?' I stammer.

I see now that none of them are looking at the body, as if somehow making eye contact will draw death towards them.

'Is he alive? Has anyone checked for a pulse?'

It seems like such an obvious response, but their confused expressions would suggest that nobody has checked. Rod steps forward, as if he's ready to be a man of action, before turning back to me, his eyes pleading for help.

'Check for a pulse in his neck,' I command, joining him beside the body, and then encouraging him down to his knees.

Rod's hand trembles as it moves closer to the top end of the coat. The body shifts and rolls towards us so that the man is on his back, his face a mangled mess of blood and bone where it's been squashed. I have to look away and supress the urge to retch. His head is covered by a burgundy-coloured bobble hat, but it's impossible to estimate his age.

And suddenly it's like I'm back on the road outside of school, and it is Saul who lies lifeless on the wet road.

'I-I can't feel anything,' Rod whispers, as his fingers fumble around the stubble-covered neck.

'Stop trying; he's dead,' I say, still unable to look back. Nobody could have their face damaged to that extent and survive.

'He's so cold,' Rod says, and if he's been out here all night then the ice-cold air certainly won't have aided his survival.

Avoiding looking at his face, I unfasten the buttons of the

overcoat he's wearing, searching for any kind of identification. Beneath the coat he's wearing a thick woollen shirt, but it's impossible to tell the original colours or pattern as it's stained through with blood. I reach inside the coat, checking the internal pockets for any kind of wallet or phone, but find nothing. His trouser pockets are also empty, almost as if someone has deliberately removed any means of him being identified. He could be anyone. Someone's father, brother or son. Twenty-four hours ago he was a living, breathing person, and now he's the victim of a car accident.

'We need to phone the police,' I say, standing. 'Has anyone got any signal?'

I check my own phone as I say this, and see the words 'No Service' at the top of the screen.

I'm met with shakes of heads. I try dialling 112 just in case, but my phone fails to connect to any network. I stand and join Lily, pulling her into my arms as she shivers uncontrollably.

'I think we need to get back in the car while we figure out what we're going to do,' I suggest, but nobody moves.

'Does anyone remember... the accident?' Rod asks as he moves closer to us.

'I don't remember leaving the party,' Lily shivers.

'I don't remember getting in the car, but I was pretty wasted,' Bella adds.

Our stares turn to Dan, who is now looking back at us.

'I think someone must have spiked my drink,' he says, bowing his head. 'I was on juice and water all night, but I have no memory of even getting in the car, let alone how we got this far.'

I can hear the fear in his voice, and I desperately want to believe him, but he sounds like he's making excuses. Why would anyone want to spike his drink?

'What about hitting...?' Rod's words trail off.

Dan throws his arms into the air, his tone frustrated. 'I woke up in the car like the rest of you with a banging headache and no recollection of anything after the party. I didn't even know we'd hit anything until Bella screamed.'

This is so bad. Although I don't want to see Dan getting into trouble, this man has died at his hands, and we need to report it. If Dan is right and his drink was spiked in some way, then maybe a blood test will prove that, and he won't be held wholly accountable for what's happened.

'We need to phone the police,' Dan says.

'None of us have any signal, do you?'

He passes his phone to me.

'Battery's dead.'

'Well, what are we going to do?'

'We're on a road, right?' Lily tries. 'So, maybe someone will drive by and we can ask them to call the police, or—'

Dan interrupts. 'We've been here all night and not seen anyone, so what are the chances we'll see anyone now?'

'We'll have to try and get to higher ground,' I determine. 'We're on the side of this mountain, right? So if we follow the road up, eventually we should make it nearer the top, and the signal should improve.'

'What are we going to do with the body?' Rod asks.

'What do you mean?' I reply.

'Well, we can't just leave it in the middle of the layby for someone else to find.'

'We can't move the body until the police arrive,' I remind everyone. 'They'll want to take pictures and collect evidence.'

'Tell me you weren't planning to walk up the road until you find a signal. It could be miles. I don't think we have any choice other than to drive somewhere and phone the police. Which brings me back to the question about what we do with the body in the meantime.'

I know he's right, and I hate it when Rod is right about things. It's freezing cold out here, so it's not like a couple of us can hang around with the body while the others go for help. And we can't just leave this guy in the middle of the layby to be hit by some other unsuspecting driver.

'What do you suggest?' I say reluctantly.

'We lift him over the side of the dry wall.'

It's such a cold and calculated response, and I'm certain Rod hasn't come up with it on the spot; he's been thinking about it for a while.

'How will we know where we've left him?'

'We leave some kind of marker on the wall. That way, when we come back, we'll be able to see.'

I look at Lily and Dan, hoping one of them will propose a better alternative, but Dan is so pale that he looks as though he may keel over in shock, and Lily can't take her eyes off the overcoat.

'Come on,' Rod says, as if herding cattle. 'If we each take an arm and a leg, we'll get him over in no time.'

Rod moves to the man's head, and reaches down, grabbing hold of both his arms.

'Dan, grab his legs. I'm sure we can lift him between us.'

Dan does as instructed, and as they hoist him up, the man's head falls back and the bobble hat drops to the road. They carry him the short distance to the wall, and then manhandle him up and over the side, before Rod clambers over the wall and adjusts the body.

'Chuck me the hat, will you?'

I collect the burgundy bobble hat from the road and see now

there is fresh blood inside it. I pass it to Rod, who pulls it over one of the stones in the wall.

'There we go. Shouldn't be too hard to spot when we return.'

He pulls himself back over the wall, and we return to the car, but I notice Dan makes for the back seat. Lily climbs in behind the wheel, with Rod joining her in the front. We're all shivering as the doors are slammed shut, and we wait for Lily to start the engine and get the heater going.

'Can you pass me the keys, Dan?' she asks.

I watch as he searches his trouser pockets.

'I don't have them,' he says. 'Aren't they in the ignition?'

'Nope.'

Rod and Bella make a show of checking themselves, but neither locates them.

'We're not going anywhere until we find the fucking keys,' Lily says.

I lean down and check the floor between my feet, and Dan mirrors the action, but there's no sign of them back here.

'Maybe they fell out on the road,' Dan suggests.

Lily, Rod, Dan and I all exit, and check the road around the car without success.

'What's that in your pocket?' Dan asks, pointing at my coat.

'Nothing,' I say, knowing I don't have the keys. And yet, as I reach into my pocket, my eyes widen as my fingertips brush against something cold and hard. I pull out the car keys with no explanation for how they got into my pocket. Unless one of these four slipped them in when I wasn't paying attention.

10

EXTRACT FROM SAUL'S DIARY, DATED 2
NOVEMBER 1999

Today was the class trip to the old waterworks as part of our History A-Level. Mrs Adams said the post-trip project – a write-up on how the Industrial Age is still influencing modern society – will count as 20 per cent of our overall grade. And although looking at pipes, filtration systems and sewers sounded like a yawnfest, it was ultimately a day when we wouldn't be trapped inside the usual grey prison. And it also meant we didn't have to wear school uniform. I wonder if prisoners on day release experience a similarly euphoric feeling.

I think I actually spent longer choosing my clothes than I did learning about the Industrial Age, because I know Zoë will be there and I am sure the feelings I have for her aren't just from my side. I caught her watching me in Chemistry the other day, and our eyes met for the briefest of seconds, but it felt like a lifetime, and as I replay the memory in my head, I'm sure the corners of her mouth curled up ever so slightly. Of course, she had to quickly look away in case Dan spotted her. But I reckon there's definitely something there. Not that I could ever betray Dan like that, but if they broke up, then I'd tell him I've never felt this way about a girl before. I'd tell him that he had his shot and now it's time for someone else to step up to the plate.

It's true they make a cute couple, but they don't seem to share any of the same tastes. He likes punk rock, but she's more RnB. He likes playing football, but she prefers tennis. She loves books and poetry, and he barely stops talking about how he's going to buy the PlayStation 2 next year. She's so much more refined than he is. And she's so beautiful too.

I had a dream about her last night, and it was like a vision of what our future will be like. We were just hanging out at the ice cream parlour chatting shit, and other people just started congregating around us, because we were the cool couple and they were attracted to us like magnets. Half the girls in school won't even hang around with Zoë now in case Dan stops by and lowers the tone.

Don't get me wrong, I like Dan. We've always been close, but something changed when he started going out with Zoë. It's not that he changed, but the dynamic in our relationship did. Until then, I'd always been the one to do things first or fastest. I learned to ride my bike three months before he did. I was picked to start in the Under 8s football team before he did. I grew hairs under my arms before he did. But he's the first of us to have a proper, long-term girlfriend. And I want to be happy for him, but if only it wasn't Zoë he loved.

What made today more exciting was knowing that Dan wouldn't be there because he doesn't do History. It meant I got to sit next to Zoë on the school bus. We didn't speak for ages, because she was listening to music on her minidisc player. I eventually plucked up the courage to ask what she was listening to and she said Destiny's Child, and then she passed me one of the headphones so I could listen too. I wanted to ask her whether she likes me too, but I was so nervous that I didn't. I wanted to hold her hand but mine were so hot and sweaty that I thought she'd think I was a freak. But it was cool, the two of us listening to the album, lost in our own little world.

But as soon as we got off the bus, little lapdog Lily came over and dragged Zoë to one side, asking what she thought she was doing, and that Dan wouldn't like it if he found out about her chatting to me. I don't think we exchanged more than five words, but Lily looked furious. Zoë told her it was none of her business and that if she liked Dan that much she should just ask him out instead. Lily did not like that. She didn't respond, but as my dad always says, if looks could kill, Zoë wouldn't have survived.

I don't get the two of them. I know they've been friends forever, but it's like Lily hangs on her every word. I swear to God if Zoë told her to jump, I think she would. And yet what does that kind of submissiveness do to a person? Will she always be the sheep, or will she just snap one day?

And to be honest I'm glad Lily saw me and Zoë together. Maybe if she lets slip to Dan then it will result in Zoë having to decide whether she does like him or whether I would be a better choice. But then I don't want to lose my friendship with Dan either. What would be perfect for me is if Dan broke up with Zoë, because then he wouldn't be able to accuse me of coming between them.

And I know Zoë is right about Lily fancying Dan. She thinks she isn't obvious about it, but she spends so much time avoiding him that anyone else can see how much she's into him. But Dan isn't interested, and why should he be when he's got the most beautiful girl in school on his arm?

I didn't see much of Zoë for the rest of the trip, and she sat next to Lily on the journey back, probably to keep her onside and make sure she didn't grass us up to Dan. If she tells Lily to keep her mouth shut, then she'll get her own way regardless.

But what today has taught me is that there is definitely something between us. I don't want to say I'm in love with her, but I don't know how else to describe the ache in my heart every time I see her with Dan. One day, hopefully she'll come to her senses, and then I'll be ready to step in. I just hope she manages to keep Lily under her spell too.

11

DAN

If I was in the driving seat and killed that man, why the hell did Zoë have the car keys? It doesn't make any sense. I have been desperately trying to remember what happened last night, and at what point someone slipped something into my drink. I'm now more convinced than ever that I was spiked, though speaking to the others, their short-term memories also seem to have been impacted. Were we all drugged in some way? But by whom, and for what reason?

We're now parked outside the Airbnb, and still nobody has admitted they've managed to find a phone signal, which means we're still the only people who know the victim is dead. I hate how ill that makes me feel. And I don't know whether it's the thought that I killed him or that Zoë did and was ready to allow me to take the blame.

I need to get inside and get my phone charging and get hold of Jem, and check that Mam is okay. One of the others can report what happened. And when the police turn up and start questioning us, I'll tell them everything I remember, which is very little. And the more I think about it, just because I woke in the driver's seat doesn't necessarily mean I was the one driving when the guy got hit. I was the designated driver, but if I'd hit him, I would have had the keys. But am I really suggesting that Zoë was driving, hit the man, and then somehow lifted me into the seat, and climbed into the back? I don't understand why she would do that. Or why she'd choose me to take the blame. Out of all of us my bulk would have been the most difficult to manoeuvre; it would have been far easier to move Bella or Lily; even Rod weighs less than me. Plus, given our history, it doesn't make sense why she would throw me under the bus.

Unless she knows more about what happened to Saul than she's previously said, and knows I'm responsible.

There are too many variables, and my head is pounding, so as soon as the car is stationary, I leap out and hurry into the house to locate my charger, plugging in the phone and waiting for the screen to fire up. The 'No Signal' message appears at the top, so I lock the phone and drop back onto the bed in frustration.

I should go in search of something to calm the pain in my head, but I can hear the others loudly debating downstairs, and really don't want to get dragged into the conversation. They all assume I hit the victim, and it should be easier for them to report the incident without me staring at them. If they're right and I was driving, then I'll face the consequences. A blood test will probably confirm what was in my system at the time, and although it's not an excuse, I am not going to beat myself up over something I had no idea about.

I close my eyes and try to push through the fog of amnesia for any snapshots of conversation or images from last night. I remember we crossed over a small bridge, and being worried that it would be too tight a squeeze. And then we had to drive through a moat of some kind, huge volumes of water splashing up and the windscreen wipers having to work double time. The Land Rover was one of a dozen cars parked in the muddy field, and I remember Bella cursing that her shoes were caked in shit, and... I think she jumped on my back, and I carried her to the barn.

Another flash of memory slices through that one like a cleaver and I see Lily. We were standing at the table waiting to order drinks. She said she needed to speak to me privately, and I was worried she was going to bring up our one-night stand again, and I tried telling her not to, but she couldn't hear properly over the music. And then she pulled me down to her and I thought she was going to try and kiss me, but instead she put her hand to my ear and said, 'I have a secret to share.' But I don't know if she divulged it. I don't know if I spoke to Lily again after that. I can't remember what she wanted to share. Maybe it was about Zoë. They'd been whispering to each other most of the journey and I kept catching sight of them chatting when we were driving to the party. Was it that Lily had been wrong earlier, and Zoë does still like me?

My hands shoot up to my head, and I search for any other memories. I vaguely remember seeing Rod with his top off, standing on a bale of hay and shouting something, which got the rest of the crowd cheering along, but then what? I don't remember seeing Zoë for the rest of the night. I was desperate to speak to her, and I think I kept searching, but couldn't find her.

I sit bolt upright, and it's like someone has spun the bed beneath me, because I immediately fall backwards, the ceiling spinning overhead. Saliva fills my mouth, and my stomach turns, and I know what's about to happen. I barely manage to drag myself off the bed, and crawl to the wastepaper basket before I vomit up a mixture of bile and what looks like half-digested bread.

I stay beside the bin, my throat burning, and my nostrils filled with the smell of what I've just expelled. The pain in my head is overwhelming, and I'm worried I might pass out, so I crawl back to the bed, and heave myself up, keeping the bin on the carpet within easy reach.

I can't remember seeing the barmaid after we reached the barn. She certainly wasn't in the car when we woke this morning, so I guess that means we didn't offer to give her a lift back to her village. We must have just left her there, or she caught a lift from someone else. We should find out what happened to her. Maybe she could be a witness to what happened to the rest of us. Maybe she saw someone messing with our drinks when we weren't looking.

I need something to wash away the taste of vomit, and so I drag myself off the bed, leaving the bin where it is, and carefully make my way downstairs, the voices lowering when I enter the room.

'Are the police on the way?' I ask, acknowledging the elephant in the room.

'We haven't phoned them,' Lily says, coming over and offering me her arm. 'You don't look so good.'

'I've just been sick,' I admit.

'Yeah, we heard you. Sit down and I'll get you a drink of water.'

I practically fall onto the sofa and feel all eyes on me.

'Let's ask Dan what he thinks we should do,' Rod says.

'What's the point?' Zoë sighs. 'He's the one most likely to suffer, so he'll agree with you anyway.'

'What's going on?' I ask.

'Rod doesn't think we should phone the police,' Zoë says, glaring at him, and I now realise what all the raised voices have been about.

'We have to,' I concur. 'It's the law. If we caused this man's death, we need to report it.'

Zoë's face perks up at this statement, but I didn't say it to curry favour.

'But what are we going to tell them?' Rod says. 'Do you remember driving into the man?'

'I don't remember shit,' I say, as Lily hands me a glass of water.

'Exactly. Nor do I, nor do any of us. I assume you were driving, Dan, as you said you would and were in the driver's seat, but I don't even remember getting in the car I was that wasted. I didn't see you hit anyone, and I don't remember us leaving the party.'

'I also can't remember leaving the party,' Lily adds. 'I didn't think I'd had that much to drink, but I haven't felt a hangover like this in donkey's years.'

'I think our drinks may have been spiked,' I offer. 'I only remember drinking juice and water all night, but my memory is hazy at best.'

'Nobody else knows we were in that car on that road at that time,' Rod says. 'Who's to say we weren't somewhere else altogether?'

Lily, Zoë and I exchange glances; it's like we're back in that wood all over again.

'A man has died, and that is tragic, but why should it ruin the rest of our lives?' Rod continues. 'What good comes from one of us facing imprisonment for an accident that wasn't our fault? If Dan is right and our drinks were spiked, then we weren't in control of our actions. The person who should be held accountable is the one who spiked our drinks.'

'Are you suggesting we just move on like it didn't happen?' I ask.

'No, not like it didn't happen. I think we all learned a lesson last night, and none of us will ever allow ourselves to be in this position again. But no good comes from us phoning the police. It won't bring the victim back to life.'

'What about justice for the man we killed, and for his family?' Zoë says.

'Who's to say he had any family? Did you see the state of him? He was probably a drunk tramp, and whilst he didn't deserve to die, we didn't mean to kill him.'

'We should put it to a vote,' Bella calls from over by the window. 'I say we don't phone. Rod?'

'I agree. When the dust has settled, I'll find out who his family is and make a generous donation to them in his name.'

'You lot are monsters,' Zoë says. 'I don't want to get Dan into trouble, but it's morally wrong not to report what happened.'

I want to speak up and say I agree, but if the police do arrest me, what happens to Mam's care?

'I'm also a no,' Lily says, squeezing my hand in solidarity, 'so that's three to one, but ultimately Dan should have the deciding vote. We've already left the scene, so we'll all be in trouble if we report it now. But as Rod says, nobody knows we were there. There's no point crying over spilled milk.'

I don't look at Zoë's disappointed face as I say, 'We should pack up and get the fuck out of here.'

12

ZOË

Is this what he's been hoping for this whole time? Pretending that we should report the accident, whilst all the time praying we would change our minds? Is that why he disappeared as soon as we got back here? Did he suspect that we'd come together to protect him if he wasn't in the room? I never had Dan down as someone so manipulative, but maybe I've been underestimating him all this time.

Legally, I know leaving the scene of the accident is a big no-no, but the likelihood is we wouldn't get more than a slap on the wrist for that. Given the state of us, and the shock of seeing a dead body, I wouldn't expect the CPS to seek a formal charge against the rest of us. Dan, on the other hand, as driver and killer would face a harsher sentence. Whether he intended to hit the victim is beside the point. He killed a man and legally – morally – he should face the consequences.

That is assuming he *was* the one who was driving.

I don't like that the finger of suspicion has been potentially thrust in my direction as well. Someone put those keys in my pocket; of that I have no doubt. But who and why are unanswered questions.

We all got out of the car when Bella found the body, so any of the four of them could have slipped them into my coat pocket without me knowing, but which one? The obvious candidate is Dan. But why would he throw me under the bus? He could have pointed suspicion at any of the others, so why choose me? Given our history, I would have expected greater loyalty; but then, maybe I've also underestimated how bitter he feels about me breaking up with him. We never did talk about it, and I've done my best to avoid the awkwardness of such a conversation. So, maybe this is some kind of revenge on his part.

But then, maybe I'm doing Dan a disservice, and the pair of us are just pawns in someone else's game. If Dan wasn't driving, then one of Bella, Lily, or Rod could have been, but which of them, and why? I try to recall if I remember standing next to any of them in particular, but my mind is a blur. The hangover, tempered with the shock of seeing the remains, is not a good recipe for long-term memory retention. There was a moment when we were huddled around the victim, but I can't remember who I was standing beside. This is pointless; for all I know the keys were slipped into my pocket while I was still asleep.

Dan has approached Rod, and I can see he's trying to get him away from the group. What's that all about? Rod is nodding along to whatever Dan is saying, and then the two of them head out of the room and into the kitchen. What are they up to? Bella is standing by the window, her back to me as she stares out at nothing in particular. Lily is pacing the room, waving her arm over her head, the phone in her hand failing to find any kind of signal. Neither seems to have noticed the absence of the two men, and I feel obliged to point it out, but sense neither will realise the potential consequences.

In my head, I can only draw two conclusions. Either Dan is trying to win Rod around to his way of thinking, forming an alliance of sorts. Or they both know a lot more about last night's incident and they want to discuss it privately. I casually stand, and walk quietly towards the hallway, straining to hear anything over the creaking laminate flooring as Lily continues to pace backwards and forwards.

'Maybe try upstairs,' I whisper, not wanting Rod and Dan to realise how close I am to the kitchen.

If Lily hears me, she doesn't acknowledge it, but a moment later hurries upstairs, allowing me to creep closer to the partially open kitchen door.

'When's the last time you remember seeing her?' I hear Dan say quietly.

'Fuck knows, mate. She got us into the party, and then I don't remember seeing her after that.'

Who are they talking about? Me? Lily? Bella?

'I think I saw her arguing with a hooded figure,' Dan continues, 'but I can't be sure if that's a genuine memory, or something my imagination has conjured to replace the gaps in the fog.'

'You really did get fucked up last night, didn't you?'

'That's the thing: no, I didn't. I swear I didn't touch anything alcoholic, but my head feels like a herd of elephants are tapdancing; it's like the worst hangover I've ever had. And if I was in this kind of state when we left the party, there's no way I would have agreed to get behind the wheel. I'm a teetotaller when I know I've got to drive.'

My gut instinct tells me that Dan means every word of that, but I know I still care for him, and I can't allow that to cloud my objectivity.

'I didn't see her with any hooded figure, but once we got

inside the barn, there was no need to stay in touch. Why do you care what happened to the barmaid anyway?'

So that's who they're talking about.

'Because she took us to that place, and maybe she knows who or how they spiked our drinks. I don't think it was just me who suffered. Everyone else is struggling to remember much of last night as well.'

'What good will it do to know who spiked the drinks?'

'Because that person is the one responsible for that guy's death. Regardless of which of us was behind the wheel, if someone drugged us, then it's their fault.'

'Wait, you don't think you were driving?'

There's a pause, and I lean closer, desperate to hear Dan's response.

'I know my own mind and I wouldn't have driven if I was that fucked, and if I was driving, why didn't I have the car keys?'

Son of a bitch!

This is his ploy. Dan was the one who deposited the keys in my pocket so he could plant a seed of doubt in everyone else's minds. He's already working on Rod in the kitchen, and next he'll be trying to convince Lily and Bella. But not if I beat him to it.

I tiptoe away, and move towards the stairs, taking them two at a time.

'You know I love you more than life itself,' I hear Lily saying, and realise she must have managed to place her call.

I don't want to interrupt this intimate moment, so I stay behind the door, and wait for her to finish.

'No, baby, I can't come home yet, as much as I wish I could. What's that? I can't hear you properly... the signal here is awful. I'll try and call again later when I have better reception. Hello? Can you hear me? Bloody phone!'

I take this as my cue to push the door further open, and smile apologetically at Lily.

'Everything okay?' I ask, hoping this will be the moment she comes clean about whoever she's been speaking to.

'The sooner we get somewhere with a decent signal, the better.'

'Trouble at home?'

She looks at me as if trying to read my mind, but then shakes her head dismissively.

'Nothing to worry about. Are you all packed?'

I take a step closer and close the door behind us, so that we're now alone in the room.

'This whole situation is pretty fucked up, isn't it?'

She stares past me, her attention fixated on the wall over my shoulder.

'I certainly never thought I'd find myself in a situation where we need to sync our stories to cover up a crime again. I don't know about you, but it's giving me real déjà vu vibes.'

I didn't come in here to talk about Saul, but I can't ignore the similarities between that situation and this one. That night I swore I would never allow myself to face such a decision again, and yet only hours after meeting up with the same group and here we are, back where we started.

'Can we talk about something else? I wanted to check what you remember about last night. Specifically, what you remember about when we left the party.'

She shakes her head, her brow tight as she continues to stare at the wall.

'Um, nothing really.'

'You don't remember us piling into the car?'

She shakes her head again, this time forcing her eyes to meet mine.

'No, nothing.'

'What about whether or not Dan was driving?'

Her eyes narrow at the mention of his name.

'What? Of course Dan was driving. He was behind the wheel when we found the body.'

At least she's on my side in that respect, and if she believes Dan was driving then that might explain her willingness to go along with not reporting the accident. She always had a soft spot for him.

I'm about to ask her if she'd back me in calling the police when I hear a creak on the staircase. Turning, I see that Dan is standing there, a ringing phone in his hand. Our eyes meet, but he shakes his head dismissively, and rushes back down the stairs. Did he hear what we were talking about? Is he angry that I've figured out his plot against me?

13

DAN

I don't like the look Zoë fires me as I reach the top of the stairs, something between anger and mistrust, maybe? And then I spot Lily cowering at the back of the bathroom, and realise that Lily must have told Zoë about our one-night stand. I don't have time to hang around and explain that we were both heavily under the influence and that it meant nothing to either of us, because my phone is ringing in my hand. Although it's been plugged in since we got back, there's barely 15 per cent charge. But the call is coming from Jem's phone, and I need to know that Mam is okay.

The ringing stops as I reach the bottom of the stairs and I see that I've lost all signal again. I grab my coat from the peg by the front door, before hurrying out and scanning the horizon for any high land where I might have a better chance of getting a signal. I fasten the zip of the coat as the cold wind whips around me. I'm tempted to try and drive somewhere higher, but after last night I'm reluctant to ever get behind the wheel again.

Until this moment, I haven't really considered the prospect that my driving killed someone, but it drops on me now like a tonne of bricks. Rational me would never drive if I thought I was in no fit state, but who's to say what my brain was doing when under the influence last night? Could I really have thought my twenty-four years of driving experience would see us safely home? The guy we found this morning was in a dark grey over-coat, with nothing bright to distinguish him from the darkness, so it may have been impossible to see him until it was too late.

I turn on the spot, surveying the land. My best shot is the uprise in the field to my right. It's not high, but certainly higher than the farmhouse, so I stalk across to the wooden fence and hop over it, landing in a squelch of mud. I don't have time to think about the state of my trainers, and march purposefully up the muddy stretch of grass. There are sheep in a neighbouring field, only a wall separating us, but I can't see any other animals in this stretch.

The ice-cold wind scratches at my face, and I wish I had a hat, gloves, and scarf right now. I pull my arms across my chest, and persevere, keeping one eye on my phone, willing it to locate a signal. There is a large tree at the peak of the hill, its thick branches stretching several metres in all directions. I stand at the base, holding my hand into the air, but the signal bar flashes in and out.

I need to get higher.

Zipping the phone into the pocket of my puffer jacket, I search for any kind of foothold that will help me elevate myself enough to grab one of the lower hanging branches. The tree has lost most of its leaves, so I can't tell whether it's an oak or a sycamore. If Rod was here, he'd be able to give me a boost up, but I don't have time to go back and ask him to traipse up here with me.

I find a knob of wood in the bark of the tree, and place my foot onto it, my muddy trainer immediately slipping off. I need more grip, and lean back against the trunk, removing my trainers one at a time and bashing them against the bark to try and knock off as much mud from between the tread as I can. My muddy footprints stare back at me from the trunk, but I place my foot on the knot again, and use it to propel myself up. My grasping fingertips narrowly miss a branch, and I land back on the leaf-covered ground, almost losing my balance. With a deep breath, I take a second tour around the tree, looking for an alternative means up, but the knob is the only obvious option.

I size up the angle between that and the branch, and then with a deep breath, I charge towards the tree, throwing my right foot at the knob and then leaping with all my might. My hands grab the branch, and I quickly swing my legs back towards the trunk, and scurry my feet up the bark, using the momentum to pull my arms over the branch, and swivel my body around until I'm lying flat across it on my belly. I let out a sigh at the exertion, and take a moment to compose myself, before unsteadily dragging myself into a sitting position, and then bringing my legs up so that I'm kneeling on the branch. I crawl towards the trunk, and carefully place my hands around other branches, using them to pull myself into a standing position, and then slowly climb higher into the tree.

When I'm as high as my fear will allow, I sit on a branch, with one arm wrapped around the trunk for safety, and then pull out my phone. I have a single bar of signal, but it should be enough. I dial Jem's number.

The call is answered on the second ring, but it isn't Jem's voice I hear on the other line.

'Monsieur Willis, I'm so pleased to see you've finally returned my phone call.'

I recognise the shrill French accent of the woman who runs the finance department of the nursing agency. I've been avoiding her calls all week, while I searched for anything else I could sell to make a contribution towards my mounting bill. She must have figured I'd be more likely to answer the call if I thought it was Jem.

I can't avoid her forever, but I don't know whether Rod agreed to lend me the money last night. But I know one way or another I will get hold of some cash by Monday, even if it means doing something that sickens me to my bones.

'Mrs Moreau, how wonderful to hear from you,' I say, laying it on too thick, but desperate to keep her on side. 'I've been trying to reach you for a few days now, but the line has been engaged every time I call.'

'I need to know when you are going to settle your outstanding bill, Monsieur Willis.'

'Did Jem not mention? I'm planning to pay you on Monday. All my assets are tied up, but the cheque should clear by—'

'I am afraid we cannot wait until Monday, Monsieur Willis. You are three months in arrears, and until we receive payment, we will not be sending any nurses to your mother's house.'

I hear Jem's voice in my head, telling me that the bailiff would have forced entry yesterday had she not been there.

'No, please, she's vulnerable and I am away until Monday morning. Please, just maintain the care until then, and then I'll be back and we can settle what I owe. I just need a couple of days.'

'No, I am sorry, Monsieur Willis, but we cannot do that.'

'Please, I'm desperate,' I say, my voice cracking under the strain. 'I will find the money on Monday. I promise. I just need a couple of days. You can't leave her knowing nobody will be there to help for the next two days. Don't you have a duty of care or something?'

There is a pause on the line, and I can just about hear the low rumble of voices, and I can picture Jem there fighting my corner; although if she knew the truth about me, she wouldn't bother.

'Monsieur Willis, are you there?'

'Yes, yes, I am.'

'You promise you can settle your bill on Monday, yes? You will come and make payment in cash or by card?'

I swallow hard, but hope it isn't audible on the line.

'Yes, I promise. It'll be the first thing I do, as soon as I'm back. I promise.'

The line crackles as she sighs.

'Very well. Then we will continue to provide care for your mother, but – and I cannot stress this enough – if you do not settle your bill on Monday, we will cease care until payment is made. Is that clear?'

I close my eyes and offer a silent prayer of thanks.

'Understood. I will see you bright and early on Monday.'

The call ends, and I return the phone to my pocket. I have no choice now but to return from Scotland with the money I need to at least settle the care bill. And if I play my cards right, enough to settle the impending bill from the site accident. This call has bought me time to figure out my next steps. And if all else fails, I will ask Rod for his help at the wedding when he'll find it harder to say no.

But in the meantime I need to figure out who spiked our drinks last night and who made sure I would be in the driving seat to take the blame for the accident. I know in my heart that I would never get behind a steering wheel knowingly under the influence. It just isn't in my nature. So if I was already intoxicated, there is no way I would have got near the front seat, let alone started the engine.

And out of the other five, I know that at least one of them has been caught driving under the influence before, and if I'm right about them, then I need to watch my back. *We all do.*

14

EXTRACT FROM SAUL'S DIARY, DATED 11
DECEMBER 1999

If I ever see Dan again, I swear to God, I will fucking kill him!

It was the Youth Cup Semi-Final today. We were up against Horbury Hamsters, the team who narrowly beat us to the title and promotion last season. But today was supposed to be the day we exacted revenge and pipped them to the cup. At least that's what would have happened had Dan not fucked it all up for the rest of us.

With seconds until the final whistle, we were one-nil up and all we had to do was keep hold of the ball. But what does that lanky prick do but lump it up the field with no purpose or direction. I tried chasing after it, but after ninety minutes of chasing after every wasted pass, I was knackered, so it was no surprise it rolled through to their keeper, who promptly punted it back up field. Their centre forward got hold of it and shot from miles out, but rather than just blocking it, Dan stuck out a leg and it went for a corner. And he had the fucking audacity to have a go at me for not getting to his original shit pass. I told him to fuck off and concentrate on marking the centre forward who towered over me, but is almost the same height as Dan.

That's his role in the team: mark the opposition's lankiest players.

But then the ball was swung into the box, an outswinger, away from the keeper, and I threw myself at it, but it was way over my head, and who should get to it but the centre forward who had a free header. Our keeper stood no chance. I looked up from the muddy field and saw the ball nestling in the back of the net and Dan nowhere in sight. The whistle blew and when the coach called us over ahead of extra time he demanded to know what had happened.

'I told Saul to stand in front of him,' Dan piped up.

The nerve of the fucking guy!

'No, you fucking didn't,' I shouted back. 'He was your man to mark.'

'You said you had him,' Dan lied again. 'I was covering the back post.'

I looked at the coach, expecting him to back me, but instead he rolled his eyes, and started trying to motivate the team for extra time. Inquisition over, and the blame left firmly at my feet. The coach took me off with cramp five minutes into extra time, but they were all over us by that point, and I wasn't surprised when Dan lost the ball to that lanky centre forward again, and he buried his effort beyond our keeper.

When the full-time whistle went, the coach threw his hands up in desperation and simply said we'd have a better chance of winning the league after Christmas without Horbury Hamsters to battle against. What kind of an attitude is that to have? We should have been in the final, but for Dan's lame-arse decision making. Never takes any fucking responsibility, that one.

And when we were in the changing rooms, he was making claims that we would have won had I played better, and I fucking lost it with him.

'We didn't lose this game because of me, you prick,' I shouted over the din.

'Goals win games, Saul. If you'd finished either of the two chances you had we wouldn't have been clinging on at the end.'

I'm not proud of my actions but I went for him. Both hands aimed at his jugular, but he'd just come out of the shower, and my hands slipped against his skin, and he easily batted me away, landing a punch of his own, which connected with my nose. That only made me angrier, and I leapt at him again, this time rugby tackling him to the ground. And I reckon I'd have put him in his place once and for all if coach hadn't come in and dragged us apart.

'What the hell is all this? You're supposed to be a team,' he said, staring us both down.

'Coach, Saul went for me because he couldn't take the truth that he's not good enough to play up front.'

'Fuck you, Dan, you can't defend for shit.'

Coach told us both to be quiet and for me to get my bloody nose looked at by the nurse. I returned to the bench to continue drying off, but I could see Dan glancing over every now and again, laughing with those closest to him. I know he was probably making little jibes about me.

He's not been the same since that school trip to the waterworks. Although I don't know for sure, I reckon Lily let something slip to him and he now knows he's got a rival for Zoë. We've not been nearly as close since that trip. Whenever I've messaged him about hanging out, he always has an excuse. He'll reply saying, 'Me and Zoë are doing this or that,' like he's trying to rub it in that she's hanging out with him instead of me.

I've barely seen her since that trip as well. I don't know for certain that she's avoiding me, but she hasn't been at any of the usual parties. She claims she's too busy revising for her exams, but I reckon Dan's warned her to stay away from me. Either that or little lapdog Lily has threatened her.

But the thing is, they don't realise how strong my feelings are for her. And I plan to get her alone very soon and tell her exactly what she means to me. And if I'm right she'll tell me she feels the same and we can leave those others behind once and for all.

15

ZOË

Bella and Rod have disappeared upstairs, and with Lily still moping in the bedroom, and Dan God knows where, I'm alone in the living room with nothing to do but think about the terrible crime we're committing by not contacting the police. Even if we don't report *exactly* what happened, someone should inform the authorities that a man is dead and hidden behind the drystone wall on whatever road that was. He can't be left there to slowly rot away, exposed to the elements; though, to be honest, the cold climate will probably keep his corpse in near pristine condition for the foreseeable. But that doesn't make it right.

I'd make the call now if I had any kind of phone signal. I could do it anonymously. Phone and report where they can find him and then hang up before they start asking questions about how I know and who I am. But I'm also conscious that mobile phone numbers and locations can be traced. If I called them on my phone, and they were able to trace the signal, it wouldn't be long before they triangulated that I was on the same road most of the night, along with four others.

But which of them would have most to gain from casting

doubt on my innocence? It's Lily's dad's car, and she is the most familiar with the controls. What if, in his unfit state last night, Dan was struggling to negotiate the tight roads, and Lily insisted on taking over? If Dan was in the front with her, and passed out, maybe she could have dragged him into the driver's seat to protect herself, and then deposited the keys into my pocket to stop us from holding him totally accountable. But Lily was my best friend for so long that I just don't want to believe she would act that way.

So, that leaves Rod or Bella. Given Rod has been the most vocal about not reporting the crime, maybe he should be top of the pile of suspects. He may be worried that if the police investigated they'd find evidence that he was the one behind the wheel. He'd certainly be strong enough to move a comatose Dan. But I don't know if he can really be that calculating.

And then there's Bella: the mysterious stranger who is crashing our party. We know so little about her. Maybe she's some kind of con artist, and this is all part of some long-term plan she has: trick us into thinking we killed someone and then blackmailing Rod to keep it all quiet. It feels farfetched, but within the realms of possibility. One thing's for sure: there's more to Bella than I think any of us have really considered.

I stand, needing to clear my foggy head. At least the lack of signal here means I am not being pestered by Evan. There's no sign of any new messages, and deep down I'm hoping the penny has finally dropped for him. There's no way I'm going to continue things, especially after all his threatening messages and calls. I don't know whether he was bluffing when he threatened to tell the senior partners about what we did, but I sincerely hope he isn't prepared to detonate a bomb under both of our careers.

I start at knocking at the front door, and as I'm the only one down here, I cross to open it. Dan seems almost as surprised to see me staring back at him.

'I was making a call,' he quickly explains, even though I didn't ask. 'Where's Lily?'

I don't know why it annoys me that he's asking after her.

'Uh, she's upstairs packing, I think.'

'You too had a good chat, did you?'

I don't understand the edge to the question, but assume he thinks I was trying to persuade her to join my side and report the accident.

'We were just catching up,' I reply defensively, even though I'm the one who should be demanding to know why he planted the keys on me.

'Well, we can't go anywhere until we get the car cleaned up. It's pretty obvious we've hit something. The car's bull bars are badly dented. I think we're going to have to remove them if we don't want anyone asking questions.'

Rod's suitcase crashes against the floor at the foot of the stairs from where it's just been thrown. Bella's case follows next and then the two of them descend, though she appears to be having a go at him for the mistreatment of her luggage.

'Are you both packed?' he asks, no longer his usual playful tone.

'We need to fix the car,' Dan says. 'It's obvious it's been involved in an accident, and it'll only take one curious cop to pull us over and start asking awkward questions.'

'Well, I know fuck all about fixing cars,' Rod declares. 'Can't we just tape it up?'

Dan shakes his head. 'No, I think we're going to have to try and remove the bull bars. We need to find...'

His words trail off as Lily descends the stairs next.

'I'm going to need some tools if I'm going to detach them. Help me search for them?'

'I'll help,' Bella pipes up, before Dan has the chance to respond. 'I grew up in a house full of boys, so I know my way around a car.'

They head outside, leaving me with Dan and Rod and an awkward silence.

'Rod, listen,' I say, as he moves towards the lounge, 'I know you're not keen on calling the police, but don't you think we should do something about the man we hit? We could phone the ambulance service anonymously to report it. I hate the idea that he's left out there to slowly decompose.'

'And how do you plan to phone them when there's no mobile service?'

'Dan has service,' I pipe up. 'You just made a call, right?'

'The only place I could get a signal was up a tree. I'll point it out if you fancy a climb.'

Why did I even bother trying? It's in his worst interests to report the accident, because clearly he was the cause of the hit and run. If I was in his shoes, I'd like to think I'd be more likely to accept accountability, but I may just be lying to myself.

'Okay, so maybe we call once we're away from the farm and we have a signal.'

'They'll be able to trace the number that made the call,' Rod says. 'You might as well write the word guilty on your forehead.'

'Okay, so what if we stop at a payphone and make the call instead?' I try again, fixing Dan with a pleading stare and hoping to appeal to his better nature.

'And if we don't pass a payphone, then what?' Dan asks. 'Why are you so desperate to bring trouble to our door?'

I scoff in shock.

'You've changed your tune! When we found the body *you* were the one who wanted to report it.'

'Yeah, well, that was before I knew someone was trying to frame me for what happened.'

'What?' I shout. 'Now you want us to think you weren't driving?'

'If I was driving, why didn't I have the keys?' he snaps back.

This is it. This is his play: plant the keys in my pocket so he can deflect responsibility and cast doubt on his own reckless behaviour.

'Maybe because you put them in my pocket.'

He scoffs this time, and I can't tell why he's putting in so much effort just for Rod's benefit, when I'd have expected this level of theatrics with Lily and Bella here to witness it too.

'Oh, sure, Zoë, and when exactly am I supposed to have done that, huh? When we were all still under the influence of whatever narcotic we were spiked with? When we discovered the body? Tell me, Zoë, at what point during that five minutes were you and I even close enough for me to slip something into your pocket? And why didn't you feel it and call me out about it then?'

I stop as these questions punctuate the racing thoughts in my head. He's right: surely I would have felt someone slipping the keys into my pocket. And my memory is too hazy to recall who was standing where when we were looking at the body on the ground.

'That doesn't mean you didn't slip them into my pocket while I was passed out.'

He raises his eyebrows for dramatic effect.

'I woke up seconds before you did. You'd have felt the car shift if I'd climbed out, opened your door, put the keys in your pocket, and then got back in. You'd have heard doors opening and closing too. And ask yourself this, Zoë; given our history and the fact I've never stopped loving you, why the fuck would I try and stitch you up?'

The admission stuns me, and I don't know how to respond.

He still loves me? He doesn't know anything about me.

I scour my brain for a cutting response, to show the admission hasn't spun me sideways, but my shoulders sag when my mind remains blank.

'I don't know,' I say, sighing with resignation.

He turns and faces the front door, but makes no effort to open it; maybe hiding his own embarrassment about exposing his feelings. I stare Rod down instead.

'And what's your excuse for not wanting to phone the police? Were you driving?'

'Of course I wasn't.'

'Well then? Were you the one who spiked our drinks?'

His cheeks flame at the question, but it looks more like anger than guilt.

'Oh, and I chose to drug myself as well? To achieve what?'

Again it comes back to motive. Rod has just as much reason to drug us all as I do, which is to say, no reason.

'So why are you so against us reporting the victim's passing?'

'Because I don't want to give the police any reason to tie any crime back to me or to you, my friends. And unless you have forgotten, Bella and I are getting married tomorrow afternoon, and I don't want anything to ruin that.'

The fact that we're all struggling to come to terms with what happened – what we did – has already spoiled any revelry I was feeling, but I don't share this thought.

The inner turmoil I'm feeling now is unlocking so many memories of the time I last felt this lost and dejected. I can still hear Saul's dying breaths on that wet street. He was staring directly at me, his soul crying out for help, but I didn't move;

frozen by fear of losing him, and the repercussions of what we'd all done. And then I ran. Desperately wanting to put as much space and time between me and reality, and in truth I don't think I've ever stopped running. Even now, when I hear him calling to me in my nightmares, when I wake, I don't allow my mind time to process what the nightmare meant, and busy myself with work.

Tim once asked what has me crying out in my sleep and I've never told him the truth. I tell him it's just the stress of work and the fear of losing the next big case. But he doesn't know that my mind replays that night over and over, looking for how it went so wrong; the steps I should have taken instead to avoid the onrushing train of fate.

Even now, I hear Saul's voice: *I'll do it for you. I love you, Zoë.*

That's what Dan and Lily don't know: it was my fault that Saul died that night. If I hadn't been so chickenshit scared, or if I hadn't allowed him to persuade me...

'It's already after nine,' Rod states, looking at his watch. 'We need to be leaving for the Kennacraig ferry terminal by ten at the latest if we're going to catch the 1 p.m. crossing to Islay. You need to stop all this talk about phoning the police, Zoë. Okay? It's not good for any of us. The best thing we can do right now is forget any of this happened. We should swear a pact: *this never happened.* It's not like this will be the first time you've all sworn a secret, is it?'

He doesn't hang around to wait for either of us to ask what he's talking about, but the glance that Dan and I now share shouts the message clear: Rod knows what we did.

16

DAN

Zoë remains statuesque for several moments before hurrying away, and up the stairs. The bathroom door closes a moment later and I'm sure I can hear the gentle sound of her crying. I should go up and check on her, but I don't. I'm frozen to the spot. Rod saying the word *pact* instantly dragged me back through my mind to the night three of us were standing in the forest, praying we'd all wake from whoever's nightmare we were trapped in.

My heart was racing so quickly that it felt as though it would burst through my ribcage at any second. In the forest, there was so much foliage overhead that only slivers of moonlight managed to breach the canopy. And I remember it being so mild for that time of night that even though I'd been running for hours, searching for a means of escape, there was no visible sign of my breath.

I remember I paused when I spotted Lily by the well. It was so dark I couldn't be sure it was her at first. She looked so scared, and when the moonlight caught her face I could see she was crying. I'd always liked Lily but I knew how insecure Zoë could be about other girls fancying me that I didn't want her to mistake my fondness for Lily for anything else, and so I always tried to keep distance between us. I think deep down I suspected she liked me a bit, but would never have dared go behind Zoë's back. And so I just stood there watching her for what felt like a lifetime, but was probably only a few seconds. And then I thought about turning around and heading straight out of the forest. I thought I should just go home and sneak back up the drainpipe and in through my open window before my parents realised I was gone.

I knew that only Lily and Zoë could place me at the scene of Saul's accident, and if they were to come forwards they would implicate themselves in the crime we conspired to commit. I was still contemplating my options when Zoë suddenly appeared behind me, and I knew then the chance to escape was gone. We were in it together whether any of us liked it or not.

It was a huge risk for the three of us to meet up that night, but I don't think any of us would have got any sleep if we hadn't come back together to share our thoughts and feelings about what had happened. But choosing the forest, where we'd spent every summer with frisbees and footballs and playing games of hide and seek, seemed safe somehow; familiarity bringing a sense of security. Yet we'd never been in the forest after sunset, and I couldn't help picturing the crazed killers and opportunist sex pests who could be lurking in the shadows of the tall oaks and sycamores.

I'd kept looking over my shoulder on the way to the forest that was the heartbeat between our three addresses, and felt confident nobody had seen me enter, but I couldn't say the same for the other two. I kept having visions of the police seeking out witnesses and some oddball coming forward to question why I was out so late at the forest on the night one of my closest friends had been mown down and left for dead. I could picture the police asking the same question and seeing through my deceit when I claimed to know nothing about what had happened.

Zoë started asking the two of us if we knew what had gone wrong, why the alarm had sounded and why Saul had raced out into the street at the wrong moment and been struck by the speeding car. I told them I arrived after it had happened, even though I knew it would mean they'd want to know why I hadn't been there to collect Saul at the prearranged time. The truth was I did see Saul come racing out of the grounds, frantically looking left and right for me, and I should have signalled or waved him over to where I was parked down the street, but I could hear the alarm and I could see two overweight figures chasing after Saul, and I panicked. I hoped he would turn right and run down the pavement away from the security guards, and then I would drive up behind him when there was enough distance. That way they wouldn't see me or my parents' car collecting him. But I didn't do that, and Lily and Zoë never asked me outright what had delayed me arriving that night.

To this day they don't know why I was late getting to the rendezvous. Nobody knows that I was stuck in traffic because I'd driven miles to purchase an engagement ring. I'd planned to propose to Zoë the night after our final exams. I didn't have much of a plan, but I wanted to show her how much I loved her, and how I'd be willing to do whatever it took to make her every day the best it could be. I kept the ring hidden for weeks afterwards, in all the fallout, the police investigation and finally Saul's funeral. I wasn't mature enough to see my friend lowered into the ground, nor to deal with the intense feelings of grief and regret that followed. I barely saw Zoë much after that. The summer came and went and I barely left my bedroom. Mam was worried that I was depressed, and I suppose that's the closest description of how I was suffering. And then we graduated and Zoë declared she was heading south for university, and I just kept telling myself it was for the best, and that she deserved better than someone who had failed his friend when he needed me most.

I sometimes muse over what our life together would have been like had that night not happened in the way it did. Would Zoë and I have married and started a family? Maybe I would have moved south with her, and set up a business down there. Or maybe I'd have convinced her to come back to Wakefield and we'd have worked hard to put Mam in the kind of facility she now needs. And every time I catch myself thinking like this, I realise it is pointless.

It was obvious the police would ask us questions after what happened. They'd learn where Saul was running from, and I've no doubt the two overweight security guards would confirm he was the intruder they were chasing.

I told Zoë and Lily that it wasn't worth the three of us admitting our parts in Saul's escapade, even though both didn't want to allow him to take the full blame. But I knew that if I told them that was what should happen, Zoë would agree to it, and if Zoë agreed then Lily would quickly fall in line. I couldn't let the two of them suffer because of my failure, and so I told them to bury all memories of what had happened. We would be safe if none of us spoke about it. And twenty-four years later, my prediction has been true.

At least, I thought it was until Rod said, 'It's not like this will be the first time you've all sworn a secret, is it?'

The fact that Zoë stared at me at that exact moment before hurrying away to the bathroom to cry means she thinks he knows too. And yet it's impossible that he *could* know what we agreed in the forest that night. It was only the three of us there, and Saul was the only other living person who knew what we'd planned earlier. There's no way he would have told Rod beforehand because of the implications it would have, and he couldn't have told him after he was mown down in the middle of the street. Which leads me to only one other conclusion, Zoë or Lily must have said something to him.

I remember we weren't that close to Rod before Saul's death. He was Saul's best friend, and so more of a friend of a friend to us. But after Zoë left for university, I would run into Rod every now and again, and we'd chat about our memories of Saul, and I realised he wasn't as bad as I'd always thought. He'd ribbed me and the others throughout school, and Saul had always defended him, saying his jokes were a sign of respect, but I didn't really see it until after Saul's death. But if Rod now knows that we lied to cover our own involvement in the events that unfolded that night, then the chances of him agreeing to lend me the money to settle Mam's care bill just took a massive nosedive.

I need to know what he meant, whether one of the others has told him, and if they have, why now. And I can't help thinking that it is more than just a coincidence that I was the one to wake in the driver's seat this morning. What if the events of twenty-four years ago are somehow the reason lightning has struck again, and we find ourselves in a place where we need to work together to bury another crime?

17

ZOË

Rod's words echo over and over in my mind: *It's not like this will be the first time you've all sworn a secret, is it?*

I grip the edges of the basin, my eyes closed, and my head bent over, waiting for the retching to start. A thousand voices race around my head at once, all begging the same question: how could he know?

That night in the forest, it was just the three of us. It was Dan's idea that we deny any knowledge of what Saul was doing at the school; the only way to protect ourselves. Dan's logic was that Saul was already gone and his sacrifice would protect our futures. It felt so callous, but once I woke from a sleep-deprived night, I could see the sense in what Dan was suggesting. Questions would be asked about why Saul broke into the school, but the only thing tying the three of us to the intrusion was our friend-ship with Saul. The teachers would undoubtedly tell the police that the four of us were part of a friendship group, and so we *might* know what Saul was doing there. And with Saul unable to contradict us, outright denial would leave them at a dead end.

And so, against my sense of right and wrong, I pretended I'd never left the house that night. My parents had been away at a wedding and Lily had been due to stay at mine, so all I had to do was make sure she didn't crack and spoil everything. And I don't think Dan knows how hard that was.

When she emerged from my parents' bedroom that next morning, her face was gaunt, huge circles beneath her eyes revealing she'd spent most of the night crying. Her first question was whether any of it was real, and I could see she was in a state of shock. I made her drink sweet tea, I forced her to eat a plate of toast, and then I made her have a hot bath. And then I made her tell me what she was thinking.

She was terrified that the police would find a witness who would place us at the scene, and that if they learned we were lying, we'd face an even greater punishment. And she didn't think it was fair for Saul to take full culpability.

'They need to know why we were there...' she kept saying. 'They need to know what we wanted to achieve.'

I slapped her at that point, and told her I would never forgive her if she ever uttered a word of the truth. I hated myself for using emotional blackmail, but it was the only thing that would stop her. For days and weeks afterwards, I was still terrified that she'd crack and let something slip, but eventually the investigation slowed and quietened, and then I was eagerly packing my bags to leave. Even after a year at university, I still kept one eye looking back over my shoulder, half-expecting to feel the hand of the law on my back.

I can't think of any reason Lily would have told Rod, so that just leaves Dan. I know they became closer after I left town, and maybe one drunken night, Dan revealed more than he should have. That's the only thing that makes any sense right now. And maybe if he and Rod are in cahoots, then maybe it was Rod who slipped the keys into my pocket. I don't remember feeling it happen, but I remember being closest to Rod while we searched for the victim's pulse. We were both distracted by the shock of finding the body, so I might not have noticed him slipping them in.

And if Dan has told Rod what we were doing there, but painted himself as some kind of innocent victim, then it would make sense that Rod would want to exert some kind of revenge on me and Lily. One thing's for sure: I'm going to have to keep an eye on the pair of them, and one eye on Lily in case my faith in her is misplaced.

A loud commotion downstairs has me reaching for the door handle, and by the time I make it to the bottom of the stairs, I see Bella, her skin pale, with Dan and Rod staring at her in disbelief.

'What's going on?' I ask, unable to read the room.

'On the car stereo,' Bella begins, slightly out of breath as if she's just finished a race, 'there was a news report. The police said they found a body on the road between... I think they said... Linwood and Craigends. Do those names ring a bell with any of you?'

'We're in Craigends now,' Rod confirms solemnly.

'And do you know where the party was last night?' she asks, before all eyes fall on Dan.

He meets each of our stares, before puffing out his cheeks and shrugging.

'I have no fucking clue where we went last night. I have glimpses of scenery, but it's all shrouded in fog in my head.'

'It doesn't necessarily mean it's the same person we left this morning,' I reason, but not even I'm convinced by the argument. How many bodies are realistically found on roads in this neck of the woods?

'The reporter said the police are appealing for witnesses as they believe the man was killed in a hit and run incident. They have a team of forensic experts scouring the scene right now.'

'Oh, fuck!' Rod screams out, starting to pace. 'That's just fucking brilliant, isn't it? How long before they find tyre tracks they can match back to that monster of a car? Why didn't we check the victim's coat for signs of paint transference?'

I've never seen Rod looked so rattled about something. Even the time he set the chemistry lab on fire back at school, he simply laughed about it.

'This isn't *CSI*, Rod,' I say, trying to calm things, so we can think clearly. I don't add that I was against the idea of leaving the scene and hiding the victim behind the wall, but if the police do come calling at some point in the future, I'll be the first to turn on the others for self-preservation.

'Me and Lily have got the bull bars off, and we've stashed them in the barn under a blanket,' Bella says. 'We've also cleaned the car and can't see any traces of blood. It's the best we can do. Lily says we need to get going sooner rather than later.'

'It isn't too late to phone the police and hand ourselves in,' I say calmly. 'The longer we wait, the more likely whatever is in our system will vanish without leaving a trace. Now, I know that none of us want Dan to face prosecution, but—'

'Fuck you, Zoë,' he shouts at me.

'Dan, now isn't the time to lose your shit,' I say back, in an even tone.

'But we don't even know for sure that I was the one driving when the accident occurred. You're assuming it was me because I was in the driver's seat, but there's two anomalies you're choosing to overlook—'

'You or Rod could have slipped the keys into my pocket when I was distracted with the body,' I say to cut him off.

'Hey, I didn't slip anything anywhere,' Rod says defensively.

'Or you had the keys all along,' Dan continues, 'because *you* were the one driving. Did anyone else notice that Lily didn't need to adjust the seat when she drove us away from the scene? If I'd been driving, the seat would have been further back, because my legs are so much longer than the rest of yours; even Rod's. I wouldn't have been able to drive because my knees would have kept bashing the steering wheel.'

Nobody responds, and I hadn't noticed, but now that he's mentioned it, I don't remember Lily adjusting the seat. Could that mean Dan has a point, and someone else was driving? Maybe that's the real reason Lily is still outside trying to clean the car: she's trying to cover her own tracks.

'So, before anyone phones the police and turns us all in,' Dan says with a sense of finality, 'don't you think we should figure out exactly *who* is responsible?'

'No, I don't,' Rod says, calmer now. 'I think that's a really shit idea. We came together to celebrate our wedding, and that is precisely what we should do. The ferry leaves at one, and if we don't leave soon we won't make it in time. And I, for one, don't want to hang around this dump any longer, waiting for the police to come sniffing around.'

He stomps off in the direction of the living room, and Dan says he is going outside to help Lily finish cleaning the car. I'm about to hurry after him, worried he's going to try and convince her to turn on me, when Bella grabs my arm to stop me.

'I need to speak to you urgently,' she says. 'It's about Lily. I think she's keeping secrets from the rest of us.'

18

EXTRACT FROM SAUL'S DIARY, DATED 10
JANUARY 2000

As days out go, today's is certainly not one I ever care to relive. A trip up to Newcastle for a tour of the university there, and what I had hoped would be a chance to spend a bit of time alone with Zoë, but Dan's insistence on tagging along, even though he isn't applying to UCAS, spoiled everything.

I had planned to go up on the train, as who needs to deal with traffic and a two-hour-plus journey along the A1(M), but after Zoë let it slip that the two of us were going to go up and check out the Law campus, Lily said she'd tag along to check out the literature vibe and insisted on driving her dad's second-hand Land Rover. I could have stuck to my train plan, but Zoë said a road trip would be fun. Just the three of us talking shit and listening to music didn't sound too bad, but then Rod also caught wind and said he'd accompany us; not asking if he could tag along, just assuming nobody would mind. And, of course, none of us challenged him.

But even so, the four of us in the car with music and banter still sounded okay. And then when Lily stopped to collect Zoë from her place, who should be there but fucking Dan. He claimed he was there for moral support for Zoë who had yet to decide whether she wanted to move so far away from home. It didn't seem to occur to Dan that I would be going to the same welcome lecture and tour as Zoë. Or maybe it did occur to him and that's more likely the reason he insisted on coming. And because he also insisted on sitting next to her, it meant he took the middle seat in the back so there could be no interaction between us without him seeing and hearing every word.

Because of an accident on the motorway, we were late arriving in the city, and missed the welcome lecture. I was so angry with myself for not taking the train. It meant Zoë and I had to try and catch up with the group as they were touring one of the Halls of Residence. And Dan kept coming out with stupid, blatant comments about how it would be a tight squeeze in the single bed when he came up to visit her. Could he be more desperate? He might as well have put a big sign around her neck saying, 'Spoken for'. I could see she was getting frustrated by some of his shit too, but she bit her tongue.

When we eventually hooked up with the others, Rod had bought a box of lager, and said Zoë should take the front seat so the boys could drink in the back. By that point I was so pissed off about Dan getting in the way and ruining the experience for me that I was the first to crack open a can and knock it back. My mood did lighten by the third can, and Rod made it clear that Newcastle University definitely wouldn't make his final UCAS list.

With our bladders full, Lily had to stop on the return journey, pulling into some random services, and I finally got two minutes alone with Zoë when Dan went off to buy her some food. She was quick to apologise about his behaviour and said she doesn't know what's got into him recently. I didn't tell her how crazy I am about her as I was worried Dan would come back and interrupt, but I know I'll get a chance one day soon, and I plan to tell her all the ways that I would be a better match.

She did say she liked the Newcastle campus and may add it to her list of choices. But she also said she's thinking about heading to Southampton University as well, but her parents aren't keen on her being so far away. I'm not sure I could cope with being at the opposite end of the country to her either. Whereas, if we're both on the same Law course at the same university, then surely it will only be a matter of time until we hook up.

We had to stop talking when Dan and the others returned, but I definitely sensed she saw today as a missed opportunity as well. We hurried back to the car, and resumed our previous positions, but as little lapdog Lily was backing out of the parking space, her foot slipped, and we shot backwards into the front of a parked Jaguar. I can still hear the crunching of metal on metal when I close my eyes.

Lily cursed, and we all bundled out to survey the damage. The Land Rover didn't even seem to have a scratch, but there was a huge dent in the bonnet of the Jag where the tow bar had crumpled it.

Lily couldn't stop swearing, saying her dad was going to kill her for taking his car (turned out she hadn't asked to borrow it), and that there was no way she could afford to pay for the damage to the Jaguar herself. She moved the car to a free space further away and was about to start writing the other driver a note when Rod suggested she not bother.

'If his car hadn't been sticking out so much, you wouldn't have hit it,' Rod said. 'Fuck him; it's his own fault for not parking properly.'

I was quick to point out that it was Lily's fault, and it was only right to leave her details for insurance purposes, but the seed Rod had planted had already sprung roots, and instead of getting out, she drove away. You think you know somebody and then they do something like that. I can't help wondering what else she'd do to avoid getting into trouble.

19

DAN

I find Lily hosing down the front bumper, the damaged bull bars nowhere in sight. I'm glad she wasn't inside when Zoë started all that claptrap about someone slipping the car keys into her pocket. Surely, she's not crazy enough to think we'd believe she wouldn't have felt someone doing it? And now I see she's started accusing Rod as well. Where will her blame-game end, before she finally admits she was the one who hit the guy. I know she wouldn't have struck him on purpose, and we'd all corroborate that she was unknowingly under the influence, so I'm not sure how the police could prosecute. Plus, she's a criminal solicitor herself, so I'd imagine she knows people who'd be able to defend her if it came to it. I don't understand why she's so desperate to shift the blame to someone else.

Lily's head is down, her black hair tied into a tight ponytail, and she won't meet my stare. She looks visibly upset, and I want to comfort her and tell her everything will be okay, but I'm not sure I believe that myself. The others always saw Lily as the more emotional of the group, and whilst I'd agree with that conclusion, I don't see her empathy as a sign of weakness. If anything, her ability to absorb the group's emotion means she's like a sponge cleaning up a mess.

I sense it may be my presence here now that is upsetting her, and I hope I'm wrong. I should find Rod and ask him about lending me the money, but the mood he was in when I left means he probably won't be too receptive right now, and I hate seeing Lily upset. I always have. And maybe if things had been different when we were growing up... if she'd approached me before Zoë did, then maybe it would have been the two of us falling in love. But there is no point thinking about what could have been. I take a step closer to the Land Rover.

'Hey, Lil, the car's looking good.'

'Thanks,' she says, her eyes not leaving the trail of spray as it hits the bonnet.

'In fact, you'd never know it had bull bars on the front,' I add, scrutinising where the damaged bars once hung.

She doesn't respond, moving away from me and pointing the hose towards the roof. Maybe she's upset that the three of us left her to clean the car.

'Can I give you a hand?'

'No, you'll only get in the way.'

Still she won't look at me. There's definitely something wrong, and maybe I should just leave her to it, but curiosity is getting the better of me.

'I'm a bit taller than you and can probably reach the roof better if you're planning to use a chamois leather to wipe off the excess water.'

'I'm just trying to get rid of any blood and mud. It's not a fucking valet service.'

Is she angry with me about something?

I move behind her and pry the hose from her hands,

switching it off and allowing it to drop to the now wet muddy track.

'Have I done something wrong?'

She shakes her head, but her eyes are clamped shut, and it looks as though she's trying to fight back tears. Instinctively I wrap my arms around her and feel hers coil around my back, and then her shoulders bob gently as she lets go of her emotion. Aside from our brief exchange at the services, I've been avoiding Lily. It was wrong to assume that she'd make things awkward after the one-night stand. Zoë said she's got a new guy, and actually maybe she's just missing him.

'Are you missing home?' I ask, placing a hand on the back of her head, and holding her face to my collar bone.

She doesn't answer, so I try again.

'It's been a crazy twenty-four hours, hasn't it? I don't think I've even started processing everything that's happened since we crossed the border. It's okay to be upset though. There's part of me wishes we'd just phoned the police to begin with. Is that what's upsetting you?'

Her shoulders stop bobbing and she forces a hand between us, wiping at her eyes.

'No, that's not it.'

'What then? Is there something I can help you with? I'm happy to finish cleaning the car if you want to head inside and get your stuff together. It was wrong of us to leave you with the sole responsibility of getting rid of the evidence of what happened.'

I feel her head shaking against my chest.

'Is it just that you're missing home and the new man in your life?'

She briefly glances up at me.

'You know about him?'

'Well, no, but I overheard you and Zoë talking when we were in the car. I think it's great that you've met someone new. Who is he? What does he do for a living? Most importantly, does he make you happy?'

She looks like she wants to say something, but she's holding back. I guess it would feel weird discussing a new partner with someone you've slept with. I try to change tack.

'I'm sorry, I can see you don't want to discuss him with me. Forget I asked. But hey, you know, if speaking to him will help take your mind off everything else, you should just call him. Obviously, best to avoid telling him what's going on here in case the police one day manage to get hold of the call.'

I'm gabbling because I'm trying to be supportive, but am out of my depth.

She's still looking at me, as if weighing up whether to confide in me or not, and I want her to feel free to be open and honest. I've always considered Lily a friend. We've drifted apart since school, but I only want what's best for her.

She looks as though she wants to unburden herself, but is holding back.

'Do you think it's possible that good can come from bad?' she asks, and I'm not sure what she's getting at.

'I don't think any good comes from a hit and run,' I say honestly, talking about yesterday, but haven't I tried to do everything to make things good since Saul died? The fact that I'm in the financial mess I am would suggest I've failed miserably, so maybe the answer to her question is no. Or maybe she's talking about the night we spent together after Zoë's fortieth party.

I've tried to repress the guilt I felt the following morning, knowing that I was jealous of the life Zoë had built without me, and looking for anyone I could sleep with to spite her. I probably should have zoned in on anyone but Lily, but she was wearing a leopard-print mini dress that night, and I was blown away by how beautiful she looked. I wanted her, but the guilt of sneaking out of her hotel room that next morning without even saying goodbye has eaten away at me ever since.

It's the reason I knew things would be awkward on this trip; the reason I panicked when she approached me in the services. I've been lying to myself for years, saying that we both knew it was just a one-night thing, when in truth we didn't discuss what it would mean. We both wanted something to happen, but I've never really considered her motivation for dragging me to her bed. I did it to spite Zoë, and regretted my actions as soon as I woke and my hangover kicked in. I panicked that she'd tell Zoë and blow any unlikely chance of a reconciliation, but in truth I was kidding myself to think that Zoë would even care that Lily and I hooked up.

I lower my gaze, and lift Lily's chin with my finger.

'I owe you an apology,' I begin, looking into her tearful brown eyes.

She really is beautiful, and I think I was so scared of making Zoë jealous when we were in school that I kept my eyes blinkered. If I hadn't blown things two years ago, and if Zoë wasn't in the picture, I would definitely ask Lily out, but if Zoë is right and Lily already has a new man in her life, I don't want to scupper any chance of us remaining friends.

'It was wrong of me to lead you on at Zoë's party,' I admit. 'I knew what I was doing and why I was doing it, and you were the collateral damage. I was a dick then, and even more of a dick the next day when I snuck out of your room. I want you to know how much I regret everything that happened that day. I was a coward. I should have told you that I still had strong feelings for Zoë and that I was trying to hurt her. But instead, I ran away and have been running ever since. You didn't deserve to be treated that way, and I am ashamed of my behaviour. I am truly, truly sorry.'

I try to read her expression, but she's distant, and when she turns her head towards the car, and holds up a finger, I realise she hasn't even been listening to me. She slips out of my embrace and opens the car door, turning up the stereo, which I hadn't even realised was on.

I'm about to ask her what's going on, but she puts a finger to her lips. And then I hear the news report.

'To recap, the police are saying they are still looking for witnesses who saw any vehicles along the Barrochan Road between Linwood and Craigends in the early hours of this morning, where an as yet unidentified man was found struck down. Police are particularly interested in speaking to the owners of a 1997 Land Rover that was seen in the area at the time.'

My blood runs cold. They know it's us.

20

ZOË

Bella doesn't speak as she drags me across the carpet in the direction of the staircase, as if she's about to reveal some deep, dark secret. She doesn't stop until we reach the upstairs landing, at which point she seems to glance towards the three bedrooms to check nobody else is around, and then thrusts me towards the bathroom, closing and locking the door.

'Hey, what's going on?' I say, rubbing gingerly at my arm where the white from her handprint has yet to fade. 'You said you wanted to speak about Lily.'

'You've been friends with Lily for a few years, right?'

It's not the answer I'm expecting, and I can't tell what she's trying to imply.

'We were in the same class in junior school, but we didn't really become proper friends until we met again in secondary school. The teacher sat us together because of the closeness of our surnames, and when we got chatting, it turned out we had more in common than either of us realised.'

'And you're best friends, right? At least that's how Lily described the two of you.'

I try not to react to the question, but in my head she's telling me that the two of them have been speaking and that our relationship was the subject of the conversation. I don't feel comfortable revealing anything about Lily to a woman I met less than twenty-four hours ago.

'What else did Lily tell you?' I ask instead, trying to get a lie of the land, before I answer anything else.

'Oh, not much, but she said you and Dan dated in high school, right?'

I'm suddenly conscious that nobody knows where the two of us are, and she made such a conscious effort to ensure we wouldn't be disturbed. I need to tread carefully here. I know she's Rod's fiancée, but given what happened last night, and what Rod said about our previous pact, I'm not sure I should be so willing to trust Bella, even if everyone else is.

'Sorry, Bella, I'm sure you're well intentioned, but what exactly are we doing here in the bathroom? Downstairs you said you wanted to speak about Lily keeping secrets, but so far all you've done is ask questions about me. Now, I don't know how friendships work where you're from, but I'm not in the habit of throwing my friends under the bus at the whim of a stranger.'

I stand firm, ready to rush for the door, if she doesn't come clean about her real intentions here. For all I know, she could have been the one driving the car this morning and is just trying to throw the light onto the rest of us so we don't consider her a suspect.

She watches me carefully, considering her answer.

'Is that what you think of me? That I'm just some stranger? Rod invited me on this trip so I could get to know each of you as you're his closest friends. But hey, if you're not interested in any of that, I'll just be on my way.'

She steps back towards the bathroom door, and reaches for

the lock, but guilt overwhelms me, and I find myself apologising, and asking her not to leave. She's right; she's going to be marrying Rod soon, and although I wouldn't describe Rod as a close friend, a friend is a friend, and I should extend her the same courtesy, especially if she's going to be a bigger part of his life.

'I'm sorry, Bella, I didn't mean to be rude. Tell me a little about yourself, and then we can start to be friends too. Where is it you said you're from?'

'It's as I said, I'm kind of from all over, which is why my accent is so difficult to place. I was born in Manhattan, but my dad got moved around a lot so I've spent time in at least a dozen different states at one time or another.'

I thought there was something odd about her accent. Every now again, it seems to change, but I don't know how to explain the change as it's so subtle.

'And what is it you do as a career?'

'Didn't I say?'

I remember asking the question when we were in the car earlier, but Rod started talking about his new foundation, and I don't recall Bella ever answering the question.

'No, I don't think so,' I say, smiling thinly, in an effort to show I'm not just being nosy, although I am suddenly conscious about just how little any of us know about her.

'Oh, well, I was a yoga instructor when Rod and I met. That's how we met actually.'

'Rod and yoga?' I say, guffawing at the claim. 'I don't believe it!'

'I think you'd be surprised at what Rod is capable of these days.'

The statement stops my laughter in an instant.

'I just meant he's more in touch with his true self,' she

explains, but I'm not convinced that's what she meant. 'We're both so glad you all agreed to come to the wedding. Rod talks about the four of you all the time, and how he wouldn't be the guy he is today without the four of you.'

I'm at odds with this statement, as I was never that close to Rod. My memories of Rod in secondary school are that of a clown who made it his life's mission to make mine and Lily's lives that little more sour with his lewd jokes and pranks. I remember reporting some of his more inappropriate comments to the head of year, but when nothing happened it became clear that Rod was being protected from above, and no amount of complaining would change his behaviour. So, in the end, I stopped trying. His idea of friendship is clearly much different to my own.

'It was good of you to invite us all. It's nice being back with Lily and Dan again.'

'Bringing back lots of memories, I bet,' she says, chewing on the end of her finger.

I narrow my eyes again, still not wholly sure of the real reason she brought me up here. She claimed it had something to do with Lily, but was that just her way of getting me away from the rest of the group? All I know is that we should get going if we want to catch the ferry, so I eye the door.

'But you and Lily are still close, right? No secrets between the two of you?'

I instantly picture Evan and the fact that I haven't told Lily about him, but I don't think that's what she's getting at; I can't see how it could be.

'Well, we don't see each other as much as I'd like, but yes, I'd say we're still pretty close.' I take a breath. 'Listen, Bella, can you stop beating about the bush and just say whatever it is you want to tell me about Lily?'

'I was just curious about what big secret Lily feels desperate to tell Dan.'

She dangles the line, and I'm embarrassed that curiosity gets the better of me.

'What are you talking about?'

She takes a step closer, lowering her voice.

'When the two of us were outside cleaning the car, I received a call from an old friend, which I went off to take, trying to maintain a signal, but the line kept dropping so I gave up on it. When I was walking back towards the car, I overheard Lily talking to someone, so I stayed out of the way. She mentioned Dan's name, so I assumed that's who she was talking to, but when he didn't answer any of her questions and the conversation continued, I peeked out and saw she was talking to herself. It was like she was rehearsing what she wanted to tell him.'

I think back to when Lily collected me yesterday morning and was asking whether I have feelings for Dan still. Is she planning on telling him we have no future, so I don't have to?

'She was saying she has a secret she's been keeping from him,' Bella continues. 'She sounded upset, and kept saying sorry over and over again. Do you know why she would be so sorry and what the secret is?'

For some reason Saul's face fills my mind, and I have to chase it away.

'There's nothing I can think of,' I lie, though inwardly I'm trying to work out whether she could somehow know what Saul told me that night.

'I think it's obvious what Lily wants to apologise to Dan for,' Bella says.

I'm not following her trail of thought.

'Oh shit, you really need me to spell it out for you? I think Lily was the one driving when the accident occurred, and she wants to tell Dan she's sorry for allowing him to take the blame.'

I think back to this morning, and I'm sure Lily was squeezed in between me and Rod when I woke up, so she's the last person I would suspect of driving. How on earth would she manage to get Dan into the driving seat and the keys into my pocket and then slip herself in between Rod and me without disturbing any of us, and while under the influence of whatever we were drugged with?

'I also think Lily is lying about being drugged too,' Bella continues. 'In fact, I think she remembers a lot more than she's claimed until now.'

Again, I try to picture this morning's events. Bella was the first out of the car, and she discovered the body. Dan was next out followed by Rod, and then Lily, but was her reluctance to get out because she already knew what they were screaming and shocked to see?

'Listen, the last thing I want to do is force a wedge between the two of you, but I just think you should be careful,' Bella says. 'I know you've been best friends forever, but in my experience, sometimes best friends are the ones you need to be most careful of.'

She excuses herself and leaves the bathroom, but I remain where I am, now burdened with the possibility that I've misjudged Lily. She has been almost inconsolable all morning, but I assumed that was because she's always been so empathetic, but it's also possible that guilt is causing her upset. All this time I've been assuming Dan was the one who slipped the keys into my pocket, but it would have been easy for Lily to slip them into my coat when she was in the car. But can the woman I've known since we were twelve have pulled the wool over my eyes so easily?

My mind is all over the place, and I need to gather my

thoughts before I accuse her of anything. I run the basin tap until it's hot and then I splash handfuls of water onto my face, using the hand soap to wash the fatigue out of my skin. I then wash it away with more hot water, before reaching for a towel and slowly drying my face, but I freeze when I see what's staring back at me in the mirror. Someone's words have been smeared into the glass, but it's what the message says that has me statuesque. Four words stand out from the steam on the glass:

I KNOW YOUR SECRET.

21

DAN

Police are particularly interested in speaking to the owners of a 1997 Land Rover that was seen in the area at the time.

The words of the radio news reporter echo through my mind as we rush from the car to the house, in search of the others.

They know it's us.

We've spent the morning arguing over whether the police will be able to find evidence that ties the scene back to Lily's dad's car, but none of us stopped to think that a witness would place us at the scene. The road we woke on this morning seemed fairly deserted at the time, but who's to say how many other vehicles passed by while we were passed out? Maybe this same witness saw us hit the man. And if that's the case then it's only a matter of time until the police are at the door, dragging us – dragging *me* – away for manslaughter.

I barge through the front door with Lily hot on my heels. Rod is in the living room, rifling through his case for something.

'They're onto us,' I tell him quickly, crossing to the window and peeling back the net curtain to check whether there are any police vehicles already on the track.

'What are you talking about?'

'On the radio,' Lily picks up, 'on the news, they said the police want to speak to a group travelling in a 1997 Land Rover. My dad's car has an "R" plate. That's 1997.'

Rod's eyes widen.

'That bitch!'

I'm confused at first; does he know who reported us to the police? Does he think Zoë's conscience has got the better of her? I hadn't even contemplated the possibility that one of our own could have betrayed us. The fact that she's nowhere to be seen right now speaks volumes. But if she was the one who was driving, would she really invite the police to find us? Maybe she's gambling that the others will choose her side and say I must have been responsible as I was the designated driver for the night, and woke behind the wheel. It's a huge gamble to take.

'Zoë,' I call out, wanting to see her face when we put the accusation to her.

'Hey, what's going on?' Bella asks, emerging from the kitchen with her phone in her hand.

My eyes snap back to Rod. Was I wrong: did he mean he thinks Bella turned us in?

He looks at her for a long moment and my eyes flit between them.

'I think that barmaid who took us to the party must have told the police we were there,' Rod says aloud, and I now see where his mind has taken him, and actually that makes a lot more sense than either Zoë or Bella calling anonymously. She was in the car when we drove to the party, but noticeably absent when we woke this morning. Would she have seen the police report and put two and two together? Or is there some other unseen antagonist messing with us?

'Did anyone get her name?' I ask, not that it will do us any good.

I'm met by three blank faces.

'We should go back to the village pub and wait for her there,' Rod says, practically foaming at the mouth. 'I gave that bitch two hundred quid and this is how she pays us back?'

'Whether it was the barmaid or not doesn't matter,' Lily says evenly. 'If it was her who reported us, she'd be able to tell them we're here. You told her we were staying on this farm, Rod, so if it was her then it's safe to say they're probably already on their way. If it wasn't her, then we have a little more time, but it's almost ten and I think we just need to get going.'

'Lily's right,' I concur. 'The plan was to get to the terminal by half twelve to catch the one o'clock ferry, right? I say that's as good a plan as any.'

'We should gather up any supplies we can lay our hands on so we don't have to stop along the way,' Lily adds. 'Bella, can you see if you can find any bottles we can fill with water? And check the cupboards for anything we can snack on.'

I never realised Lily could be so pragmatic. The Lily I remember wasn't one for forming plans and being practical, but she's now organising us with the precision of a general. For the briefest moment I'm reminded of my own upbringing, and how my mam would organise Dad and me. I don't know how Lily can be so cool under such pressure, but it's a relief that someone is, and is ready to take charge of the situation.

'Rod, the Airbnb host was supposed to leave a welcome box with supplies, right? See if there's any bread for making sandwiches. We'll need fuel at some point, but I'd suggest we get as far from here as possible before stopping to fill up. Ideally, somewhere relatively remote without security cameras on the forecourt.'

She claps her hands, snapping us into action.

'I'm sure when I was looking for tools in the barn earlier, I saw a set of old plates. I think we borrow those – stick them over what's on the Land Rover – and suddenly we have a "T" reg, instead of an "R". It may not be enough, but it may help us hide in plain sight. We only need it to get us to Jura, and then we can come up with a new plan. Find Zoë, and tell her we're off in five minutes.'

She doesn't wait for us to answer, marching out of the house and in the direction of the barn. I race up the stairs, finding the three bedrooms empty, but the bathroom door is closed. I gently knock.

'Yes,' Zoë replies meekly, her voice lost somewhere between exhaustion and terror.

'We're leaving in five. Are you ready?'

She doesn't answer at first, and I wonder if she heard me.

'Where's Lily?' she eventually says. 'There's something I need to ask her.'

'Heading to the barn to look for alternative licence plates. Whatever you need to ask her, be quick.'

I don't wait, hurrying back down the stairs, and find Rod alone in the living room. This is my chance. I need to be brave and just ask him for the money. If he agrees, then I'll phone Jem and reassure her that I'm going to fix things. And if he doesn't, well, it doesn't bear thinking about.

'Hey, Rod, have you got a minute to chat?' I ask, suddenly aware I don't really know how to start the conversation.

He stops rifling through his case and stares at me, his manner not overtly welcoming.

'I was just wondering what you remember from last night,' I continue, hoping he tells me he remembers us discussing my financial woes and has already transferred the cash.

He puffs out his cheeks.

'If you're asking whether I remember if it was you or Zoë driving, then I'm as clueless as the rest.' He pauses, and pulls a sympathetic face. 'You were the one who volunteered to be the designated driver, so I get her point.'

'But do you remember seeing me drinking anything last night?'

He looks up at the ceiling in silent contemplation.

'Honestly, I don't, but I really don't remember a lot of anything. There were a lot of drinks. I vaguely recall a tray of shots of something luminous, but I have no idea what it was.'

I figured this would be his response, but it should only help my cause if I can get him feeling sorry for me.

'I just can't believe that I would have knowingly got behind the wheel of the car if I'd been drinking. I've never done it before, because I know how much of a lightweight I can be, and I tend to get quite clumsy after a couple of pints, so I've never trusted myself to drive after any alcohol.'

He nods empathetically, before his attention is diverted back to his case as if he thinks the conversation is now over.

I take a step closer, because I don't want Bella or Zoë to over-hear what I'm going to say next.

'There was something else I was hoping to ask,' I say, willing the words to get past the lump in my throat, knowing that I'm crossing a line in our friendship from which there will be no return. I hate that things have come to this, but I need to swallow my pride.

'The thing is...' I begin, willing myself just to blurt it out. 'The thing is, I'm in a bit of trouble, mate. I, um, I'm having some financial difficulties, and I hate to ask – believe me, this is soul-destroying – but do you think you'd be in a position where you might be able to lend me some cash for a few weeks?'

He watches me without speaking.

'I'd pay it back with interest,' I add quickly, really wishing I'd spent more time rehearsing what I wanted to say.

'Sure,' he replies flatly. 'What do you need? A couple of hundred? I should say all the drinks are paid for at the reception tomorrow, so you don't need any cash for that, if that's what you are worried about.'

I didn't expect him to be so willing, but two hundred pounds isn't nearly enough to pacify Mrs Moreau at the agency.

'Oh no, it wasn't for tomorrow. The thing is, Rod, my business is in dire straits, and everyone seems to have a hand in my pocket. I'm in real trouble.'

He eyes me suspiciously.

'How much do you need, Dan?'

'Do you think you could lend me a couple of grand? Five at most?'

I instantly regret settling for such a low figure. That will be enough to ease Mrs Moreau's concerns for now, but it's only delaying the inevitability of bankruptcy. I see now that what I should have done is waited until we got to his house later, sat him down and presented my case more formally, explaining the issues I'm facing because of that on-site accident that really had fuck all to do with me.

Five grand is probably not even a drop in the ocean for someone with Rod's family background, and I'm sure if I'd asked for the amount to settle the court case he'd have probably considered it.

'I'm not a fan of discussing financial matters with friends and family,' he begins, his tone so flat I can't tell if he's going to agree or reject the proposal out of hand. 'I saw how it affected my father's relationship with his family. I won't go into the detail, but when he married into Mammy's wealth, his own brother came begging cap in hand, and it didn't end well for the two of them. Have you asked the bank for a loan?'

I've asked every bank, I don't say.

'It's not something they can help with,' I tell him, not wanting to admit just how awful my credit score is with the previous issues I've had.

'Hmm...' he muses. 'Can you give me some time to think about it?'

I don't know how to answer. I'd rather know now so I can search for an alternative, but I don't want to pressure him into saying no.

'Of course,' I say passively.

'And are you happy if I discuss it with Bella? She is soon to be my wife, and I don't like the idea of starting our marriage with secrets.'

The thought of others in this group learning the truth about my mess is the last thing I want, but I find myself nodding.

We both stop at the sound of footfalls on the staircase. Zoë stares back at us from the foot of the stairs.

'What are you two discussing?' she asks warily.

'Nothing important,' I quickly retort, before Rod can drop me in it. 'Are you ready to go?'

She raises her eyebrows at the two of us before shaking her head and marching out of the house, slamming the door behind her.

22

EXTRACT FROM SAUL'S DIARY, DATED 30 MARCH 2000

Rod Astor really is a dick sometimes. I mean, he's my best friend, and I don't expect him to be perfect all the time, but one of these days his shit is going to get him into serious trouble. And if I'm not careful, I'll be the one who pays the price.

I know his dad is the headteacher, so how much trouble can he really get into, but I just think he's going to go a step beyond his dad's ability to cover for him.

There's a rumour going around that Mr Astor had to co-fund the new school swimming pool because a witness came forward and said Rod was the reason the chemistry block burned down. Rod outwardly denied it but admitted it to me last summer. He said his dad was pretty pissed off, but the school governors were prepared to turn a blind eye in exchange for a 75 per cent contribution to the costs of building the pool and repurposing the old chapel into state-of-the-art changing facilities.

But they must have argued about something last night, because all day Rod has been searching for something he could do to get into more trouble. Talking back to the form tutor at registration earned him a scathing look; turning up late for assembly earned him a lunchtime detention; and refusing to hand in his History assignment resulted in the threat of a letter home. None of it was enough. It was like he had a death wish all morning. I didn't see him at lunchtime as he was serving his detention in the school library, but I saw him again in the changing rooms ahead of games afternoon, and he had this mischievous look in his eye. I should have stayed well clear. In fact, I regret not just avoiding him all afternoon. But curiosity got the better of me, and I wanted to know what he was up to. He told me we would sneak off during cross country, and I assumed he was planning to go and have a crafty cigarette, but he dragged me back to school, and to the swimming pool.

He told me to wait by the changing rooms, and to keep watch for anyone coming in. I asked him what he was going to do, and he just winked. I should have known something was up when he went inside, returning two minutes later with a large black sack. I chased after him as he ran into the small wooded area at the far side of the playing fields.

'This is perfect,' he said, when we got to the clearing where most of the smokers hang out during breaktimes.

I asked him what was in the bag, and he kept watching me with this huge grin on his face, like he was trying to assess how likely it was that I'd grass him up. I had to convince him I could be trusted, and then he threw the bag towards me. It landed open on the ground, and I saw several girls' blouses and T-shirts fall out.

'I pinched the girls' clothes,' he said with glee. 'When they get out of the pool, they'll have to stay in their swimming costumes for the rest of the afternoon. There'll be tits everywhere.'

I couldn't help laughing out loud, imagining how shocked they'd be returning to the changing rooms to find their clothes gone. I asked him when he planned to return the tops, and he said he had no intention of giving them back and wanted my help to bury them amongst the trees. I told him I'm all for a joke, but not giving the tops back would be tantamount to stealing. He didn't seem to care. I told him it was fine to keep the clothes this afternoon but we should put them back in the morning because then the teachers would be even more confused about what happened. But then he struck a match and dropped it on the pile. The flames caught immediately, and I found myself backing out of the woods in time to see the first of the cross-country runners passing, and promptly joined the group. I should have realised that somebody was bound to have seen us, and sure enough, at the end of the day, and with most girls covering them-selves in their wet towels, Rod and I were sent to the head-teacher's office.

I was fucking fuming with Rod, and whilst we were outside, waiting to be called in, I gave him a piece of my mind. It's all right for him having a dad who can bend the rules, but I was unlikely to escape punishment so easily. I kept thinking about what my parents would say. I knew Dad would hit the fucking roof, so I told Rod he needed to step up and accept responsibility. I told him he was to say it was all his idea and that I tried to talk him out of it, which is sort of true. He said he would, but the second we were called into the office, he was a totally different person, crying and begging his dad not to believe the so-called witness.

Instead, he claimed he and I were running the whole time and that someone has it in for him because they're jealous of us. He even suggested it was probably Glynn who stole the girls' tops. I thought there was no way his dad would buy it, but he did.

I wanted to speak up and tell the old man that Rod was lying, but to do so would have meant admitting to my own part in the endeavour. And I figured Rod would say I was as much to blame. So, when Rod's dad told us to go home and say no more about it, I knew it was my 'Get Out of Jail Free' card, and I went along with it.

And now I feel hugely ashamed, especially because I saw how pissed off Zoë and Lily looked as they huddled in their damp towels.

One thing's for sure: I need to stop hanging around with Rod when he has that mischievous look in his eyes, as I might not be so lucky next time.

23

ZOË

I think she remembers a lot more than she's claimed until now.

Bella's words fire off every synapse inside my head as I march downstairs, finding Dan and Rod conspiring again in the living room. I've no doubt Dan has been busy telling Rod that I'm to blame, and I'm angry that I ever trusted Dan. I'm clearly a bad judge of character, as Evan's last message attests. I should just block his number, but if I do that he'll drop me in it with Mae at work, and I need to stay ahead of any fallout. I've taken screen-shots of his messages so I can show Mae how he's been trying to blackmail me, in the hopes that my coming clean might buy me a stay of execution.

I slam the front door so Dan knows just how angry I am at his continued betrayal. I don't want to believe that Lily could be capable of similar deception, allowing the finger of suspicion to swing between Dan and me whilst all the while knowing she's the one the spotlight should be shone on.

And I also don't know which of them scrawled the message on the mirror, claiming to know my secret. It would be typical of the sort of prank Rod would have played back in school, and maybe it was him who wrote it, but I also don't know for certain that I was the party intended to read it. I wiped it from the mirror with a towel. I sense there is a game at play here, but I'm not going to take any steps to start playing until I know who my opponents are.

My thoughts return to Lily as I reach the barn and find the door ajar. I can understand why she would struggle to come to terms with what happened. Killing someone with a car is a huge burden to accept. And if she was struggling to admit her actions and saw the rest of us not suspecting her, I can totally understand how easy it would be just to go along with the flow. In that way, it would feel less real, and she could almost allow herself to believe she imagined being the one who caused the accident.

It would certainly explain why she was so keen for us not to report it at the scene. I'd originally assumed it was because she's still a bit sweet on Dan and that her motivation was to protect him. But given what Bella said about Lily rehearsing a speech to reveal a big secret to Dan, it all makes sense: she didn't want to report the crime because then they might uncover the fact that she was responsible.

I hang back at the large wooden doors, taking a deep breath to steady my nerves. I can hear Lily moving about inside, but I need to approach this in the right way. Ultimately, she's my friend, and if our roles were reversed, I'd want her to take a gentle approach with me; to let me know that she isn't judging me for what was ultimately an accident. I've no doubt that she didn't want to hit the guy, and the deceit that has followed can easily be explained by her fear about what she did. And if she's rehearsing how to tell Dan the truth, then that means she's already on her way to accepting what she did and making amends.

It's possible that with us all a bit worse for wear after the party, Lily volunteered to drive us home. After all, she's the one most familiar with the car's handling, and she did take over driving from me yesterday when I was struggling with the steering. I could just imagine her suggesting that she'd be able to navigate the narrow roads back here better than any of the rest of us, even under the influence.

I take a second deep breath, before rolling around the door and into the tall open space. Strands of straw litter the concrete floor and there's a draught blowing through the gaps in the wooden wall panels. Directly in front of me is a mud-strewn tractor, the windscreen caked in dirt and dust, which looks as though it's been a relic here for years rather than weeks. There's a large wooden worktable running the length of the left wall, and shelving units along the back, until the large rectangular bales of hay looking like a large Lego set.

I can't immediately see Lily, but then spot her rummaging through the shelves at the back of the barn. She is mumbling something that I can't quite make out, but then she stops as she sees me and freezes.

'Oh, hey,' she calls out, as if suddenly realising who I am. 'Did you hear the news?'

I'm about to ask about what Bella said she heard, but the question throws me.

'What news?'

'The police are now looking for an "R" registered Land Rover.'

My mouth hangs open.

'Rod and Dan reckon that barmaid turned us in.'

Wouldn't she have told the police our names and descriptions, rather than just the vehicle type? And I'm sure she'd be able to tell the police we're staying at this farm, and yet they haven't come by to question us.

'I saw some spare plates in here earlier,' Lily continues, 'but for the life of me I can't remember where. Can you help me look?'

If Lily was the one driving, she'd be the keenest for us to get away and cover the fact that her dad's Land Rover has an 'R' registration number.

I cross to the worktable and begin to search amongst the various tools and clamps covered in cobwebs, but there's nothing obvious.

'So, I was talking to Bella,' I say as casually as I can manage, failing miserably, 'and she mentioned overhearing you talking while washing the car.'

In my periphery, I see Lily freeze, but she doesn't look over, and it's only temporary before she continues opening and closing drawers in the filing cabinet she's beside.

'Oh, really, what did she think I was saying?'

'She said she thought you were talking to Dan at first, but then realised he wasn't there. She said it sounded like you might have been trying to apologise to him about something or other.'

I'm trying to extend an olive branch in the hope that she takes it, but she doesn't answer, closing the final drawer of the filing cabinet, and moving back towards the tractor.

'Lily? Did you hear what I said? Bella said she thought you were rehearsing an apology to Dan, and I just wondered—'

'You shouldn't put too much faith in what Bella says. She can't even get her own story straight, so why should you trust her to recall what others have said?'

I turn to face her.

'What do you mean?'

'Do you remember when we first collected her and Rod at the

airport? She said she grew up in New York, right? When we were washing the car, she kept telling me about her upbringing in California.'

'Ah, yeah, but she told me her dad served in the army and they were always moving about.'

'It's not just that,' Lily continues. 'Do you... I don't know how to explain it, but I just get a weird vibe off her. Do you know what I mean? I can't say why, but there's something not right about her and Rod.'

'If you mean the age gap, Rod has always chased after younger women.'

'No, it's more than that. I feel like she's up to something. Playing games.'

'So, you're denying rehearsing an apology to Dan outside?'

'You're damned right I am! She's making it up.'

'But why would she? What does she have to gain?'

Lily shrugs.

'Who's to say why any of us do anything? Maybe she's trying to drive a wedge between you and me. She knows that you and Dan used to be an item, and maybe she senses unresolved feelings there and is trying to paint me as an obstacle. I don't know why she'd lie to you, but I don't trust her as far as I could throw her.'

'What else did the two of you talk about while you were removing the bull bars?'

'She was the one doing most of the chatting. Well, interrogating would be a more apt description. She kept asking questions about the rest of you.'

'Like what?'

'She asked all sorts of questions about you and Dan: when you broke up; how long you were together; that kind of stuff.'

'And what did you tell her?'

'At first, I said it was none of her business, but she kept on and on, so in the end I told her the basics: how you were going away for university and didn't think a long-distance relationship would work.'

It strikes me as odd that Bella would have any interest in that kind of detail, particularly as she could easily get that information out of Rod if she needed. But I can't see why that history would be of any interest to her anyway. And yet Bella's voice continues to echo through my head now: *I think she remembers a lot more than she's claimed until now.*

'Hey, how's your head after last night?' I ask Lily next.

'More or less recovered. How about yours?'

'Still full of holes.'

Lily sighs heavily.

'There's something I should tell you,' she says, staring down at me from the cabin of the tractor. 'I don't think I was drugged like the rest of you.'

I stare back at her, surprised by this admission.

'When we first woke up in the back of the car, I genuinely had no idea of how we got there or any memory of leaving the party,' she says. 'But over the course of this morning, things have started to return. I was pretty wasted. It's been ages since I was properly drunk, and so it didn't take more than a couple of beers and then I vaguely remember Rod ordering shots, and most of the rest is a blur. I do remember falling into the back of the car. I think Rod must have been carrying me, because he squeezed in next to me and fastened the seat belt around me. I was definitely too wasted to have driven, and I'm pretty sure I passed out in the back not long after. But the thing is, what I distinctly remember is the rest of you all stealing Dan's water to drink. I didn't have any, but I can picture all four of you drinking from it. So, what I was thinking was maybe the drug – whatever it was – was present in Dan's water bottle.'

She jumps out of the cabin, landing in a hunched position on the hard floor.

'You think someone spiked Dan's water?' I say, no recollection of Dan even having a bottle.

'Hold that thought,' she tells me, throwing herself under the tractor and reaching for something, before pulling her arm out and holding two plates in her hand. 'Found them! I knew I'd seen them in here somewhere.'

'Why would someone want to spike Dan's water?' I ask as we head out of the barn, towards the Land Rover.

'That I can't answer, but it's the one thing you all drank from that I didn't.'

'Where is the bottle now?' I press.

'I can't tell you. I've searched the car from top to bottom, and I can't find it.'

'Maybe it fell out when we were stopped on the road, or maybe it was thrown away before we even left the party.'

'Or maybe someone removed it to cover their tracks.' She raises her eyebrows at me as she says this.

'Who?'

She shrugs gently.

'I know it wasn't me, and by the look on your face, I'm fairly confident it wasn't you either. That leaves three others, two of whom we've known for more than two decades. But there's one person we don't really know, who also volunteered to help me remove the bull bars and clean the car.'

We both turn and look back towards the house as the front door opens, and Rod and Dan emerge, slowly followed by Bella. I know instinctively that we need to find out a lot more about the stranger in our group.

We leave the confines of the barn, heading back towards the car, but Lily stops us as she spots the piece of paper flapping in the wind beneath the windscreen wiper.

'What's that?' I begin to ask, but as we close in, I instantly realise what I'm staring at. It's a printed image of the five of us passed out in the Land Rover. And I'm the one behind the wheel.

24

DAN

'Is this your idea of a joke?' Zoë demands, as we near the car.

I don't know what she's referring to, but then she points at a printed page beneath the driver's side wiper blade.

'I didn't put that there,' I snap back defensively. 'I swear I've no idea what that is or where it came from.'

I find myself turning to look at Rod over my shoulder, expecting that impish grin of his, but he looks as shocked as the rest of us.

'Wait, is that... is that a picture from last night?' he eventually asks.

'I assume so,' Zoë says between gritted teeth. 'Which of you did it? Thought it would be funny to stir up shit? Well, ha fucking ha. It was a stupid prank.'

'I was with you in the barn,' Lily replies, holding her arms up passively.

'And the three of us were in the house,' I counter.

Although I didn't see Bella inside, the fact that she emerged with us proves that she was there.

'Well, if it wasn't you three, and it wasn't us two, then who the fuck left it there?' Zoë says, and I feel a shiver run the length of my spine.

'Who gives a shit?' Lily replies nonchalantly. 'We should just throw it away and get going if we want to catch that ferry.'

She moves to snatch it from beneath the wiper blade, but Zoë tells her to wait.

'It could be evidence,' she says. 'We shouldn't touch it. It's obviously some kind of warning from someone who saw us on that road this morning; probably the same person who reported seeing a Land Rover matching our description there too. This just means we have no choice but to phone the police and turn ourselves in.'

I look closer at the image, and my eyes widen.

'Are you sure you want to do that, Zoë? Correct me if I'm wrong, but that photo puts you behind the wheel of the car, and not me.'

I think I can be forgiven for the tone of indignation in my voice.

'I know it does, but we don't know where or when it was taken. I think the bigger question is who took it and left it here, because whoever it is, they know who we are and where we're staying.'

She glances around the surrounding fields and woods, and rubs her hands against her forearms.

'Wait, you think whoever it is, is here now?' Lily asks, also now eyeing our surroundings. 'Then I think we just need to get going. I've seen enough horror movies to know it's those who hang around and wait for the antagonist who wind up in trouble.'

I almost laugh at Lily's logic. This isn't a movie, and whilst leaving the printed page on the windscreen is pretty creepy, it can only be one of us who did it.

'Wait, this is ridiculous,' I say, 'nobody else knows we're here, do they? Hell, even *we* didn't know where we were staying until Rod told us in the car. Stop fucking around, Rod, and just admit it was you. Look, you're really freaking out Lily and Zoë.'

'I swear to God that picture is *nothing* to do with me. I mean, I'm in the fucking picture, so how could I have taken it?'

It's a fair comment. All five of us appear passed out in the car. Zoë and Bella are in the front, with the rest of us asleep in the back, with Rod and me sandwiching Lily. If those were our positions when the accident occurred, Zoë would only have needed to manoeuvre me into the driver's seat before claiming mine.

'Also, unless it's escaped your attention,' Rod continues, 'where the hell would I have found a printer and paper? Did you see one in the house, because I certainly didn't. And it isn't something I tend to carry in my luggage to Amsterdam either.'

I allow my eyes to fall on the trees up the hill where I spoke to the care agency earlier. Could someone be hiding up there now, watching their game play out?

'The picture doesn't prove anything,' Bella declares, 'apart from that we got wasted last night. You can't see where it was taken, and there's no sign of the victim, so I say chuck it away, and we get going to Jura.'

'Agreed,' Rod declares, moving closer to the car.

'Wait,' Zoë calls out. 'What if the person who left the picture is the same person who drugged us all last night?'

'Who?' Rod snaps.

'I don't know, but there's something else,' Zoë now says. 'When I was in the bathroom earlier... the tap was running and there was a load of steam, and... I saw a message. Someone had smeared *I know your secret* on the glass.'

I look at Zoë, trying to work out whether she's adding this for effect, but her expression doesn't change. Maybe she's just become a better liar; she is a solicitor, after all. Convenient that she should be the one to discover the paper under the wiper *and* a mysterious message in the mirror that nobody else noticed, and she failed to mention sooner.

'I want to see it,' I say, spinning on my heel in the direction of the house.

'You can't,' she calls after me, and I stop. 'I wiped it off. I thought it was Rod playing silly beggars, which is why I didn't say something sooner, but now... maybe whoever left this page also left that.'

'But who and why?' Lily asks, her voice quivering.

'I think someone might be trying to set us up, or to at least make us think about other historic things.'

Zoë fires a cold stare in my direction as she says this, but doesn't elaborate when Bella asks what she's talking about.

Is she suggesting that what happened last night is somehow connected to what happened to Saul? Surely not. The only people who know about that night and last are me, her and Lily. Is she suggesting that Lily left the picture and the message? And then the penny drops: she thinks I left both.

'None of us could have taken that picture because we're all in it,' I reaffirm. 'I don't like any of this, but I also don't want to hang around and wait for the police to turn up. We need to get going.'

This time Zoë doesn't argue.

Lily tells us all to get into the car while she secures the spare registration plates to the front and rear of the Land Rover. I move ahead of Bella and Rod, and target the rear passenger side door. I want to be as far from the driver's seat as possible. There's a part of me that questions whether I'll ever be able to get behind the wheel of a car again. I still have no memory of what happened in the early hours of this morning, and whilst deep down I want to believe that Zoë was driving when the collision occurred, I have to accept that there is still a chance it was me.

Maybe the amnesia is a blessing, maybe I could hear the echoes of the impact, and if so, I definitely wouldn't be able to live with the guilt. As it is, there is a tiny part I can cling to that says *maybe* it wasn't me.

Bella piles in beside me, with Rod the other side, leaving Zoë to take the front passenger seat.

Lily lifts the wiper and pulls away the piece of paper, but then she pauses as she turns it over in her hands. She remains frozen to the spot before slowly raising her face, and turning the page so we can all see the phone number scrawled on the back.

25

ZOË

I don't recognise the handwritten phone number on the back of the paper, as Lily hands me the page and climbs in.

'What do you think it means?' she asks the group.

'I'm guessing it means whoever left the fucking picture wants us to call them,' Bella says, rolling her eyes.

My mind can't keep up with any of this. I was so sure that Dan or Rod left the picture under the wiper, and whilst they both appear to be passed out in the image, who's to say they didn't use some kind of tripod and timer on their phone in order to capture it? Or maybe they asked someone to take it and they were just pretending to be asleep. As wild as these theories are, they're easier to stomach than the prospect that someone out there knows what we did and now they're trying to taunt us about it.

'Type the number into your phones,' I suddenly say as inspiration strikes. 'If one of us knows this person then their number would appear in our list of contacts.'

I'm met with shakes of heads as everyone follows my instruction and we receive no matches. Well, at least that tells us that whoever this is, we don't know them. But then, that's probably a worse position to be in. Oh, God, my mind is all over the place!

'This changes nothing,' Rod declares, waving his hand dismissively. 'The plan is to get to Kennacraig to catch the ferry. That's what we should do.'

'But what if this person contacts the police and reports us?' I say.

'It is just a fucking picture, Zoë,' he replies. 'You said so yourself; it proves nothing.'

'Yeah, but what if this isn't the only photograph they have? What if they have pictures of the body outside the car too?'

'You're letting your imagination and paranoia get the better of you,' he says.

'Am I, Rod? Am I really? Maybe that's because we killed someone with this car in the early hours of this morning, we have no memory of who was driving, no idea who drugged us, and now some fucker knows and could report us to the police. It's all right for you, but if I'm arrested and charged with a crime – and leaving the scene of an accident is a crime – then my career is down the pan.'

I don't know where the tirade came from, and I'm left panting by the exertion of shouting at him. I sit back in my seat, no longer wanting to look at any of them. It doesn't matter how much I argue, there's no convincing them. Maybe it would just be better if I got out of the car now and phoned the police; take the decision out of their hands. But in truth I still can't escape the feeling that whoever left the picture is watching us right now, and that their intentions aren't pure.

A hand shoots out and snatches the page from Lily.

'To hell with it,' Rod declares, 'I'm just going to phone the number and see what happens. Better than just sitting here like lemons.'

Silence descends while we wait to hear Rod engage with the person on the other end of the number.

'There's no answer,' he finally says. 'See, it's nothing to worry about. Now, can we just...'

He doesn't finish the sentence as his phone beeps twice. 'I have a message from the number. It says: *I know what you did. Five grand or I phone the police.*'

My heart sinks. If only we'd called them the moment we got back to the farm, we wouldn't be in this mess right now. And every second we waste reduces the chance the police will discover whatever is in our systems and who put it there.

'Well, that's it then,' I say. 'Phone the police and let's get this over and done with. If we're honest about not knowing which of us was behind the wheel, and that we left the scene because we didn't have a signal and were in shock, they might show leniency.'

'Don't be fucking ridiculous!' Rod snaps back. 'Whoever this is, if they really had something concrete on us, they'd be asking for more than five grand. I reckon we call their bluff. I'll reply and ask where they want to meet for the exchange, and then the five of us can see who they are and put an end to this nonsense.'

My eyes flick to the rearview mirror. I don't like how sheepish Dan looks and he's been unusually quiet in the back, when usually he's full of big ideas.

'Right,' Rod says, 'I've written back to them to say I don't know what they're talking about.'

Silence returns again as we all wait for a response with bated breath. I rack my brain for any clue as to who could have taken the photo and knew we were here. It has to have been someone at the party, but the only person we knew was that barmaid, but I can't see that she'd do something like this.

Rod's phone beeps.

'What have they said now?' Bella asks.

'Um, I'm not sure,' Rod says. 'It's a link to something.'

'Careful, it could be malware,' Lily says. 'I have a friend who was sent a message from HMRC, but when she clicked on the link they stole her identity and took a load of credit cards and personal loans out in her name. She's still fighting to get it resolved.'

'I don't think we have a lot of choice,' Rod replies. 'There, I've clicked it. It's loading a webpage. It's a Glaswegian news site... it's an article about the body discovered on the Barrochan Road between Linwood and Craigends this morning. Fuck!'

'Tell them we'll pay the money, and then we can get the fuck out of here,' Bella tells him.

'No,' he replies. 'I want to know who this is, and whether they know what happened last night. The fact they snapped this picture and have connected us back to the hit and run means they might know who drugged us and why. I'm telling them we should meet.'

I watch Dan, seeing him slowly reach into his pocket and pull something out, but he keeps it down by his leg so I can't see what it is.

Rod's phone beeps again.

'They said I need to transfer the money wirelessly. No, I'm not doing that. I'll tell them we meet or there is no money.'

'And when they phone the police?' I ask.

'For all we know, they already have. Or they haven't, but will as soon as I transfer the money. Either way, we have to assume the worst. Relax, I've negotiated bigger deals than this.'

The phone beeps again.

'Good. They've said we should meet them in the village. Aim for the car park we were in last night.'

Lily starts the engine and drives us away from the Airbnb.

We're taking a huge risk using this car when the police have made it clear they're looking for it. If we're stopped and they find we've tampered with the plates, we'll be in even more trouble.

Fresh mud splashes up at the windows as we traverse the narrow and bumpy track back to the main road into the village. I don't like how out of control things have become in such a short period. In my own life I thrive when in charge, and yet merely hours after falling back in with this group I hate that I'm allowing myself to yield to their wants, rather than fighting for my own.

At least I've not received any more messages from Evan since yesterday. Maybe the jerk has finally got the message, and it isn't just the intermittent signal in these parts. I'm determined that when I'm back home on Monday – and even though I have Monday booked as holiday – I'm going to tell Mae that I need an urgent meeting with her and I'm just going to lay everything out: the fling with Evan, the inappropriate behaviour in the work-place, and how he's been blackmailing and threatening me in the weeks since. I'll also come clean to Tim, as it's the least he deserves. And then when the dust settles, we'll have to see what's left to salvage of my marriage and career. If this weekend has taught me anything, it's that I only have one life to lead and I shouldn't allow others to dictate how I do it.

The atmosphere is subdued, with nobody speaking and the stereo switched off. Maybe what occurred the last time we were all inside this vehicle is playing on everyone's mind. I close my eyes and heighten my other senses, focusing on the bounce and rhythm of the seat I'm in, willing it to stir fresh memories of last night. I still maintain that I never would have got behind the wheel of the car if I'd been drinking. I just wouldn't risk it. That's not who I am.

I can feel every bump and pothole we skirt over, and the lack of suspension is painful, but nothing stirs any fresh recollection. I don't want to be in here though. My stomach is turning with each jolt.

I glance over at Lily, wondering what's going through her mind right now. Is she wishing she hadn't agreed to drive us in her dad's car? The worst part is, I could have flown from Heathrow to Islay and arranged for Rod to pick me up from there. I naively thought it would be good to be this close to the others again; I should have known the feelings of guilt it would have stirred. Every time I look at Dan and Lily, I can't help but think about Saul and the pact we swore in the woods in the hours afterwards.

We pass the village sign, and I notice a crow sitting atop it, and with a sense of foreboding Lily pulls us into the small car park, parking in the same space she did last night.

'I don't remember seeing any banks in the village,' Dan says, the first words he's spoken since we left the Airbnb. 'Where are you going to get the money from?'

Rod doesn't answer, instead climbing out of the car and moving around to the large rear door, opening it and rifling through his case, before emerging holding a large wad of notes. Dan's mouth drops when he sees it.

'Here you go,' Rod says, handing it to him. 'This is what you were after, wasn't it? Five grand to tide you over.'

Dan's cheeks blaze in an instant.

'Come on, don't act so coy, Dan. It was all very elaborate: the picture, the phone number, and the messages. I suppose you were about to send me one that said I should arrange for one of my friends to leave the money in some designated place and for the rest of us to drive away, right?'

'I... I don't know what you're—' Dan protests, but Rod cuts him off.

'Oh, please, do you really think I was born yesterday? You

come to me this morning asking to borrow five grand and I say I'll think about it and suddenly there's a threatening message demanding the exact same figure and threatening police involvement. You wanted five grand, here you go, now call off this bullshit charade so we can continue to the ferry.'

I can't take my eyes off Dan in the rearview mirror. So that must have been what he was doing behind his leg, thinking Rod wouldn't notice, but now he's been found out. I am disappointed that Dan would sink so low, and I'm annoyed that Rod realised who the mole in our ranks was before I did. I can't believe all the stress he's caused this morning, and I want to lash out and smack him for it.

'I swear to God: the picture and messages are nothing to do with me,' Dan says. 'I asked to borrow that money in strict confidence,' he adds through gritted teeth, 'but that has nothing to do with this. And if you're so sure it's me, call the number now.' He hands over his phone. 'And check this too for any messages. You won't find anything.'

'You could have a second phone,' I pipe up.

'Search me,' he glares back at the mirror.

Dan pushes open his door and moves in front of the car, emptying his pockets until we can see the lining.

'Fucking frisk me, if you don't believe me,' he yells at Rod, who proceeds to pat him down, stepping back with a shake of his head.

'He doesn't have another phone,' he says, and we all freeze as Rod's phone bleeps.

It definitely didn't come from Dan's phone, as Rod is holding both.

'The message says we should knock three times on the pub door and hand over the money to the person who answers it.'

We all turn and stare at the village pub, where this nightmare began.

26

Someone has been reading my diary. I'm certain of it. I've been
keeping it hidden beneath the extra panel in the drawer in my
bedside table, but just now when I came to get it out, the wooden
panel was facing the wrong way. I'm always so careful when I put
it away and the grain of the wood was reversed. Mam and Dad
are away for the weekend, so it can't be either of them, so it must
be one of the others, and I reckon I know which.

Mam and Dad said we could have a few friends around, a
maximum of five each, so I invited Rod, Zoë and her little lapdog
Lily, and of course Zoë's shadow Dan tagged along. Rod brought
vodka and so we were just planning to chill in the living room
watching horror movies. But Rod must have let slip that I had a
free house, because the house was suddenly full of people I
barely know, and the television was switched off and music put
on instead.

I should have told them all to just fuck off, but I didn't want to
be *that* guy. And I figured when Reuben got home he'd make a
big thing of it and kick them out instead. But it got to eleven and

he wasn't back, and because the numbers had dwindled, and I was a bit drunk, I no longer cared as much.

I desperately wanted to get Zoë away from Dan. He had his tongue down her throat most of the night, apart from when he was playing pool in the conservatory. She looked so stunning in a red mini dress that accentuated every curve of her body. I doubt I was the only one who couldn't keep my eyes off her. I like to think she made that effort because she knew I'd be there. I've caught her watching me more and more in class at school, and when we're in History, we usually sit next to one another.

I still haven't told her how I think about her every morning when I wake up and how she's the last thing on my mind when I go to sleep at night. I don't want to come off as some kind of obsessive. I'm just trying to bide my time, watching Dan's jealousy slowly tear them apart. She deserves so much better than him.

Reuben eventually rocked up, but he didn't say anything about the noise or people at the party. He brazenly walked towards Zoë, held out a rolled spliff and asked if she'd like to join him outside. I thought Dan was going to go mental, but then Reuben is so much taller than all of us, and being twenty-one, he's about to graduate university and just has this air of superiority about him. He didn't wait for Zoë to answer, and headed outside to spark up. He knows how much shit I could get him in if I told Mam and Dad that he brought marijuana into the house, but he was so nonchalant about it.

I followed him outside and told him he should stay away from Zoë because she has an insanely jealous boyfriend.

'So?'

That was what he said.

'And then there's the obvious age gap between you,' I pointed out, because he clearly wasn't getting my message that she was off-limits.

'Age is just a number. And girls do mature a lot faster than guys. You've got to admit she's fucking hot.'

I made sure Zoë wasn't within earshot and told him that I'm in love with her, and he needs to back off, and he simply laughed.

'You don't know what love is, little brother. And a girl that smokin', she's not interested in guys like you. No disrespect, but you don't actually think you have a shot with her, do you?'

I lost my cool and I went for him, but he barely moved, before swiping me into the side of the shed with a thump. He was laughing at me, and I desperately wanted to wipe the smile from his face, but then Zoë appeared, and came over to check if I was okay. She helped me to my feet, and her perfume filled my nose, and massively turned me on. It was all I could do to control myself and stop the impending erection.

'He's just a bit drunk,' Reuben said, offering the spliff to her.

And I couldn't believe it when she accepted it and took a long drag, coughing as she exhaled.

'I've got something harder in my room if you want to take a look,' he said shamelessly, without a single care about me or Dan who was still lurking inside.

'I have a boyfriend,' she said.

'And? I'm not looking for a threesome. I tell you what, when you get bored of messing about with little boys, you come and find me. I'll bet you a hundred quid I can make you orgasm four times in a row with just my fingers.'

I don't know which of us was more embarrassed, but Zoë was the first to head back inside, with Reuben watching every step.

'I'll give you a month,' he said, looking down at me. 'If you've not hooked up with her by the time I finish uni, then I will sleep with her. It's time to man up, little brother, because life's too short to let a fine piece of ass like that pass you by.'

I thought he'd go off to bed, but he stayed downstairs, never more than a few feet from Zoë, and making no secret of his interest. And the worst part is she didn't tell him to back off again. I think she liked that three of us in the room couldn't keep our eyes off her. She was revelling in the attention.

So, when she'd gone, I came up here to write in my diary and that's when I noticed the hidden panel facing the wrong way. I'm going to have to find a better place to hide my journal as I dread to think what would happen if it fell into the wrong hands.

27

DAN

I'm so fucking angry right now that I'm tempted to snatch the money from the seat where Rod left it and catch a taxi back to Glasgow and the first train back to Wakefield. I cannot believe that my friends thought I would be capable of something so vicious and elaborate. And I'm even angrier that Rod has now revealed that I asked him for money. I didn't want the others thinking less of me, but the way neither Lily nor Zoë leapt to my defence tells me exactly what they really think of me.

I shouldn't have rushed the conversation with Rod. I can't believe that he had the money I asked for in his case but still couldn't make a decision. What does that say about how he sees our relationship?

I start at the ringing of my phone and when I see Jem's name on the display, I quickly answer, and move away from the others for privacy.

'Hello?' I say, uncertain whether this will actually be Jem, or Mrs Moreau at the agency.

'Dan? Thank God, I've been trying to get hold of you for ages.'

'Sorry, signal here is shit. How's Mam?'

'It happened again, Dan.'

'What? Say that again. What happ—'

'I've just arrived at the house and the front door was open.'

'Wait, where's Mam? Is she okay?'

'Yes, listen, she's fine.'

I breathe a sigh of relief. It wasn't all that long ago that I was late returning from work, and Jem said she found Mam wandering about in the street, unsure which our house was. I said at that point I wanted to change the locks to stop her getting out, but was told she needs to be able to get out in case of a fire. So, that's why I ended up increasing the frequency of the nurse visits.

'I went in and she told me a man came to the door and forced his way in. She became scared and went into shutdown, so she didn't see where he went or what he did. She was in her chair rocking when I came in. It was only when I saw the television gone that I figured that bailiff must have returned earlier than yesterday. I know it's none of my business, but how bad are things if you've got bailiffs calling?'

'I told you before: all my assets are tied up, and this is just a timing thing.'

'With all due respect, Dan, it takes more than a couple of unpaid debts for bailiffs to be instructed. I'm not having a go, but I have a duty of care towards your mam, and I hate that she was in this position this morning.'

This is my fault. Reading between the lines, that's what she's saying. If I hadn't allowed our finances to get so out of control, Mam would be safer.

'And given what's happened these last couple of days... I don't like to say it, but I think it might be better – safer – if your mam was now in somewhere with 24/7 care.'

'I can't afford that.'

'If you sold this place, it would cover the cost.'

I close my eyes to hold the tears back. She doesn't realise that that's the only home I've ever known and that selling it will only serve as further evidence of how much I've failed my parents. Deep down, I know she's right, and Mam's health has deteriorated in recent months. It's meant I've been having to start work later and finish earlier, to make sure she's safe, and that isn't helping our finances either.

'I'll stay on today for as long as I can, but if you have any friends or relatives you can call on to be here with her, I'd recommend you give them a call.'

She hangs up, and I hurry after the others with an intense feeling of dread. I really shouldn't have come away, and it might just be best if I tell them I need to head home.

'Are you all right?' Lily asks when I fall into line with her. 'You seem upset.'

I presume the question is driven by the guilt she's feeling for not standing up for me earlier.

'Problems at home with my mam,' I say. 'Dementia.'

'Oh, Dan, I'm so sorry to hear that. Your mam was always kind to me when I worked at the local Co-op. Whenever she came in she'd always ask how things were going at school, and she was always volunteering at the library and fêtes when we were in school. Life really isn't fair sometimes.'

Maybe I misread what Lily really thinks about me, and that only makes me regret our night together even more. No, I don't regret the night, I regret the way I handled myself in the aftermath. I'm tempted to ask if she's told Zoë yet, but to be honest, I'm not sure I care any more. Zoë isn't the passionate crusader for justice that I remember. And actually, when I now look back at those years when we were going out, I think I've been viewing them through rose-tinted spectacles. I was in love with her – or at least the idea of her – but I don't remember too many laughs we shared. And she certainly doesn't appear to regret leaving me behind when she headed south for university.

Rod stops when he reaches the pub door, but when he pushes against it, there's no movement so he raps his knuckles against it instead. When nobody appears within thirty seconds, he knocks again.

'Bar's closed,' a female voice hollers from behind the door.

'We've come about the photo,' Rod calls back, and a moment later the door is unlocked and opened, and we see the barmaid from last night, whose name I still can't remember.

Her dark brown hair is squashed into a messy bun, and where she barely looked seventeen last night, in the cold light of day I'd say she's several years older, her skin pocked with acne scars.

'Oh, it's yous lot,' she says. 'I wondered if you'd show. You got my money then?'

I can't see the wad of notes Rod had earlier, but Bella is beside him, and I assume he must have hidden it in her bag.

'So you were the person who took the photograph of us in the car?'

'Sure. Hand over the cash or I'll phone the police.'

Zoë steps forward, so she's between Rod and the door.

'Wait a minute, we had nothing to do with any of that. That's why we've come here. We think someone slipped something into our drinks, and we wanted to ask what you recall from last night and whether you saw anyone messing with our glasses.'

She frowns, as if considering Zoë's question for a moment before stepping back from the door and allowing entrance. I close the door once I'm through and join the others at the largest table in the centre of the room.

'I don't know nothing about your drinks being spiked,' she says.

That's what she would say, especially if she was the one responsible. But I still don't understand why she would.

'But you know whose party it was?' Rod asks.

'Why does that matter?'

'Because that person might be able to tell us how we all ended up drugged.'

'Listen, I wouldn't say yous was drugged. Drunk, yeah, but I wouldn't have said you was acting stoned.'

'None of us can remember leaving the party, and we're not heavy drinkers,' Zoë says. 'The first thing any of us can remember is waking in the car this morning. When did you last see us?'

'Oh, I don't know, I was getting smashed myself.'

'Did you see us get into the car?' Zoë asks.

'No, I remember this one acting like he was fucking William Wallace, but nothing after that,' she says, nodding at Rod.

'So how did you take the photograph?'

She looks away from us as if she's just caught something out the corner of her eye.

'Okay, let's cut the bullshit. I didn't take that picture. Some guy turned up first thing and offered me a hundred quid to walk it up to the farm and put it on the windscreen.'

My shoulders tense at this.

'Who was he?' Rod demands, and the table shakes as he leans on it.

'I don't know. Just some bloke.'

'What did he look like?' Zoë asks next.

'I don't know. Average height, average build. A bit like your man over there, but much younger. No offence.'

She's looking straight at me as she says this.

'Hey, I didn't pay her to deliver the picture,' I say before any of them can accuse me again.

'No, it wasn't him. You're Dan, right?'

I nod.

'Yeah, well, it wasn't Dan here, but this guy looked a wee bit like him; more handsome though. More self-assured.'

I'm not sure whether to be offended or grateful that she's pushed me out of the spotlight of suspicion.

'This guy, have you ever seen him before?'

She shakes her head.

'So, he's not local?' Zoë presses.

'No, never seen the man before.'

'And yet you were willing to do as he asked?'

'He paid me a hundred quid! That's more than I earn here in a night. He said all I had to do was take the picture up to the farm, with my number and when yous phoned to say I wanted five grand or I'd call the cops.'

'And what would you tell the police?'

'That the five of yous drove me to my mate's party. I got yous in. Y'all got wasted. And then when drivin' home, you knocked and killed that guy they found on the Barrochan Road between Linwood and Craigends.'

'But you didn't see us drive away from the party?'

'No, but I didn't stay until the end. Your car was still there when my old ma came to pick me up. There was no sign of yous.'

At least that explains why she wasn't in the car when we woke this morning, if her story is to be believed. I am inclined to believe her though as, if anything, she's talking herself out of the money in Bella's bag.

'You didn't see this guy at the party last night?' Zoë tries again.

'No, I've told yous, I don't know who the fuck he is or why he wanted me to give you the picture. Okay?'

Silence falls across the table. I can't think of why anyone would be so keen to rile us like this.

'Can we look at the CCTV to see if any of us recognise him?' I ask, spotting a ceiling camera in the corner of the room above the bar.

The woman pulls a face, and I see she has a cracked incisor.

'It isn't real. The camera, I mean. It's just a precaution to stop any of the locals kicking off. Sorry.'

'Then can you provide a fuller description?' I ask instead.

'Like I said: he was fit, probably late twenties, dark hair, a bit taller than me and I'm five eight, so maybe five ten, but not six foot.'

I look at the others around the table to see if there is any momentary recognition, but she's not given a lot to go on. I can think of clients who match that description, but none who would want to spike our drinks.

Rod reaches for Bella's handbag, opens it and extracts the money.

'I will give you this on two conditions: first, I want confirmation that you haven't already spoken to the police?'

Her eyes are glued to the money.

'I haven't.'

'And that you won't be speaking to them once we've paid you off.'

'I won't.'

'I need your word on that.'

'Trust me, with my reputation with local law enforcement, they probably wouldn't listen to me anyway.'

I'm not sure what she means by this, but given the nature of the party she took us to, I suppose it's possible she may have had run-ins with the police before now.

'Secondly, you have my number now. I want you to phone me

if this man returns. Okay? Ideally, get a photo of him to send to me. Do that, and I'll pay you a further five grand. Understand?'

'Aye. If he comes back, you'll be my first call.'

Rod hands her the money, and my heart sinks when I think of how much that would aid my situation back home.

Rod checks his watch.

'We're cutting it fine, but we should still make the 1 p.m. ferry if we leave now.'

28

ZOË

The Kennacraig ferry terminal is not what I'm expecting. Having travelled from Dover to Calais a number of times as a child, in my mind's eye I'm expecting something far grander than the small hut at the side of the road before the road itself disappears into the sea. It looks more like a small motorway service station than a lifeline to the people on the island of Islay.

It's almost one o'clock, and we should arrive at Port Askaig on Islay by three, and then it's a ten-minute crossing to Feolin on Jura. Rod reckons we should make it up to his family's manor house in Tarbert by half past four at the latest.

The wind whips my hair around my face as we head to the deck of the MV *Finlaggan* vessel. The boat itself reminds me a lot of the ferry we once crossed to the Isle of Wight on during a school trip. I remember our teachers pulling their hair out as they tried to control thirty nine-year-olds running all over the boat. At least today's crossing should be less stressful.

Bella and I head inside, as the air is damp with the threat of rain, and it's too cold to stand on deck with Lily, Rod and Dan.

There is a small restaurant-cum-cafeteria, and we both order strong coffees and find a table.

'Do you ever suffer with seasickness?' Bella asks, taking a sip of her drink.

'No, never have so far,' I reply.

'Hmm,' she muses, 'I thought you would.'

I can't tell if that's supposed to be some kind of dig.

'Why would you think that?'

'I'm sorry, I wasn't trying to cause offence. You just struck me as someone who might not cope well on water. There's something... delicate about you.'

Well, there's something very false about you, I want to shout back, but bite my tongue instead and sip at the coffee, but grimace at the bitter aftertaste. It feels like the word *delicate* is somehow insinuating weakness, but I could just be overreacting because of the message I saw in the bathroom mirror.

I study her as she withdraws an emery board from her bag and files her glossy nails. There really is so much I don't know about her, and after she questioned Lily's loyalty to me and the group, I feel like doing some digging of my own.

'You said you and Rod met at yoga,' I say, smiling thinly.

'That's right. I was working as a yoga instructor at a hotel in Manchester when he joined one of my classes, and we got talking afterwards, and then he invited me out for dinner, and I guess our love grew from there.'

Her accent is patchy again, and I remember what Lily said about some of her past stories not quite stacking up.

'And now you're set to marry less than a year after meeting?' I say, intentionally leaving the innuendo hanging.

'And you're happily married too, right?' she hits back, avoiding my question altogether.

'Yes, that's right.'

'And did I hear you say Tim is a teacher?'

The question stops me dead in my tracks.

'He is, but I don't remember telling you that,' I say, frowning.

'No? Oh well, maybe I overheard Lily and Dan talking about it.'

I can't immediately tell if she's just saying that to cover her tracks, or whether she's deliberately trying to drive a wedge between Lily and me again.

'When was this?' I ask, rising to the bait.

She raises her eyebrows, and puffs out her cheeks.

'I honestly can't remember. Maybe it was last night, because I can't immediately place it. Weird, right?'

There's no other way she could know about Tim and me unless she'd managed to get onto my social media feeds, or overheard it from someone else. Given our limited mobile phone signal since crossing into Scotland, I don't know how she would have been able to get online.

'And the two of you don't have children, right?'

This feels like a dig at mine and Tim's failings, but I could be reading too much into it.

'Being a parent isn't for everyone,' I say. 'What about you and Rod? Are there children planned for the future?'

Her smile turns downwards momentarily.

'We honestly haven't discussed that yet. I'm much younger than him, so we still have plenty of time before any long-term decisions have to be made.'

I do not trust this woman. I can't say why but there's something about her that feels off. Given the age gap, the whirlwind romance, and Rod's wealthy background, instinct tells me she's marrying him for his money, but I shouldn't project my own insecurities about my marriage to Tim onto others.

Lily and Dan appear inside the deck doors a moment later,

though there's no sign of Rod in tow. I wave and Lily says something to Dan before handing him some money and pecking him on the cheek. At first it seems like such an innocent exchange, but their eyes linger for a moment longer than is necessary before she starts walking towards our table.

'Dan's just getting some drinks. Do either of you want anything?'

Is she deliberately avoiding eye contact with me?

'No, but you can have my seat. I need to dash to the ladies' room,' Bella says, standing and moving away from the table.

Lily drops onto the chair and I study her face for a long moment, while my mind slowly connects the dots. I don't know how I didn't see it before. They both still live in Wakefield; they've been friends for years; Lily's been trying to stop me hearing when she's speaking to him on the phone; refusing to tell me who he is. And that might also help explain why Dan has been acting so shiftily around me. He kept asking about whether I had a boyfriend and I assumed that meant he wanted to get back together, but maybe he was just checking I'd moved on so he could come clean. Of course Lily hasn't told me she's seeing Dan, because she must know how I would react if I found out the two of them were together. What if it's more than just them fooling around and they're in love? I don't know that I could handle seeing the two of them marrying and starting a family. It feels as if the rug has just been ripped out from beneath my feet.

I still care for Dan, and I guess I will always love him in some way. And I desperately want to see Lily happy, but why do they have to find that happiness together? I don't think I would have a problem if Dan was dating someone I didn't know. How would he feel if I'd hooked up with Rod after we broke up?

No, I must be reading too much into it. They wouldn't do anything behind my back.

'Everything okay?' Lily asks now. 'You look lost in a world of your own.'

'No, I'm fine,' I lie. 'Was just thinking about something Bella said.'

'Oh, was she giving you the Spanish inquisition now as well?'

'No, not exactly.' I pause and take a sip of my drink. 'If I ask you a question, will you give me an honest answer?'

I see her swallow, before she responds.

'Sure. That's what friends should always do.'

'What do you make of Bella and Rod?'

Is that a hint of relief when she puffs out her cheeks?

'Um, I'm not sure. They are a bit of an odd fit, but I really don't know that much about her.'

'Did she tell you how the two of them met?'

'Um, I think she said something about him buying out a company she was working for or something. I'm not sure; I wasn't really listening to the answer.'

My ears prick up.

'So nothing about a hotel in Manchester?'

Lily shakes her head.

'Not that I recall. Why?'

My eyes fall on the clutch bag Bella has left on the table, and I quickly snatch it up.

'What are you doing?' Lily asks, almost choking on her gasp.

'I need information about her,' I say, locating her purse and extracting it. 'I told you, there's something off about her, and we owe it to Rod as his friends to find out what her true intentions are.'

If I've convinced her with the half-lie, she doesn't show it.

There is a small plastic insert containing credit cards, but there's no sign of a driving licence, but I vaguely recall her mentioning that she doesn't drive, so I shouldn't be surprised not to find one. But it's the names on the cards that have me blinking twice.

'What did Rod say Bella's surname was? Do you remember?'

'Sure, McDonald, like in the fast-food chain.'

I lift up the insert and show her the American Express credit card.

'Then why does she have a card in the name of Bella Walker in her purse?'

Lily shrugs.

'Shit, quick, she's coming back.'

I catch sight of Bella emerging from the toilets, and quickly shove the purse back into the bag, as Lily stands and says she's going to go and see what's taking Dan so long with their drinks.

'Was it something I said?' Bella says casually, nodding at the hastily retreating Lily.

'No, she's just thirsty, I think.'

I want to immediately demand to know why she has a card in someone else's name in her purse, but I don't want her to know I'm on to her little game before I have more that proves she's not who she says.

'Can we cut the crap, Zoë?' she suddenly says, and I realise now she has fixed me with a hard stare. 'You don't have to pretend to like me. I get it. You're not the first woman I've met who dislikes me. It's a common reaction. I guess there are some insecure women who can't handle comparing themselves to someone like me. It's no sweat. I don't need you to feign interest in me.'

I can't believe she's just accused me of that!

'How dare you? I'm not insecure.'

She smiles back at me as if I'm complimenting her.

'Okay, if that's the lie you need to tell yourself, then so be it. Makes fuck all difference to me.'

'I'm not jealous of you. I have a good career, a man who's head over heels in love with me, and am perfectly happy with my life, thank you very much.'

I know I'm laying it on thick, but I don't want her accusing me of such shallowness. I don't care that she knows I dislike her, but I'm not going to be painted as a jealous prude.

'Good for you, Zoë. It's great that you've managed to make something of your life, especially after what happened to Saul.'

I freeze at the mention of his name.

'Rod was telling me about what happened that night, and,' she raises her eyebrows, 'it's a good thing that you've managed to put all of that behind you.'

My cheeks blaze as I try to think of what Rod would have told her. If he has told her of his suspicions, then I'm going to have to tread carefully when I finally out her for who she really is, because there are some secrets I can't afford for the others to know.

29

DAN

I am expecting our arrival in Feolin to be a far grander affair than it turns out to be. The Land Rover is one of only six cars to disembark the blue car ferry, but there is no welcome party for Rod. Zoë, Rod and I are in the back, with Rod's legs spread across ours in an effort to make himself more comfortable.

The road from the port is single-track, making progress slow as we occasionally have to pull in to allow a car in the opposite direction to pass. To our right, the water comes right up to the edge of the road, and to the left, all we can see is a steep incline of moss-covered rock. The sky overhead is a dull grey, and this is how the journey progresses, in stony silence, the strain of the last couple of days showing on everyone's faces. It's almost as if we've all forgotten the reason we're here: to celebrate Rod and Bella's marriage. Not a single person in this car looks as though they want to be here.

The single-track A846 continues as we head further inland, but our view left and right is still dominated by hills and peaks. And aside from the occasional car coming the other way, there is no sign of life here. The area is so remote, and technically we're now trapped here until the boat returns.

I haven't been able to stop thinking about Mam. I stayed on the deck of the ferry with Rod for as long as I could manage, but didn't dare bring up the loan again with Lily present. The fact that he also didn't mention it suggests to me he has no intention of helping, and frankly, I know what I now need to do, and unfortunately that means putting Mam's house on the market. There are so many complexities to the choice, such as where I'm going to live, and how quickly it will sell. The one benefit of being good with my hands is that it's in a good state of upkeep, which will hopefully help. And now that I've had time to think about it, it's only a house, and with Mam's memory worsening every day, it probably won't be that long until she doesn't even remember living there with me and Dad.

The road is taking us above sea level now, as we continue to move in a southerly direction. Rod doesn't say, but I sense this may be the only main route around the island, as I can't see anything else resembling a road in either direction. There is a drystone wall separating the road from the fields to our right now, and it brings back memories of the wall we had to lift the dead guy over. We definitely intended to return and report the accident, I tell myself, but my memory of those hours is still so hazy. I'd hoped glimpses would start to return at some point, but there's been nothing yet. My lack of decent sleep and food since probably isn't helping. None of the others have managed to offer any further insight into what happened, though Lily did snag my arm when I went to order our drinks to say she wants to speak to me privately later, so maybe there's more she remembers than she's let on so far.

We cross over a cattle grid, and slowly but surely, small dirt tracks start spurting from the side of the road, leading down to the occasional cottage or manor house. And finally, after almost forty minutes of silence, we see a tall iron fence, laced with barbed wire at the top, stretching for the best part of half a mile. Large wooden gates separate the fence at the centre, and the words 'Tarbert Manor' have been hand carved into the gates. Lily pulls the Land Rover to the right, and lowers her window at the intercom.

'Tell them the eagle has landed,' Rod calls out from beside me. 'That's the passphrase.'

Lily relays the message and a moment later the gates slide apart, and we're able to progress forwards. The gravel of the track crunches like cereal beneath the tyres, and I'm gobsmacked by just how large the estate appears to be. All I can see is green fields eventually leading towards a small forest at the far side of the property, and then as we follow the track around the bend, the manor house comes into view, and I'd swear it's bigger than Buckingham Palace. I always knew Rod's family were wealthy, but this is something else. No wonder he didn't bat an eyelid when the barmaid demanded five grand. Would he even notice if I borrowed thirty grand's worth of heirlooms to clear my debts?

I hate that that's where my mind has gone, but I'd do anything so as not to sell the family home. The truth is I know nothing about antiques and antiquities, and wouldn't openly betray a friend like that.

Lily pulls up outside the large double doors, which open almost immediately and two men dressed in black suits appear, with one coming to my door to open it while the other waits by the main door.

'Welcome home, sir,' he says, and sounds like he means it.

He then makes his way around the car and opens Bella's door

for her. The rest of us climb out, and collect our bags from the
boot, and congregate by the double doors until the second man
invites us to follow him inside, where we're met by a man dressed
in a red-and-green tartan kilt. He introduces himself as
Belvedere, though it isn't obvious if that is his first or last name.
He walks with strong posture, moving seamlessly through the
house, announcing different rooms as we pass until I'm dizzy.
Large gold-framed paintings hang from every wall, and there are
garish-looking statues and monuments on every flat surface. He
deposits each of us at a different room, but we're essentially all on
the same corridor, so at least we shouldn't get too lost in finding
one another.

'And this will be your suite, sir,' Belvedere tells me when we
reach the end of the corridor. 'I will leave you to freshen up for a
few minutes, and then I will come and collect you all and escort
you to the drawing room.'

He bows and departs, closing the doors behind him. The
room is bigger than mine and my parents' rooms joined together.
A four-poster bed is the centrepiece, and there are more framed
pieces of art on the walls.

There is a freestanding bath in the middle of the bathroom,
with marble worktops around the edge of the room and gold-
coloured taps and cupboard handles. It feels more like a hotel
suite than a guestroom in a friend's house. But with it getting
closer to five o'clock, and my stress levels dangerously high, I
head out of my room in search of a drink. There's no sign of
Belvedere as I reach the corridor, and the doors to Lily's and Zoë's
rooms are closed, so I head back to the main entrance in search
of a kitchen where I can ask for a beer.

There's no sign of any staff to ask for directions, and from the
size of the house from the outside, I sense maybe we're in a guest
wing, though I've no idea which corridors will lead back to the

main house. I stop when I hear a woman's voice coming from a room to my right, and soon realise this must be Rod and Bella's room when I hear her talking about how he doesn't need to worry and that she has everything under control.

I'm about to knock and ask Rod for directions to the kitchen when I hear a man's voice I don't recognise.

'I'm worried about you, Lou,' he says, and I assume there must be somebody else in the room when I hear a woman with a Devon or Cornish accent respond.

'I told you before, you have nothing to worry about. The plan is working and tomorrow we will have what we need.'

'And you're sure the others don't suspect?'

My shoulders tense at this question.

'Of course not. They still think they're here to witness this sham of a wedding, but they'll know the truth soon enough.'

I'm about to push through the door and demand to know what the two of them are planning, when the English woman speaks again.

'We need to watch Zoë; she was asking all sorts of personal questions on the ferry, and I think maybe she suspects that I'm not who they think.'

Wait, the English woman was on the ferry with Zoë? That doesn't make any sense. Zoë was sitting with Lily and Bella. My eyes widen as my mind takes a huge leap, and I stumble backwards, my mind whirring with questions and doubts about everything we've heard so far this trip.

Bella isn't from the US.

Then why would she pretend to be? I don't understand what is happening here, but if they're worried about what Zoë might suspect, then she's my next port of call. Both her and Lily need to know what I heard.

I'm hurrying back along the corridor in what I think is the

direction of Zoë's room when I hear a voice I haven't heard in over twenty years.

'Hello, Dan, I've been looking for you.'

30

ZOË

Bella knows something about the night Saul died. She didn't say it in so many words on the boat, but I am sure she was hinting at it. But what can she know really? Rod had so many questions for all of us in the days and weeks that followed the discovery of Saul's body in the street outside the school, but we never let anything slip. We stuck to the pact and we denied everything. There were even moments when I denied to my parents and teachers that I was ever that close to Saul. It felt like the ultimate betrayal, but I was so scared that people would otherwise see through my veil of lies. I needed them to stop asking questions, and denying that I knew him seemed the easiest option.

Even now my heart still flutters when I hear Saul's voice in my head: *I'll do it for you. I love you, Zoë.*

I clamp my eyes shut and force the memory away as I always do. I'm not ready to tear down the wall I've built around that truth. I've covered it with lie upon lie until I'm not even sure what the truth is any more.

But still it eats away at me, like an earwig burrowing further and further into my subconscious. When we met later that night under the canopy, neither Lily nor Dan seemed to realise that Saul and I had switched places, and that it was he who entered the school when it should have been me. I don't know why they never questioned me about it. When we first decided to get our revenge, we drew straws for which of us would enter the premises, and I lost.

Dan was the one holding the straws, and I was certain he would somehow fix it so that I wouldn't have to go in. He even let me draw first, and somehow, I managed to withdraw the wrong one. When Dan and Lily both saw how worried I looked afterwards, I was sure Dan would volunteer to take my place, but he didn't. As far as he was concerned, we'd all chosen fairly and to be honest, had our roles been reversed, I wouldn't have offered to swap places with either of them, so I was probably expecting too much.

In my immature mind, neither Dan nor Lily had as much to lose as me. If I was caught breaking into school property, and the school pressed charges with the police, that would have been the end of my university placement, and my future practising law. Lily was going off to read English Literature, and Dan was already preparing to take over the running of the family business following his dad's stroke.

They left me there in the street, facing a task I didn't want to go through with, and that's when Saul arrived. He'd always been kind to me, and when he saw how visibly shaken I was he put an arm around my shoulders and asked what was wrong. I couldn't hold back and ended up sobbing into his chest.

He told me he couldn't believe that Dan hadn't offered to take my place, and how he didn't deserve to be with someone like me.

I hear his words in my mind now: *I'm crazy about you, Zoë. Let me show you how much you mean to me.*

And I guess I was flattered that he'd been carrying a torch for me. In that moment, I knew I should have told him I wasn't interested and wouldn't cheat on Dan, but then Saul kissed me, and it was like a firework exploding in my mind. Here was a guy who was prepared to break all of the rules to be with me, and that was the kind of love I felt I deserved.

I can still feel the pain burn in my gut when the silver car came out of nowhere and knocked him up into the air. It all happened so quickly, like a tenpin being flattened by a ball. I remember swallowing my scream, because I didn't know what else to do. Our romance was so fleeting; I loved him for exactly one hour and then he was snatched away from me.

I bow my head, angry that I've allowed Bella to get inside and make me relive the agony. Deep down, I know Bella can't really know what happened as I've never told a living soul.

She said, 'It's great that you've managed to make something of your life, especially after what happened to Saul.'

That doesn't necessarily mean she knows my role in those events. She could just mean the emotional impact of losing a friend at such a young age. And yet the way she then raised her eyebrows suggested she knows more.

I don't like how on edge she has me with one simple judgement. It feels like she's playing a game of chess, provoking me into revealing my strategy. But what she doesn't know is how practised I am in the art of misdirection. I have battled wits with some of the greatest solicitors and barristers the UK criminal justice system has to offer. I know how to get what I want. And right now, I know I need to better understand who my opponent is, so that I don't underestimate what she's capable of.

So, I abandon my luxurious sleeping quarters in search of Lily. She shares my suspicions and two minds are better than one, so I knock at her door and wait for her to answer.

'Have you seen the bathroom?' she says when she realises it's me. 'This place is off the scale, Zo.'

I head in, quick to close the door, not wanting anyone to over-hear our conversation.

'I think you're right about Bella,' I say, dragging her over to the bed, 'and I need your help to figure out who she really is. You saw the American Express card in a different name. That isn't right.'

Lily claps her hands together.

'What do you need me to do?'

'Help me check for any social media accounts. You focus on the name Bella McDonald, which is how Rod introduced her, and I'll go with Bella Walker.'

'Maybe it's just a married name though,' Lily says frowning. 'Like, maybe Rod isn't her first husband, and she hasn't changed her name back yet.'

I like that Lily's mind has focused on the probability that Bella is some kind of gold digger, maybe lurching from one rich partner to another to fund her lifestyle. And whilst that's a possible reality, I can't help thinking there's more going on here than simple fraud. I don't share my suspicions about Bella's interest in Saul yet, as I don't want Lily thinking I'm still so fixated on his death, because that will lead to awkward questions from her.

We both perch on the end of the bed running the names. According to my phone, there are over one hundred Bella Walker profiles, but some of these are overseas, so I narrow the search for the UK, but this then removes those who haven't listed their country, so I return to the original list, clicking on each name one by one, studying the profile picture, searching for the woman who is down the corridor.

I don't know what I'm expecting this to achieve, as if her

privacy settings are engaged, I won't learn much, but if we do find a profile for her as Bella Walker, it will confirm she's lied to Rod about the McDonald surname. Whether that will be enough to save him from marrying her is another question altogether.

'Any luck?' Lily asks, thumbing her screen.

'Not yet,' I admit, knowing this search is fruitless if Bella doesn't use Facebook, but not sure where else to start.

And then a fresh idea strikes me: if this was a new client or the defendant in a criminal case, I wouldn't be wasting time searching social media for the individual. I search my contacts list and when I find Jasper's name, I call him.

'I know it's the weekend, but I have an urgent favour,' I say to him.

'What do you need?' his gruff voice replies.

One thing I can always rely on is Jasper's refusal to waste time with pleasantries and small talk. He prefers life to be more efficient.

'I have two names for you, but both relate to one person. Her name is either Bella McDonald or Bella Walker,' I say, spelling the surnames for him.

'Age?' he says back.

I look to Lily for help.

Any idea how old Bella is? I mouth to her.

Lily considers the question. 'Early thirties?'

I relay the information to Jasper.

'It's going to take me longer to find her without a date of birth,' he warns, and I know he's right. It's not the first time we've had this conversation.

'I will try and find some more information and update you,' I say, although short of ransacking her bedroom, I'm not sure how I'll achieve that.

'UK based?' he asks next.

'Yes, she is now, but born in the US, we think. She said she was born in Manhattan, but that she travelled a lot as a kid, but definitely US. She flew into Leeds Bradford Airport from Amsterdam yesterday, if that helps?'

'My contact at the airport is away for a few weeks, so that's a no-go at the moment,' Jasper replies. 'Anything else you can share?'

'She's supposed to be marrying my friend Rod Astor tomorrow, so maybe look for recent marriage application requests?'

'When do you need the information?'

'ASAP, please.'

'It will be the usual rate,' he warns, and I tell him I'm happy to pay double if he gets me answers within the next two hours.

'See what you can find,' I add before hanging up.

Bella passes me her phone.

'What about this one?' she asks, and as I stare at the screen, I see a woman in a Panama hat and large sunglasses, but it's difficult to see much of her face as she's hugging some photogenic guy.

'I'm not sure,' I tell her, thumbing through the limited detail in the profile that's not protected by security settings. 'It doesn't say where she lives.'

'I know,' Lily says, 'but she's the closest I've found. No idea who the guy is she's hugging, but it certainly isn't Rod.'

I continue scrolling through the page, when Lily's phone suddenly erupts to life and I see a picture of Lily hugging a baby appear on the screen with the name 'HOME'.

I lift it up so she can see, and she opens her mouth as if she wants to say something, before she snatches the phone away and carries it over to the window to answer.

'Hi, Mam, yes, we've made it to the house now... Oh, is he? Um, now's not a great time,' she adds, turning back to look at me with a frown of concern. 'Um, yeah, it's just I'm with someone at the moment... Can you give me five minutes and I'll call you back?'

She hangs up the phone with me watching on, and I'm expecting her to ask me to leave, and that the picture is her holding a friend's baby, but the more I replay the memory of the image, I can't ignore the familiarity of the face.

'Don't be mad,' she says, extending her palms, with fingers splayed. 'I know I should have said something sooner... but yes, I have a baby.'

31

DAN

I freeze at the sound of my own name, but when I turn it isn't the pimple-faced thug I'm expecting to see, instead the voice belongs to a man with a rapidly receding crown, a purple, bulbous nose, a cream linen suit and maroon tie covering his paunch. It takes me a moment to sync the voice and appearance.

'You don't recognise me, do you?' he says, taking several strides forward and thrusting out a hand as if we're old friends.

A ball of tension begins to coil in the pit of my stomach; I haven't felt this uneasy since those mornings in secondary school where the younger version of this man used to threaten violence unless I handed over my lunch money.

He grabs at my hand when I don't offer it and pumps it in his own.

'It's good to see you, Dan,' Glynn continues. 'Rod said he was getting some of the old gang together. Are you and Zoë still an item?'

I shake my head, my throat so dry I couldn't speak even if I wanted to. I need to remember that I'm also not fourteen and shouldn't still feel intimidated by this person.

'Oh, you're not? That's great news. Oh, sorry, not for you, obviously, but it means the rest of us can have a crack now as well. Have you seen Zoë about the place yet? I'd like to reacquaint myself with her.'

He pulls a lascivious face, and my stomach rolls.

'Um, no, I don't think she's here yet,' I say, trying to buy myself some time to warn her what to look out for.

I want to leave now, to return to my room, lock the door and then hibernate until Glynn has left. I can't say why, but it's as if forty-two-year-old me has taken a back seat and allowed my adolescent self to take the wheel. My bladder is suddenly constricted, ready to burst, and if Glynn demanded I hand over all my cash now, I think I probably would; not that I have anything to give him.

'So, tell me, what have you been up to?' Glynn continues, crossing his arms, with no apparent recollection of the living hell he made my life for so many years.

All clear thought has abandoned me, and I don't even know how to begin answering the question. All I can seem to think about is waking up in the car this morning, and the man's blood on the bull bars. Why do I feel so compelled to share that part of my life with this bully?

'I... um... not much,' I finally venture, and it takes all my willpower to keep it short.

'Oh, come on, Dan, it's been, what... twenty-four years since we last saw one another. You must have done something in that time? Are you married? Any kids?'

'Not married, and no children,' I answer, eyeing the route back to my room that Glynn is now blocking. 'W-what about you?' I try instead, hoping if I can get him talking, someone I know will wander past and come to my rescue.

'Oh, you know, married twice, divorced twice, but you can't

keep a good man down.' He laughs at this, but I'm uncertain why two failed marriages is something to gloat about. 'Still looking for Miss Right,' he adds, running a hand through his thinning hair, pushing it back over the shiny spot in his crown.

'Well, if I see Zoë, I'll let her know you're looking for her,' I say, hoping to quickly sidestep and continue on my way, but feel the weight of his hand placed on my shoulder.

'Don't rush off, Dan, I haven't finished telling you about me. I'm a detective now. Did you know that? Coming up to my twentieth anniversary on the force.'

It's an admission I'm not anticipating. How can this man who left me bruised and winded on countless occasions when I tried to stand up to him end up upholding the law, rather than breaking it? How could anyone think he could be trusted to deliver justice?

'Oh, that's amazing, Glynn, congratulations,' I say, and I swear it's my fourteen-year-old voice that says it.

'Yeah, well, I know I wasn't always... well, now, how does my therapist describe it...' He clears his throat. 'I know I wasn't always very kind to you and your friends back when we were in school and sixth form. In fact, I was a bit of a shit.'

I want to tell him what an understatement that is, but fear interrupting him.

'And so, the reason I was looking for you, Dan, was to offer an apology, and to extend an olive branch. What do you say? Can we forgive and forget?'

He thrusts out his hand for me to shake again, and I desperately don't want to, but I can't let this nightmarish trip down memory lane prevent me from finding Zoë and telling her what Bella said.

Against my better judgement, I press my palm into Glynn's giant, clammy hand and we shake.

'You don't realise how happy this makes me,' Glynn continues, yet to release my hand. 'That you are willing to let bygones be bygones tells me so much about how much we've all matured.'

I try to withdraw my hand, but he grips it tighter.

'Let me hear you say it,' he says, his voice harder.

'What's in the past is the past,' I say through gritted teeth, before wrestling my hand free.

A large smile spreads across his face.

'That is so generous of you, Dan, and I really am pleased that we can put all of that nonsense behind us and move forward as friends. Tell me, how is your dad keeping? Stroke, wasn't it?'

'Dad passed not long after the stroke.'

'No, oh, I am sorry to hear that,' he says, though it sounds sarcastic, but that might just be his manner. 'And how's your mam?'

Instinctively, I don't want to tell him that Mam is in a bad way with her memory, because it's personal, and not something I want to share with my tormentor.

'She's fine, thanks,' I say instead.

'Good, good. And what was it your dad did? An electrician or something, wasn't it?'

'Plumber.'

He guffaws at this.

'Oh, dear me, you don't want to get those two muddled up, do you? Can you imagine? It would be chaos and people would die.'

The ball of tension in my stomach tightens.

'Reminds me of all that nasty business when we were sitting our A-Levels. Do you remember? Oh now, what was his name? You remember, don't you? The kid who was run down outside the school. Oh, what was his name?'

I sense Glynn's apparent amnesia is temporary, and for some reason he is trying to force me to say Saul's name.

'Saul,' I say, caving to the pressure.

Glynn takes a step backwards and snaps his fingers.

'That's right! Saul. I remember now. He was a close friend of yours, wasn't he?'

I glance back over Glynn's shoulder, wanting to shove him out of the way and just run, but my feet fail me.

'We... uh... we weren't that close. He was more of a friend of Rod's, I think.'

Glynn pulls a confused face at this.

'That's not how I remember it. No, you lot were always hanging about between periods. There was you, Saul, Zoë, of course, and then what was that other girl's name? Dark hair, moody expression; always fancied you but didn't dare act on it in case she upset Zoë. You remember, don't you?'

'You mean Lily.'

'Yes, that's it. Dear me, I don't know what is going on with my memory today. Would probably forget my head if it wasn't screwed on. Eh?'

He chuckles, but I don't join in.

'Yes, you, Zoë, Lily and Saul were quite the group as I remember it. Well, until he died, of course. Do you still see much of Lily and Zoë?'

I can't stomach much more of this. I need to remember that we're both much older, and that he shouldn't have this kind of influence over me any more. I could probably take him in a fight these days, as he's not nearly as domineering as once he was. There's only a couple of inches' height difference now, and physically he's not sharp. I take a deep breath, and slowly swallow.

'We all went our separate ways after sixth form,' I say. 'Listen, Glynn, it's been lovely catching up, but I do need to get back to my room to change. Maybe we can have a drink and talk about old times later on, or tomorrow after the ceremony.'

'Oh, yes, absolutely, I don't want to hold you up. And yes, it would be great to catch up on old memories. Especially about what happened to Saul. I'm not sure if you remember, but it was my old man who led the investigation into that hit and run. He interviewed you a couple of times, in fact. Do you remember that?'

Why is he bringing this up now? This feels like more than just nostalgia.

'He could be quite intimidating, my old man,' Glynn continues, and I resist the urge to tell him the apple didn't fall far from the tree. 'He reckoned he could actually smell guilt on a suspect.' He pauses, chuckling to himself. 'It's funny though, I always used to laugh when he'd say that, but it turns out my receding hairline isn't the only thing I inherited from him.'

He stares at me for a long time after he says this, and I'm suddenly aware of what he can smell on me.

'I suppose that's ultimately why I ended up following in the old man's footsteps. And do you know what's even funnier? That case – Saul's hit and run – still haunted him until the day he died. He just couldn't understand what Saul was doing outside the school and how nobody else seemed to know either. He was absolutely convinced that someone covered up what really happened. He never did find the car or driver that mowed Saul down either.' He pauses. 'You had your driving licence back then, didn't you?'

If he thinks I hit Saul, he's definitely barking up the wrong tree, but the Glynn I remember wouldn't give a shit about jumping to the wrong conclusion, so long as he got his own way.

'I did, but I didn't have a car until much later.'

'No, but you used to practise in your dad's old van, didn't you? I'm sure I remember seeing you in a supermarket car park loading your mam's shopping bags into the back.'

'I occasionally drove the van, sure, but I was at home the night Saul died. My parents were there and confirmed I never left.'

He snaps his fingers together again.

'That's right. They gave you an alibi, didn't they?'

I'm sure he's deliberately making it sound like my parents lied. Whilst technically they did, they didn't realise I'd snuck out of my window and down the drainpipe.

'I really should be getting back to my room, Glynn, I'm sorry—'

'The thing is, Dan, Saul's family have been kicking up a bit of a stink about the fact that nobody was ever prosecuted for their son's death, and so my Chief Super has asked me to review the casefile. Isn't that a quirky twist of fate?'

So, that's why he's suddenly interested in digging over the past. I definitely need to warn Lily and Zoë that he's lurking. We've kept our secret for twenty-four years, and I, for one, am not prepared to give it up without a fight.

'You be running along for now, Dan, and then maybe a bit later the two of us can have a proper – informal – chat about what you remember of that night.'

'I, um, I'm not sure what else I can say about it, to be honest, Glynn. It was a long time ago.'

'Ah, but that's the beauty of time, isn't it? Sometimes it takes time for things to settle so they can be seen clearer. And don't worry, I'll know if you're lying to me, because I'll smell it on you.'

32

ZOË

I watch Lily as she tries to avoid my stare. How could I not know she is now a mam? How could she have kept that secret from me for all this time? I know it's been a while since we last met in person, but during that time we've spoken on the phone, and even had a couple of videocalls, and she could have mentioned it at any point, but chose not to. I don't understand why she would keep something so huge from me, her best friend.

On the outside, I'm keeping a straight face, but on the inside my heart is breaking. Firstly, because she felt this was news she couldn't or didn't want to share with me. And had I not seen the picture flash up on her phone, would she have even mentioned it during this trip? If she wanted to tell me, she would have by now. And that means she didn't want me to know, but I don't understand why.

'You should say something,' she says now, still avoiding my stare.

I honestly don't know what to say. The second reason I'm dying inside is the raging feeling of envy now starting to course through my veins. Tim and I tried for years to start a family, including remortgaging our house for two rounds of IVF before the doctors told us the odds of conceiving were just too stacked against us. I remember sharing the trauma of conceiving and losing the embryos with Lily over the phone. She was always so sympathetic and reaffirmed it wasn't our fault. And all that time she had a secret baby she chose not to mention.

'Please, Zo, I don't know what to say,' she says when I don't respond, her voice cracking. 'I didn't want you to find out like this. I know I should have said something sooner, but it never felt like the right time, and the longer I left it the bigger the secret seemed to grow, until it became impossible to tell you.'

It makes me think about my reckless decision to seduce Evan in the boardroom and the fallout I've been experiencing ever since. I haven't shared that news with anyone, but that's because I'm so ashamed of my behaviour. I don't want people to know how stupid I was, and his threats and verbal abuse are all of my own undertaking. I don't want others to see me as a victim. But that situation is completely different to this one. I cannot think of any reason why a real friend would keep this from me.

I still don't know what to say to her, so settle for, 'What's his name?'

'I named him George, after my dad.'

I nod in acknowledgement as I fight to keep my tears at bay.

'This is the first time I've spent any significant time away from him,' she continues. 'Mam and Dad watch him when I have to go to the shops or the rare occasions when I have to go into the office for work, but last night was the first night I haven't heard him breathing while I sleep since he was born.'

I'm trying to replay all the times we've spoken in the last year, and she hasn't mentioned anything. I think about the videocalls, but I only ever saw her top half on the screen, so I suppose she could have kept a bump hidden beneath the table. Is that why she hasn't come down to visit in Winchester? Every time I invited her, she always had an excuse, promising to make it down sooner or later. It's why I was so surprised to see her at my party two years ago.

Oh my God, was she pregnant at my party? If last night was the first time she's been away from him, then she must have been. And even then, she didn't say anything. I think of the cream dress she was wearing that night. Sure, her figure had changed since school, but then I've rounded out as well, so I didn't think anything of it. She looked healthy and happy. I never would have said she was pregnant.

'How old is he?' I ask next, now determined to know how long she's been lying to me.

'Eighteen months,' she says, which all but confirms she was pregnant the night of the party. 'He's who I was speaking to at the airport when we were waiting for Rod. I know you assumed I was talking to a boyfriend, and I didn't correct when I should have. But don't you see how that would have been the wrong time to break the news. Can you imagine? *Oh yeah, Zo, by the way I have an eighteen-month-old baby you know nothing about.* That's what I'm saying. It became impossible to tell you after so much time had passed.'

I stand and cross to the bathroom, tearing off a handful of toilet tissue and dabbing my eyes.

'You still should have told me,' I say, retaking my seat on the edge of the bed. 'You should have told me the moment the test came back positive. That's what best friends do! That's what I did when Tim and I were pregnant before the miscarriage.'

I swallow down the swelling lump in my throat.

'How could I though? After all the pain you'd experienced, I thought it would be like rubbing it in your face. You and Tim have the perfect marriage, the perfect home, the perfect life apart from the one thing you can't have that I do. I thought it would ruin our friendship; that you'd never be able to move past the fact that Mother Nature granted me something she didn't give to you.'

'That's not fair,' I snap back as a tear escapes and rolls down my cheek. 'I would have been so thrilled for you. My grief has nothing to do with your joy. I can keep the two strands separate in my head; I'm not fifteen any more!'

She lets out a deep sigh.

'You're right. I'm sorry. I was scared that you would be angry that I fell pregnant and you hadn't been able to. I never said anything because I didn't want to upset you, but I see now that was wrong, and I'm sorry. God knows I wish I'd said something sooner. You have no idea how difficult it has been living with this lie. When I picked you up yesterday, I was certain you'd see through me. I thought you'd be able to smell him in my dad's car. Dad gave me the Land Rover when George was born. I almost forgot to take the baby seat out of the back.'

There has been something different about Lily this trip, but I couldn't put my finger on it. She was so pragmatic back at the Airbnb, taking charge of the group, so unlike the meek Lily I remember in school who was always a sheep rather than a sheep-dog. And all the sneaking off to make calls, I wrongly assumed she was phoning some secret lover. And then on the ferry I thought she might be dating Dan. How wrong I was!

'Would you like to meet him?' Lily asks next. 'Mam said he's desperate to see my face, so I was going to videocall him now we're on the Wi-Fi. I'd really like it if he could meet his Auntie Zo.'

There's a small part of me that wants to refuse the offer out of spite, but I know that's the wrong voice to listen to. I nod instead, and Lily joins me on the bed, holding her phone out whilst she hits redial and switches on her camera. A moment later I see an older version of Lily's mam staring back at us on the screen.

'Oh, Zoë, is that you, love?' she says. 'How many years has it been?'

'Hi, Meg, it's been a while, yes,' I say, feeling my anger slowly starting to subside when I see the baby with the biggest eyelashes at the bottom of the screen.

'I've been saying to Lily that she ought to invite you up. We could easily put you up in the pub for a couple of nights whenever you fancy.'

I can't take my eyes off George's sweet face. He has dimples in his cheeks like his mam, and the darkest eyes. He is so cute that my heart aches for a child of my own. He coos and I find myself laughing along with Lily, and don't resist when she reaches out and takes my hand in hers, giving it a small squeeze.

'Hello, baby,' Lily says now, and he immediately responds with a chorus of 'Mama, mama, mama,' bouncing up and down with genuine excitement, though I'm not sure he can properly see us on the screen despite Meg's best efforts to adjust the phone in her hand.

'I hope you're being a good little boy for your nanna,' Lily says.

'Oh, he's being very good,' Meg confirms, 'though I think he's teething again. He had a bit of a temperature last night, and he's been chewing those cooling plastic rings you keep in the fridge.'

'Oh, sorry, he's not too much is he? I can come home if you—'

'Don't be silly! It's been too long since you had a break. Your dad and I are coping fine. I actually think he quite likes having an excuse to leave the bar and come up and check on us to be honest. You have a good time. I think Georgie is loving spending some time with his nanna, aren't you, Georgie?'

I've never been surer that this is what is missing from my life.

Evan was an attempt to sabotage my marriage because Tim couldn't give me what I wanted, but I should have spent time trying to find a solution rather than fleeing. I've got a good career and I can't complain about money, but I would swap it all in a heartbeat for what Lily now has.

When the call ends, Lily heads to the bathroom to fetch more tissue, and I unlock my phone ready to message Tim and ask if we can have a proper talk later tonight. I want to get things clear in my head before we speak, and I want to come clean to him about Evan and my suspicions of his own affair. And if there's no way to resolve our troubles, then at least I know what I need to do.

But as I'm typing out the message, my phone vibrates, and I see a notification from the withheld number again.

> There's no point denying what you did. I know and so too will your friends soon enough. Come clean or all your secrets will be laid bare.

'Is everything okay?' Lily asks. 'You look like you've seen a ghost.'

'Oh, it's nothing,' I begin to say, before cutting myself off. 'Actually, the truth is: I'm being stalked by a dick I slept with at work.' Saying it out loud isn't nearly as difficult as I imagined, and it almost feels like a perceptible weight has been lifted.

Lily's eyes are as wide as I've ever seen them, her eyebrows raised.

'Shit! Does Tim know?'

'Not yet,' I say with a shake of my head.

'And this guy, what's his beef?'

'He's the nephew of one of the senior partners – my boss, Mae – and he's threatening to tell them everything if I don't continue our fling. I've told him countless times that it was a mistake, but he has footage of us taken from the office security cameras.'

'Shit,' she says again, when I show her the latest message. 'What does he mean all your secrets will be laid bare?'

This is my opportunity to tell her about that night with Saul, but as she said it's been so long that the secret has grown into something far bigger and now it's impossible to tell her. I shrug rather than admitting it.

She offers me a hug, and while she's holding me there, I can't help thinking how well she managed to lie to my face for the last two years, and now I'm curious about what else she could have been lying about, like whether she was the one driving last night.

33

DAN

I tear along the corridor, half-expecting to find Glynn jogging along behind, no doubt aware that finding Zoë and Lily will be my first task. After all, he *could smell it on me*.

I shudder at the thought as I skid to a halt outside Zoë's door, and try to compose myself. That Glynn is here at Rod's and Bella's wedding shouldn't be too big a surprise given he and Rod were always close in school. But the fact that he's asking questions about a decades-old case that we were all implicated in feels too coincidental. And I can't stop thinking about what kind of pheromones my body was subconsciously emitting the whole time we were talking. I know it's probably just a ploy he uses to unsettle potential suspects, and I hate how quickly it's worked.

I knock twice on the door, trying to work out exactly how I'm going to tell Zoë about Glynn, without revealing my own part in Saul's death. It's one thing that we all agreed to cover up why Saul was there, but quite another to admit I'm ultimately responsible for his death. There's every chance Zoë will try to twist my words into making me look guilty about this morning's hit and run.

I take a step backwards, now wishing I'd gone to find Lily first, but there is no sound of movement inside the room, and when I open the door find it vacant. So when I reach Lily's room and press my ear to the door, I'm not surprised to hear both Lily and Zoë inside talking; probably Zoë still trying to convince Lily to side with her against me. This time, I don't knock, barging inside and demanding to know what they're talking about.

Lily looks sheepishly at me, but doesn't answer.

'We were talking about private stuff,' Zoë answers, but there's a guilty look on her face. I imagine if Glynn was here now, his nose would be twitching.

'Like what?' I ask.

'Nothing that concerns you.'

'Nothing that concerns me? I think if you're trying to persuade Lily into falsely identifying me as this morning's driver, then it *does* concern me.'

'That's not what we were talking about,' Zoë says with a roll of her eyes, followed by an audible sigh. 'If you must know, we were talking about the arsehole at work who's been harassing me with inappropriate messages.'

I don't know how to respond to this, but instinct tells me she isn't lying for once.

'Oh, I see, I'm sorry,' I eventually offer, but she doesn't acknowledge it.

Instead she turns to Lily.

'Are you going to tell him, or should I?'

Lily's cheeks instantly redden.

'Wait, what?'

Zoë turns back to face me.

'Lily doesn't think she was drugged last night. She said she was pretty wasted and thinks maybe the drugs were in the bottle of water you had on you when you got in the car.'

Lily looks relieved at the announcement, almost as if she was expecting Zoë to say something else, but now my mind is distracted by this new information.

'Did you see somebody tamper with my bottle?' I ask Lily.

'No, nothing like that,' she says, 'if I had, I would have said something sooner. No, it's just I can remember seeing you sitting in the front with the bottle and then it being passed around to everyone else to drink from. Given we were all drinking different things last night, it's the one drink everyone else shared.'

It's not a lot to go on, but if she's right then that provides a level of vindication; I knew I wouldn't have got behind the wheel if I had been drinking alcohol.

'You saw everyone else drink from the bottle?' I clarify.

'Bear in mind, I was pretty drunk myself at the time. It's been a while since I properly drank like that and was pretty tipsy after that vile glass of wine at the village inn. But I can vaguely remember Rod snatching the bottle from you because Zoë was complaining she didn't feel very well, and he thought some water would help. I can remember thinking I hope Zoë doesn't vomit in the car again, like she did after prom. Then I think Rod took a swig before passing it forwards. I don't remember if Bella drank from it.'

My heart sinks.

'But I was in the driving seat.'

'I think so. Sorry.'

I'm half-expecting Zoë to leap up and say she told me so, but she remains perched on the bed, her head slightly bowed.

'So, it *was* my fault,' I say, the penny finally dropping.

'Not necessarily your fault,' Lily adds. 'I don't remember you drinking anything but water when we got there, and if someone slipped something into your bottle without you realising, then the fault and blame lies with them, not you.'

'But who would deliberately drug a designated driver?' I

reply, frustration building. 'It just doesn't make any sense to me. We didn't know anybody at that party, so it's not like anyone there would wish us any harm. And even if they did, why drug me at all? There are easier ways to exact revenge. Is there anything else you remember? Both of you, I mean. Zoë, what else can you remember about last night?'

She frowns for a long time before answering. 'Honestly, not a lot. I've been so worried about Evan's messages and threats that I think I just wanted to get drunk and stop thinking about it all. Rod was a livewire, but then he always is, and Bella seemed to be having a good time; she kept trying to drag us up to the dance floor in the middle of the barn. I have hazy images of flashing lights; greens and reds, and then nothing until we all woke in the car. I'm sorry, Dan, I didn't see anyone go near your water.'

I roar out my anger and press my head against the wall, once again praying for a chance to wake two days ago and make a different decision about coming on this bloody road trip.

In my mind's eye, I picture Glynn with his pointy nose sniffing the air around me.

'There's something else you should both know,' I say, without turning to face them. 'Glynn O'Donoghue is here, and is asking questions about the night Saul died. He collared me a few minutes ago to let me know he's a detective now – can you believe that? – and that he's been tasked with reviewing the evidence collected for Saul's hit and run. He said he wants to discuss things later and he's looking for the two of you as well.'

'Glynn O'Donoghue joined the police?' Zoë says, exasperated.

'And he's here now?' Lily asks, biting her lip. 'Do you think he knows what we...?' Her words trail off.

'Not unless one of you told him,' Zoë snaps.

I turn back to face them, now leaning back against the door. So many times I've pondered whether we did the right thing that night. We were young, scared about what punishment might come our way, but twenty years on, are the police really going to be interested? Would our lives have been dramatically different to what they are now? I know I influenced the others to keep quiet, because I was worried we'd somehow be held accountable for Saul's death, but maybe our silence is the real reason the police never managed to find the driver of the car that struck him down.

'It all feels too convenient,' I say now.

'What do you mean?' Zoë asks.

'Glynn happening to turn up at Rod's impending nuptials the day after we're all involved in yet another hit and run. I don't believe in coincidence, and something about all of this just... feels wrong. I just can't place what is off, but there's something.'

Zoë and Lily exchange glances, before Zoë speaks again.

'What do *you* think of Bella?'

The question throws me.

'She seems nice enough, I guess. I haven't really spoken to her properly, but I figured that was just our age gap. Rod seems happy.'

'She mentioned Saul to me on the boat. She said something about how well I'd done to put all the mess behind me. It came out of the blue, and I don't understand why she would know about any of that.'

'Maybe Rod told her how he died,' I suggest.

But Zoë pulls a face of disagreement.

'I don't see how it would come up in conversation, especially given how much time has passed. It just doesn't feel like a natural subject of conversation. Have you ever told anyone?'

I shake my head.

'Exactly! I've not told my husband, because as far as I'm concerned it's all in the past and I don't want to be reminded of it.

I know Rod was distraught when Saul died, but he's had twenty-four years to process his grief, so why would he raise the subject with Bella? And, more specifically, why would he talk about us and Saul in that context?'

'What are you saying, Zoë?'

'That I agree with you, and that something feels off about this whole thing.'

I think it's the first time we've agreed on anything all weekend.

'Do you think Rod knows Glynn is reopening the case?' Lily asks, and Zoë and I both look to one another before shrugging.

'If Glynn was asked to review the case, he'd want to speak to any of the witnesses from that time, assuming they're still alive,' Zoë explains. 'We had to make statements at the time, so we shouldn't be surprised that he'd make contact and ask us whether we've remembered anything else, but he would have to do that more formally; he shouldn't be probing at a mutual friend's wedding. In fact, given his proximity to the original crime – attending the same sixth form – him being put in charge of reviewing the case feels like a major conflict of interest.'

'He said something about it being one of his dad's cases,' I say, 'and that his Chief Super had asked him to look at it as a favour.'

She raises her eyebrows sceptically.

'Given his former friendship with Rod, maybe Glynn pressured him into an invitation so he could try and catch us off-guard. Do you remember how underhand he could be when we were at school?'

I think about that ball of tension in my stomach when we were speaking.

'So, what do you suggest we do?' I ask next.

'For starters, I think we're all in agreement that there is something suspicious. Right? Well, then I think we stop running from the past, and towards it instead. I have a friend who's already doing some digging into Bella's background. The evening's festivities are due to start shortly. I suggest we change and show our faces, and while the future bride and groom are distracted, we go looking for answers.'

34

ZOË

Back in my room, I quickly change into the dress I bought specifically for tonight's pre-wedding celebration. I found it at a designer outlet, and as with most things in my life it seems more expensive than it is. Tim thinks it's hilarious that I'm always putting on this façade about who I am and where I've come from, but he doesn't realise how long I've been running from the past; so scared that someone is going to realise how much of a fraud I really am and bring the world I've created crashing down around me. It's a huge amount of pressure to carry around every day. It's no wonder I'm on the verge of a nervous breakdown.

Maybe that's why I'm not so surprised that Lily managed to hide her pregnancy and son from me so well. And yet, in her room when she broke the news, I still felt like she was holding something else back. Bella claimed she'd witnessed Lily rehearsing a speech about some big secret she needed to reveal to Dan, but it can't have been about the baby. Why would Dan care that she is now a mam? If the two of them are secretly dating, then surely, he'd already know. And if they're not, why would he care?

No, it has to be something else, and as much as I don't want to think that she was the one driving when we struck that guy last night, I can't see what else her secret might be. There was a time when I'd only have to give her a hard stare and she'd crack and reveal whatever titbit of gossip she was trying to harbour. But there's a newfound resilience to Lily; maybe a result of becoming a mam.

I jar at the sound of my phone vibrating again. And as I collect it from where it's charging on the dressing table, there's a part of me desperately hoping it's Tim just checking in on how I am. But then I see it is from the same withheld number that's messaged three times already since we arrived on Jura.

> Have you told them yet, Zoë? Do they know you're the reason Saul died that night? If you don't tell them, I will.

The breath catches in my throat, and I find myself rushing to the bathroom, and retching up what little food remains in my stomach. I haven't eaten much all day, but that doesn't stop the gurning and burning in my throat. When I've wiped my face and flushed, I return to my phone.

It's impossible. There is no way Evan can know anything about Saul or what I did that night. On dark nights when the demons visit me in my nightmares, I have doomscrolled for any content about Saul's hit and run, and never uncovered anything that names me, Dan, or Lily. The articles only ever reference Saul, and the date and time of the incident. So, there's no way he could have found out I had any involvement in any of that.

And that leads me to now question whether all these messages I've been receiving are actually from Evan at all? I assumed they were because they started when I blocked his number and the threatening tone mirrored what he'd previously been sending. And all the references to secrets in the messages I assumed related to our sordid encounters – yes, plural – in the boardroom.

I lied to Lily when I told her it was a one-off. And I've been lying to myself, claiming I didn't get any pleasure from playing hard to get and having him chase me. Part of the thrill of going back to him each time was the threat of our secret being discovered. To say the sex has been passionate would be an understatement. Animalistic is a far closer description. I can still picture the moment when we tore each other's clothes from our aching limbs and screwed in Mae's executive bathroom while she was on a videocall with a client in the room next door. It was such a thrill knowing any sound would alert her to our presence, but that only drove us on further.

And I see now how I have brought all of this upon myself. I led Evan on and then tossed him aside like he meant nothing. I shouldn't be surprised that he's hurting about it. And I think some part of me – maybe on a subconscious level – wants him to reveal all to Mae, so she can be the one who detonates my career and home life. Deep down, I know I don't deserve the life I have when I'm the reason Saul doesn't have his.

I told Evan I would leave Tim, and I hate myself for lying so purposefully to him. I wanted him to think there was a potential future where we'd still be together, so that when I ripped off the Band-Aid, it would sting that much worse. Refusing to acknowledge his messages and bow to his demands has been my way of poking him with a stick and daring him to carry out his threats. I've been calling his bluff, secretly disappointed when that's all it has turned out to be.

But this new message, this is something different. This is something I didn't expect.

If not Evan though, who else could be sending these unprovoked threats? I was with Lily when the message came through, so it couldn't have come from her, unless she has a second phone I know nothing about. And then there's Dan, the only other person who knows Saul took my place in breaking into the school that night. It's clear from the argument he and Rod had earlier that Dan has financial worries, but whoever has sent this message isn't demanding a fee for keeping quiet. So, I can't understand what Dan's motivation would be. And whilst I don't trust Bella, I didn't know her forty-eight hours ago, so there's no motive for her to be threatening to expose secrets she knows so little about. Everything she knows has come second hand from Rod, and he shouldn't know about what happened that night.

Could it be there is some other figure from the past I haven't even considered?

My mind is all over the place and I'm going round in circles. There isn't one suspect standing out to me, and I hate when I can't see what's missing from a puzzle. But I'm resilient and I don't stop churning information in my subconscious until I get to the truth; it's what makes me so damn good at my job.

I drop onto the four-poster and lie back, closing my eyes and trying to empty my head of all information, so I can start from the beginning.

Whoever is sending these messages knows who I am and has access to my phone number. So far, that could be any of the main players. They know that I was close to Saul and that he took my place that night (assuming that's the secret to which they are referring). Technically, that should rule out Evan, but then a fresh thought scratches an itch in my head: Evan has access to the same resources as me. It's been less than thirty minutes since I contacted Jasper and asked him to find out everything he can about Bella. And I know from firsthand experience just how good he is at doing that. If Evan wanted to find dirt on me, then Jasper is the perfect person to uncover it. Would it be that hard to discover there was a hit and run at my school the same year I graduated? Would it then be a huge leap to discover that Saul and I were acquainted?

The more I now think about it, the more that makes sense. I can't see why Dan, Lily, Rod or Bella would want to expose me, but Evan has means, motive and opportunity.

I have a fresh flash of thought. The barmaid at the village inn said a man of average height and build paid her to take the photograph to the farm and leave it where we could see it. Evan couldn't be more average if he tried. I wish their security cameras had been in operation so I could have seen his face.

I sit bolt upright. If he paid the barmaid, then that means he was the one who took the picture in the first place, which means he was there at the party. My skin crawls at the possibility that he followed me here from London. He was in my house when I received Rod's invitation through the post, so he would have seen we were coming to Jura. Has he been tracking me this whole time? Knowing how obsessive his messages have been in recent weeks, it's absolutely the sort of thing I could imagine him doing.

My mind makes another leap: if he was at the party and took the picture, was he also present at the time of the accident? He hasn't said as much in his messages but he paid the barmaid to leave the picture and send the link to the news story about the hit and run, so he's connected the dots. And if he knows that, it's only a matter of time until he threatens more than just my career. What if he was the one who planted the keys in my pocket in an effort to frame me? Or worse still, what if he witnessed me behind the wheel immediately after the accident?

I quickly message the number, denying any wrongdoing and

telling him I know what he's up to, and that we should talk before he does anything we might both regret. He immediately responds.

> A man died because of you, and you want to talk? It's time to come clean, Zoë, before you hurt someone else.

He hasn't denied it's him, but what if he is also the person who drugged us all? I hurt him repeatedly, and pushed him hard enough that he felt compelled to follow me to Scotland, but what if his intentions were more malicious than that? There's no way he could have known that that homeless man would be on the road at the same time as us, but what if his plan was that we'd have a car accident that resulted in our deaths?

I don't like how quickly my mind is making these connections, but this is exactly how it reacts to cases, looking for impossible clues and connecting the dots. How many times has Mae told me I should have been a detective rather than a solicitor?

I re-read the message. Who does he think I'm going to hurt by not coming clean?

I lie back on the bed, replaying these thoughts over in my head, now looking for flaws in my logic. There are so many assumptions, but no hard evidence that Evan is the person behind all of this. And what is his plan if I don't cave? How is he going to know whether I've come clean about Saul if he's not here? I could message him and say I've told them everything. But to do so would be to admit the truth of what I did to Saul, and I'm not ready to do that yet. But I need to do something. I'm not somebody who can sit idly by and wait for things to happen to me.

I unlock my phone and send him another message, asking

where he is and whether we can meet. If he followed us to Scotland, then there's every chance he's followed us to Jura. And if he dares to show his face, I'll put an end to his meddling once and for all.

35

DAN

I assume it's Zoë or Lily knocking at my door, so when I open it and find Belvedere standing there in his full tartan regalia, I'm taken aback.

'Master Astor has requested you join him to discuss an urgent matter,' he tells me.

I slip my arms into my suit jacket and follow him out of my room and along a maze of corridors, past huge artwork, and finally to a spiralling staircase that leads down into what I presume is some sort of basement. Belvedere punches in a security code at the panel beside the large iron door at the bottom of the stairs, and advises me to go in, before closing the door behind him. The room I'm in has a low ceiling, and as I step forwards, a strip of automatic lights power up in the floor following my journey.

'Rod?' I call out. 'Are you down here?'

An explosion of lights erupt overhead and suddenly I see I am surrounded by a roomful of expensive-looking cars.

'What do you think of my garage?' I hear Rod call out from somewhere behind an enormous sparkling Range Rover.

There must be at least a dozen cars, each reflecting the glare of the ceiling lights, where they've been heavily waxed to the point where I can almost see my reflection in the red sheen of a Ferrari. This is more like a car showroom than a garage. I don't know a lot about cars, but what I'm seeing before me must have cost a small fortune to acquire.

'Very impressive,' I reply as he comes into sight, sitting on the edge of a large leather corner sofa that lines the far wall.

'Do you want a beer?' he asks next, offering an open bottle towards me, which I accept, before clinking it against his bottle.

'Cheers,' I say, sitting a couple of cushions away from him.

'Cars were my dad's favourite pastime,' he says now, staring out at the collection. 'He used to spend every free moment tinkering and cleaning his collection of antique cars when I was growing up. Developing an interest in them was my only way of being able to spend any time with him. In fact, he taught me to drive in that Aston Martin over there.' He waves his hand, but I can't spot the car amongst the others. 'He told me the moment he watched *Goldfinger*, he wanted the DB5, and he spent ages searching for one, and he'd go all around the country trying to convince people to sell him one, offering ridiculous money, but eventually realised it wasn't any old Aston Martin DB5 he wanted. No, he wanted the car Connery drove in the movie. And eventually, he got it – well, at least it was one of the versions used during filming.'

'You learned to drive in James Bond's car? That's pretty fucking cool,' I say, my amazement genuine.

He's staring off into the distance, and I sense there's something he wants to tell me, but he's holding back.

'Do you get to drive many of these?' I ask, curious how fast he'd actually be able to go on the narrow roads and dirt tracks we travelled in on.

He shakes his head.

'I'm chauffeured about most of the time these days. For me, it's never about driving these cars. I know that's their ultimate purpose, but take that Ferrari 458,' he says, pointing at the red model I passed. 'It's a thing of beauty. I could sit here and look at it for hours. It cost over a quarter of a million pounds, and I had to have it delivered here because I didn't want it getting damaged on the boat ride over. A helicopter carried it over from the mainland.'

Has he just brought me down here to brag? Any one of these models could clear my debts and fund my mam's care for the rest of her life, without me needing to sell our family home.

'My dad preferred classic cars,' he continues, 'so he'd probably be appalled if he could see the upgrades I made. I still have a couple of his models stored in a different part of the house, but this here: this is for me, and me alone.'

I take a sip of my beer.

'What am I doing down here, Rod? Your butler said you had something urgent to discuss.'

He doesn't answer at first, almost as if he hasn't heard me, but then suddenly his head twitches and his attention returns. He reaches down the side of the sofa and suddenly lifts a large stack of notes, which he places on the cushion between us.

'Twenty thousand pounds, is that enough to get you back on your feet? You mentioned five earlier, but I sensed you weren't giving me the whole picture.'

I can't take my eyes off the pile, and I genuinely don't know what to say.

'I'm sorry I accused you of being behind that photograph earlier,' Rod says with shame. 'It's been a weird day, and I think seeing all of you together as a group again has brought back so many memories of school; some welcome, and some not so much. I leapt to the wrong conclusion, and I'm sorry. I'm also sorry for doing it so publicly, especially after you'd approached me in confidence. Hopefully, this will go some way towards redressing the balance.'

I take another swig from my bottle.

'I'll pay it all back,' I say, reaching for the pile, but he presses his hand over mine.

'This isn't a loan. I don't need the money; I value our friendship more. I'm sure things haven't been easy for you during the pandemic and then your dad dying and now your mam fading away. I would give anything to spend five more minutes with my parents, so I don't want you having to miss out on spending time with yours.'

'I think she's going to have to go into full-time care. It's not safe for her at home any more.'

'Oh, mate, I'm sorry to hear that. Hopefully this will help that transition though, right?'

I nod, a lump forming in my throat as I think about what the rest of us conspired to do two decades ago.

'I really appreciate this, Rod. Thank you.'

'Hey, it's really nothing. I should be thanking you for coming all this way just for my wedding.'

I look back out at the lineup of cars.

'What does your future wife think about your expensive hobby?'

'I've only brought her down here once, to be honest, and she didn't seem all that impressed. She hasn't complained about the amount of time I spend down here, so I suppose she's fairly indifferent to it all.'

'Well, I'm really pleased you found someone who makes you happy,' I say, leaning forward and clinking my bottle against his again.

He takes a long drink from his bottle and then places it between his legs.

'How is your head after... well, you know?' he asks.

'Still full of holes,' I answer honestly. 'What about yours?'

'The same. Have you any idea what we were slipped?'

I shake my head.

'Some kind of date rape drug, I guess,' I say, shrugging.

He ponders my answer.

'Can I tell you something?' he says. 'I don't want to leap to conclusions again, so I wanted to speak to you about it before I accuse her... I think Lily drugged us.'

I blink several times, trying to work out whether I misheard or he's joking.

'You think *Lily* drugged us? But why?'

'Do you remember I said at the airport that it was lucky I wasn't given a full body search at Customs? I wasn't joking when I said I smuggled something back with me. I put them in my bag when we got to the services, and when I checked for them when we arrived back at the Airbnb this morning, they were gone.'

'What did you bring back?'

'GHB. It's known for numbing the mind and can impact memory amongst other things.'

'Are you fucking serious? You brought GHB back with you. As in the date rape drug?'

He frowns.

'That's not what I use it for.'

'Then why the fuck would you bring something like that back with you?'

'That's not important, but the vial I was carrying it in is no longer in my bag, and given we all have holes in our memories from last night, my gut tells me that someone laced our drinks with them.'

'But why do you think it's Lily? How would she know it was there, and why on earth would she want us incapacitated?'

'I don't know what her motive was, but when we first arrived at the Airbnb, she said she'd forgotten to bring her phone charger. I said I had a spare in my bag, and she went and took it. I was carrying the GHB in an old nail varnish bottle. It's a clear, colourless liquid. I didn't even think about it again until we got back to the farm, which is why I then checked my bag and found the vial missing. As far as I'm aware, Lily is the only other person who's been near my bag since the services.'

It's a huge leap to make, and I'm grateful he's shared this detail with me rather than accusing another of his friends of conspiring against him.

'That doesn't mean she took it though,' I counter. 'There were five of us in that Airbnb.'

'Well, I didn't take it because it was in my possession already. Did you take it?'

'No, of course not,' I declare defensively, before realising that only enhances his argument. 'What about Bella?'

'I asked her and she hasn't seen it either. So, that leaves Zoë or Lily. And only one of them was anywhere near my bag. Wait, do you think Zoë took them?'

'No, that's not what I'm saying; I just think it's a huge assumption you're making with very little evidence. And I can't think of any reason either would want to drug us.'

'Do you trust them both?'

It's a question I can't immediately answer. There was a time when I trusted them with our biggest secret, but that was a long time ago. And if I do truly trust them, why was my instinct to immediately warn them about Glynn and his questions about Saul's hit and run? If I trust them then I should have nothing to fear.

'I take it from your silence that you don't trust them,' Rod declares when I don't say anything.

'No, it's not that, it's just... I hardly know the two of them any more. We barely talk, but I can't imagine the people I remember would do something like that.'

I'm not sure which of us I'm trying hardest to convince.

'Bella told me she overheard Lily rehearsing some speech to you when they were cleaning the car. She said it had something to do with some big secret she wanted to tell you.'

'Me?'

'That's what Bella said. She also said she mentioned it to Zoë. Has Zoë told you?'

I shake my head, frustration starting to fire at the thought of Lily and Zoë conspiring against me. But what if they have been conspiring this whole time? What if drugging me was to cause an accident so I'd be blamed and then they'd be able to blame me for Saul as well?

'You know there's always been something about those two,' Rod continues. 'Thick as thieves. Between the two of us, I've always thought they know more about what happened to Saul that night than they've ever let on.'

I hold my breath, hoping he doesn't notice the sudden change in my focus.

'I used to think that you were somehow involved in all of that as well,' he continues. 'Is there anything you've not told me about the night Saul died and why he was outside the school?'

'What? No,' I say, taking a long drink from my bottle. 'I was at home in bed,' I add when I've swallowed. 'My parents confirmed as much to the police.'

'Did you know they were each other's alibis that night? I didn't realise until Glynn told me. Did you know he's here today?'

I nod.

'Yes, our paths have crossed.'

'Did he tell you he's in the police and has been asked to review the case? Maybe he can get to the bottom of all of that once and for all.' He suddenly checks his watch. 'Oh, shit, I didn't realise how late it was. I'd better head back out or Bella is going to kill me.' He points at the pile of money as he stands. 'You'd better put that somewhere safe.'

I collect the money and force as many of the piles into the pockets of my trousers and suit jacket as I can before following him back upstairs. I'll stash the cash in my room and then I'm going to find Lily. I want to look in her eyes when I ask what secrets she's keeping.

36

ZOË

It's been an hour since I messaged the withheld number and Evan has yet to reply. I asked where he was and whether we could meet, and I'm not sure how to read his radio silence.

I've left my room twice to briefly mingle with the other party guests, and thankfully I didn't see Glynn on either occasion, so if I remain in my room for the rest of the night, with the door locked, I should be safe until morning. I haven't seen Lily or Dan and am assuming they are bunkered in their rooms as well. But I hate having to hide away like this.

And so, without wishing to waste any more time, I compose an email to Mae, asking her to meet me on Monday afternoon, once I've returned from Scotland. I tell her I've acted recklessly, and that it is in the best interests of the firm and our clients if I come clean about my actions and take a leave of absence. Before I know it, I've written an essay, explaining what Evan and I did, and accepting full responsibility. I end up deleting these parts and leaving it as a request for a personal meeting to discuss work-related matters, and then press send.

I want to make it clear to Mae that I regret my actions and

want to find a way to move past them. She is a good listener, and I like to think a fair-minded woman, but I have a better chance if I speak to her one to one, so I can put my side of the story to her. I doubt I'm the first professional to have an irrational affair, and it's not like I've broken any laws. Admitting my culpability might be the only way to save my career, but it might also destroy what remains of my marriage.

So, my next step is to phone Tim. I can't keep lying to him when my intention is to come clean with Mae and my colleagues. Tim plays squash with one of the partners' husbands once a fortnight, and I'd rather Tim hear the truth from me.

He answers on the third ring.

'Oh, hey,' he says, and I immediately notice the enthusiasm in his voice. 'How's Scotland? Are you having a good time?'

Not in so many words, I think, but don't say.

'Yeah, everything is fine here. How are you? How was your day?'

'Let's just say TFI Friday,' he says, sighing. 'I've always said the best thing about being a teacher is the students, and the worst thing about being a teacher is their parents.' He groans audibly. 'You sound less drunk than last night, I take it you're being more restrained?'

I frown at this.

'Wait, we spoke last night?'

'Do you not remember?'

'Um, actually, no.'

'That's understandable, you did sound pretty out of it on the voicemails.'

'Voicemails? Plural?'

'Uh-huh. I wish I hadn't deleted them, so I could play them back to you. In the first one all I could hear was a lot of background noise, and in the second it sounded like you were talking loudly at somebody. I assumed your phone had been dialling when you weren't aware of it, but then in the third message you started singing at me.'

I cringe. I never sing, even when drunk, but given what I may or may not have ingested at that point, who's to say what I was capable of?

'I'm sorry if I woke you.'

'Oh no, you didn't. My phone was on silent, so I didn't catch any of them until this morning. Made me chuckle to be honest. I haven't heard you that wasted in forever. And it was nice to know you were thinking of me.'

I grind my teeth together.

'Actually, I've been thinking about you a lot... well, I've been thinking about *us* a lot.'

There's a momentary pause.

'Yeah, so have I,' he says. 'Do you want to go first?'

I honestly don't know if I have the words to break his heart.

'Why don't you go first,' I say instead.

There's another pause, and I hold my breath while I wait for him to say it's time to throw in the towel.

'I love you, Zoë. I always have, and I always will. I know... I know things haven't been right between us for a while, and I'm as responsible for that as you are. I suggested the counselling because I thought it was what you wanted. That's what married people do when they're struggling, right? Anyway, it was clearly more difficult than I expected for you to open up to a stranger, and I'm sorry that I insisted we keep going.'

I release my breath.

'I had an affair,' I say, closing my eyes, but the tears are already pushing through my lashes and splash against my cheeks.

I instantly regret the confession, but saying it aloud feels as though the pressure on my shoulders has lifted a fraction. He doesn't speak, and I find myself checking the phone's signal on the display in case we've been disconnected.

'I know,' he eventually says. 'I heard the two of you in your office one day.'

My mouth drops.

'What? When?'

'I came by to see if you wanted to go out for a spot of lunch, and I overheard you on the phone telling whoever it was that you were wet and to meet you in the boardroom.'

The tears fall quicker.

'Why... why didn't you say anything before?'

'I didn't know what to say. I think I was pretending I hadn't heard it, or that I'd just misunderstood. But then I realised how distant you were; how you'd wait until I was asleep before coming to bed; how we stopped talking most of the time. I sensed the distance more after that, and figured it was only a matter of time until we had this conversation. You know, it's funny, it's so much easier talking about it over the phone than in person. At least this way you can't see how much this is breaking my heart.'

Mine too, I don't add.

'I never meant to hurt you,' I say instead, reaching for a tissue and wiping my eyes. 'I still love you, Tim, and I want you to know how much I genuinely regret the affair. It was stupid, and if I could take it back, I swear to God I would.' I take a breath, trying to compose myself. 'There are things... things you don't know about me... About who I was before we met. I feel like I've been living the life everyone expected me to lead, but I don't know if that's who I really am, or not any more.'

I picture our wedding day, and the thrill I felt when he slipped the ring onto my finger. Hearing his voice now has reminded me that what we have is special and worth fighting for.

'I know I don't deserve a second chance,' I say quickly before he can speak again, 'but if you are willing to give me one, then I swear I will spend the rest of my life trying to make it up to you, and to prove I am worthy of your love.'

His silence has me checking my phone's display again.

'Please, Tim. At least take a couple of days before you rush into a decision. I'm asking for a few days' holiday from work, and maybe we could get away for a bit, and properly talk about what we both think a marriage should be. And if at the end of that you decide that what we have isn't worth fighting for, then I won't refuse a divorce.'

When he next speaks, I realise he's crying.

'I don't want to lose you,' he says. 'I meant what I said about loving you. My feelings will never change. But you're right that we should take some time and figure out what we both want. I don't think it's a good idea to be making decisions over the phone.'

We both laugh, and my heart swells.

'That sounds like a plan,' I tell him. 'I really do love you.'

'I love you too.'

'I'd better let you get back to marking homework.'

'Oh, that reminds me,' Tim says suddenly. 'I can't believe it slipped my mind. There was some guy here asking questions about you.'

The hairs on the back of my neck stand.

'What guy?'

'I didn't catch his name to be honest. My height and build. He turned up at the school gates at collection time and asked to speak to me. So once the other children had been collected, I hung around, but it was only when he started asking questions about you that I realised he wasn't a parent or relative of one of the children.'

I immediately picture Evan in my mind's eye.

'What was he asking?'

'I'm not sure really. It was stuff about you: where you grew up, why you never returned home, whether I knew what happened twenty or so years ago. It was the oddest conversation, to be honest. I was half-expecting him to whip out some identification, but he never did, so I don't know if he was with the police or a reporter or what.' He pauses. 'Was it the guy you were having an affair with?'

'When did you say this happened?'

'Yesterday afternoon. I meant to message you about it, but it slipped my mind. What was he talking about?'

I clamp my jaw tight. It can't have been Evan if he was the one paying the barmaid to bring the printed image to the Airbnb. But who else would be asking Tim questions about me?

'I will tell you all about it when I'm back,' I tell Tim now, as I see another incoming call on my phone's display. 'I need to go, but I'll message when I'm on my way back.'

I end the call and answer Mae's.

'Your email has me intrigued. What personal matter has to wait until Monday?'

One confession in a night is all I'm capable of, and I really don't want to go into all the gruesome detail with Mae over the phone.

'I don't suppose it has anything to do with that nephew of mine, does it?'

The breath catches in my throat. Am I already too late? Has Evan already told her about our affair?

'Well, if he's away with you right now, can you tell him to call me, please? Going AWOL is not acceptable behaviour, and has left me embarrassed and making excuses today.'

'What makes you think he's here with me?'

'Oh, dearest Zoë, did you really think I hadn't noticed your outrageous flirting with my nephew? I don't care what the two of you do on your own time, so long as you keep it outside of the office. Do I make myself clear? Anyway, we can talk about it when we meet on Monday, but tell him to phone his aunt.'

She ends the call, and I stand there, certain now that he's the one who's been pulling strings in the background here. But if that's the case, then who the hell was asking questions of Tim?

37

DAN

I push open the doors to Lily's room when she doesn't answer my knocking, but there's no sign of her inside.

Good, I think to myself, closing the doors, and crossing the room to where the suitcase stands open on the small table. It's not in my nature to snoop around in someone else's belongings, but if Rod is right and Lily was the one who drugged us, there may be evidence of the empty vial Rod spoke about.

I lift the washbag out of the case, and hold the zip fastener between my thumb and finger, but I hesitate.

What am I doing here? Do I really believe that Lily could have spiked our drinks and caused the accident? I don't want to believe she could have done, but hasn't there been something off about her this whole trip? I mean, it's not like Rod and Zoë have been like the friends I remember either. And come to think of it, with everything going on back home with Mam and the bailiffs, I've also not been my old self. What I'm doing here is a serious breach of trust, and I need to be certain before I cross a line from which there is no return.

I try to think about the moments when things have felt weird with Lily, but I think that's been every time that we've been alone together. But that awkwardness is the result of us sleeping together after Zoë's fortieth; at least that's why it's felt awkward to me. But maybe that means I've been blinded to other inconsistencies in her behaviour. There have been too many times when I've seen her sneaking off to make phone calls without her saying who she's been in contact with; and Rod was right when he said Lily and Zoë have been as thick as thieves as they always used to be in school. And I don't know what it is the two of them have been conspiring over, but it's clearly something they're not happy sharing. I don't want to believe either of them caused the accident, but maybe their aim in spiking our drinks was something else – I can't think what though. But let's say for a moment that their intention was something else, but something went wrong and we hit that guy by accident. It makes sense that neither would be prepared to admit the part they played in killing someone.

My fingers tremble with the fastener between them, and then I pull it open, carrying the washbag to the bathroom, so I can remove and stand the contents on the countertop. A toothbrush, a can of antiperspirant, and a bottle of perfume, but no nail varnish bottle. And for the life of me I can't remember seeing Lily's hands, so I don't know whether her nails are varnished or not.

I zip up the bag and return it to the case, before running my fingers along the insides, searching for anything that resembles a small bottle, but there's nothing.

'What the fuck do you think you're doing?'

My heart skips a beat as I feel Lily glaring at me from the now open bedroom door. I didn't even hear it open. I slowly turn.

'I'm looking for the GHB,' I say quietly. 'Where is it?'

Her face screws into a ball of confusion.

'What are you talking about. GHB, as in the date rape drug? Why the fuck do you think I have that?' She catches herself and I see the penny finally drop. 'Wait, is that what we were... shit, makes sense... but wait, you think that I... Fuck you, Dan. Why the fuck would I want to spike your drinks? What, you think because we had sex once that I was trying to rape you?'

'No, I don't know what your plan was, Lily, but I think it's about time you started telling the truth about things. Rod said you were the only person who went near the drugs in his bag.'

She closes the door behind her as she continues into the room, her face reddening with anger with every passing second.

'So, let me get this straight. Rod told you he had the date rape drug in his bag, and claims I stole it from him, is that right?'

Hearing her say it out loud makes it sound even more ridiculous than the voice of doubt in my head.

'Did you stop to ask Rod what the fuck he was doing with GHB in the first place?'

'Does it matter? He's admitted he had it but that someone took it from him and we all ended up drugged, so what do you expect me to think?'

Her mouth hangs open.

'And you think so little of me that you genuinely believe I could or would do something like that?'

This isn't how I wanted this to go, and now I'm feeling even more guilty.

'I honestly don't know,' I say instead, instantly regretting it when she picks up a wooden coaster from the bedside table and flings it in my direction, but it strikes the curtains behind me with a low thud.

'You son of a bitch,' she says, and I can see now she's crying.

I bow my head.

'Listen, I'm sorry, but all of this is just so fucked up that I don't know what or who to believe any more. If you're saying it wasn't you, then I believe you, and I'm sorry for doubting you.'

She remains where she is, crying, and I desperately want to console her, but it doesn't feel it's my place to do so. Maybe it would just be better if I fetch Zoë and explain the mess I've made.

'Don't forget, I wasn't drugged last night,' she says. 'If I was behind it all, would I have admitted I wasn't affected? Wouldn't I have swallowed some of the water from the bottle as well so the rest of you wouldn't get suspicious?'

It's a good point, but could also be a double bluff.

'So what have the two of you been conspiring about since we got here?'

'Conspiring?'

'You know what the fuck I mean. Having your little whispered conversations; like when I came to warn you about Glynn and his dogged questions. Zoë said it was to do with your drink not being spiked, but you...' I shake my head. 'There was something off about your demeanour, like you thought she was going to say something else to me, and you looked relieved she didn't.'

I see her expression change and snap my fingers together.

'There it is again,' I say, pointing at her face. 'You're lying to me right now, and I can see it in your eyes.'

Her face drops and she collects her phone from where it's charging on the bedside table and takes several steps towards me, stopping when we're a couple of metres apart.

'Okay,' she says quietly, 'you really want to know what I've been lying about all this time?'

'If it has anything to do with the accident this morning, then yes, I think I have a right to know.'

I see her gouge her tongue into her cheek.

'Oh, you have the *right*, do you? Okay, well, if you really want to know, then I'll tell you.'

She pauses and stares at me for a long time, and my mind is whirring with possibilities about what she's going to say.

'I knew Glynn was going to be at the party,' she says.

I'm not sure what I was expecting to hear, but that wasn't it.

'Glynn – as in Detective Glynn O'Donoghue who's reviewing Saul's hit and run accident? You knew he would be here? How?'

'Because I met with him last week, and he said he'd been invited.'

It's not that big a revelation. I was expecting some dirty little secret. Okay, so she didn't warn us Glynn would be here, that's no big deal. Yes, it would have helped to be prepared, maybe I'd have thought twice about coming, but...

And then a question slams me between the eyes.

'Why did you meet with Glynn last week?'

She purses her lips.

'He came to my parents' pub a few weeks ago, and told me he's been tasked with reinterviewing all the witnesses that were approached following Saul's accident. I agreed to meet him at the police station, and he asked all the same questions—'

The ball of tension is back in my gut.

'Tell me you didn't mention the pact,' I say rhetorically.

She takes a calm breath.

'I gave him the same answers as I did originally, and he thanked me for coming in, and I thought that was that. But he came back to the pub that night, and told me he knew I was lying throughout the interview, and that he intends to prove it one way or another, and that it would be better for all involved if I just came clean about my part in what happened.'

The room is spinning and I feel like I'm going to be sick.

'He reckoned he suspects you and Zoë were also involved, and that he would offer some protection to whomever of us spoke up first. He said he hadn't spoken to the two of you yet and was giving me first refusal.'

Fuck, fuck, fuck.

'Tell me you didn't say anything, Lily. Please?'

She stares at me for what feels like an eternity. It's no wonder he homed in on me earlier, telling me he could smell my guilt.

'I think it's time we all come clean, Dan,' she says next. 'Aren't you fed up of living with the guilt? I mean, last night... seeing all of you again, and Rod, the guilt was eating me alive. That's why I started knocking back drink after drink. I live in a pub and have been sober for nearly two years, but last night it was like I was possessed by an alcoholic, because I just wanted to forget it all.'

'But admitting that we've lied for all this time, what do they call it? Perverting the course of justice. We could all end up in jail.'

'Not if we come clean voluntarily. Glynn is going to get to the bottom of it eventually. If he speaks to enough people, he'll figure out what we did, but if we come clean first we can explain why; people need to understand.'

I take a step backwards, accidentally bumping into the suitcase, and it upturns, spilling Lily's clothes across the floor.

'I can't keep lying, Dan. This isn't about just me any more. I have to protect my family too. I don't...' She takes a deep breath and exhales it. 'I don't want my son to see his mam sent to prison.'

I blink several times.

'Wait, you're a... you have a son?'

She closes the gap between us and takes my hands in hers, her phone pressing against my knuckles.

'Listen to me, Dan, I don't want *our* son to see either of his parents sent to prison.'

Her eyebrows are raised, her eyes so wide they're almost on stalks. I'm not processing what she's saying at first.

'I know this is going to come as a shock to you, but that night after Zoë's party... George was the result.'

I snatch my hands away, shaking my head.

'No, I don't have... you're lying... we don't...'

She chases after me, holding out her phone, but I brush her hands away.

'You stay away from me. This is bullshit.'

'Look at his face, Dan, and tell me you don't see yourself in him.'

The room is spinning even faster, like I'm trapped on a rollercoaster, and I push past her, diving towards the toilet in the en suite, before I vomit into the bowl.

This is like an intense dream. None of this is real. I just need to pinch myself and then I'll wake and none of the last forty-eight hours will have happened. I will my eyes to open, but when they do, all I see is the orange goo in the bottom of the bowl. I stand and flush, blowing my nose and washing my face and hands. Lily remains by the door, and offers me a towel.

'I didn't mean to break it to you this way. I'm sorry, I had a speech planned, but I could never find the right time to tell you. He's a perfect little boy, and so smart. And listen, I'm not telling you because I want anything from you, but you have a right to know that you're a father, and it's up to you how much of an interest you want to take in his life.'

I stagger forwards, uncertain what to say, and conscious that my reaction so far has been far from ideal.

'Can... can I see him?'

She offers me her phone, and my heart immediately warms when I see the image of the boy and the dimples in his cheeks, just like his mam's.

38

ZOË

I wake shaking, unable to catch my breath, and it takes several seconds to figure out where I am, and that I'm not behind the wheel of the Land Rover. In the nightmare, I watched as the figure bounced off the bonnet and was flung backwards as I tried to slam on the brakes; but the figure whose face splatted against the windscreen was Evan, rather than some homeless stranger.

It felt so real – the detail so intense – that I can't be certain it was only a dream. Is this a common effect of being dosed with GHB: imagination trying to fill in the blanks?

I push the thin sheets back and stand, but my hands are still trembling as I head to the bathroom and climb into the shower, allowing the warm spray to wash away my tears, until there are no more to cry.

I'm not sure what time the party ended last night, but I didn't leave my room after ten, and it's a relief to see the small chest of drawers is still in place behind the doors where I left it. I was determined to make sure Evan didn't get in here last night.

I keep replaying Mae's words over in my mind: *If he's there*

*with you now, then please just tell him to phone one of us and let us
know he's okay.*

The way Mae spoke, she already knew the two of us had been
fooling around, even though I was certain we'd been so careful.
But if he has followed me up here, where is he, and why hasn't he
shown himself?

I check my phone and there are no new messages from either
Evan's phone or the withheld number. There's been no response
to my request to meet and talk, and the lack of response is
worrying me even more.

I thought coming clean to Mae and Tim would ease my
conscience, but if anything it's only made things worse. It's made
the affair and Evan's negative reaction to it more real somehow.
No, that's not it. In truth, it's made my poor treatment of Evan
sink in more. I really was a bitch to him: leading him on one
moment, and then pushing him away again, and then dragging
him into the boardroom. I used him to scratch an impulsive itch
in my head, but I never told him what or why I was doing it. He
was a plaything I could get out whenever I wanted and then toss
away when he'd served his purpose. And I think that's the real
reason I didn't report his inappropriate behaviour – the
messages, the threats – to anyone sooner. His reaction was a
direct consequence of my own behaviour, and I wasn't prepared
to think of it in that way then. But now it's abundantly clear
to me.

This is all I can think about as I dress and drag the heavy
chest away from the bedroom doors. It's not long after eight and
the ceremony is starting at midday, so I have under four hours to
figure out what Evan's plan is before he ruins Rod and Bella's big
day. I follow the corridor of floor-to-ceiling artwork until I reach
the large reception area, which is a hive of activity. Figures pass
me by in a blur, some tying bouquets of flowers to the handrail of

the large staircase, others carrying large covered trays, and some manhandling stacks of chairs from one room to another. I feel in the way, but I don't know what the expectation of guests is. I should have asked Rod whether there was a planned breakfast or pre-wedding catch-up, but my mind was preoccupied last night.

I call out to Belvedere as I see him pass by the foot of the stairs, and he tells me there is food available in the dining room and urges me to follow him. I wish I hadn't as I step in and find Glynn sitting in one of the tall chairs facing us as we enter. I want to turn and head back out but Belvedere is blocking my way, pointing out where I can find cereals, pastries and juice and that he'll have someone take my order for cooked food.

'Will you join me?' Glynn asks, making half an effort to stand, and waving towards the vacant chair across from him.

He's the only person in the room, so as much as I don't want to be anywhere near him given what Dan warned us about last night, I have little choice. I pour a glass of blood orange juice and sit.

'You haven't changed a bit, Zoë,' he says, wiping the corners of his mouth with the cloth napkin.

'Nor have you, Glynn,' I say, ignoring the now obvious paunch and rapidly receding hairline.

'I understand from our esteemed host that you're a solicitor down south now, is that right?'

I don't want to be sitting here with the man now investigating the crime I participated in over twenty years ago. After my poor night's sleep and the stress of the last two days, I can't be certain my mouth won't let something slip before my brain has engaged.

'Yes.'

'I'm surprised our paths haven't crossed. I'm in the police now.'

'I focus my time on criminal cases in London, so unless you

have many dealings there then I suppose we wouldn't run into one another.'

I take a sip from the juice.

'No, I suppose you're right. Do you get back home much?'

'Not as much as I should.'

'Pity. Hey, I saw an old friend of yours last night.'

I don't know why but I instantly picture Evan; would he be reckless enough to somehow sneak into the house and mingle among the guests and talk about me?

'Oh, did you?' I reply as casually as I can manage while taking another sip of the juice.

'Well, I suppose you'd call Dan more than just a friend, wouldn't you? I mean, the two of you were inseparable during sixth form.'

I breathe a sigh of relief.

'That was all a very long time ago.'

'Absolutely. Are you married? Divorced? Seeing anyone?'

My skin crawls at the thought that he thinks he'd have any chance with me after the hell he put us all through.

'Happily married,' I say, smiling.

'To Tim, right?'

I inwardly gasp; how does he know my husband's name?

'He's a teacher, isn't he?'

This is what Dan was trying to warn us about. I need to remain calm. If Glynn is now reviewing Saul's hit and run, it makes sense that he would have undertaken a bit of research on key witnesses. I need to remember it is his job to try to catch potential suspects off-guard.

'That's right,' I reply, cooler than I'm feeling. 'You seem to know more about me than I you. Are you married?'

'Divorced. Twice. I was telling Dan last night that I haven't found Miss Right yet.'

Where is the person to take my food order? Belvedere said she'd be along soon, and I hate being stuck in here on my own with Glynn. Maybe I should have knocked for Lily or Dan before I went wandering.

'I'd been hoping to run into you... well, all three of you, in fact. Have you seen Dan or Lily since you arrived?'

This is a tricky question for me to answer. For all I know, he already knows we travelled up together, but I also don't want him thinking we're still in cahoots.

'They're around, I think,' I say, opting for somewhere in the middle.

He considers my answer.

'If you have some time, there are a few questions I'd like to ask, though it's slightly more of a formal thing. You may or may not have heard that I've been asked to review the unsolved hit and run of one of your old friends, Saul.'

I try to make a face that shows surprise, but judging by the slight upturn of his lips, I'm not sure I've managed it.

'And so I'm reinterviewing all the old witnesses who made statements at the time, to see whether they've remembered anything new. I mean, you're familiar with the legal system, so you understand why I'd want to speak to the three of you, right?'

'Of course,' I say, my voice noticeably higher. 'But surely you don't want to do it here and now over breakfast?'

'No, of course not. But perhaps we could find some time after the service, but certainly before you head home in the morning.'

'I can tell you now that I really don't remember much about that night at all, to be honest. There's certainly not been anything fresh come to mind in the last twenty-whatever years. I think Lily and I were having a sleepover at my house. We probably watched a movie, ate some pizza, drank some wine, and talked about going off to university. But I'm second-guessing myself now, because I really don't know what we did, or what I said in my original statement.'

He drops the napkin on his plate and leans back.

'I get it, and I know it won't be easy to remember. But I have your original statement here with me. If you give me five minutes, I can fetch it from my room and you can have a read of it to refresh your mem—'

'No,' I say, standing quickly. 'Actually, I've just remembered I need to meet with Lily because she asked me to help do her hair before the ceremony. I'll find you a bit later on, and then we can go through the statement and any questions. As I say, I don't really remember anything about that night, so it will probably be fairly fruitless.'

I'm half-expecting him to stand and arrest me here and now, because his eyes are telling me he knows something he's holding back.

'Oh, I hope I haven't put you off your breakfast?' he says.

I smile thinly.

'I don't have much of an appetite at the moment,' I tell him, before excusing myself and leaving the room, hurrying away but not really looking where I'm going.

I start when my phone vibrates in my hand and I see a message from the withheld number.

> Have you told your friends that you were the one behind the wheel on Friday night, Zoë?

I re-read the message. Was Evan there? If he took the photograph, did he also see what happened on the drive home? I need to know one way or another, but rather than replying, I locate Evan's number and call it. And when I hear the echo of the ringtone along the corridor, I know he's here.

39

DAN

I wake in bed beside Lily for the second time in my life, but this time the feelings of guilt are completely different to those I felt the last time. That morning, after I'd had to watch Zoë celebrating her fourth decade with her handsome husband and perfect life, I'd realised how much I'd wasted my own. In hindsight that was probably the point when I should have asked someone for help. But instead, as usual, I buried my head and just tried to work harder; like the gambler so utterly convinced that the next bet will be the one that cancels out all the previous failures.

But this time it's different because we haven't had sex. No, the feelings of guilt that are clawing at my insides now are for the last two years I've wasted, oblivious to the fact that I have a child, and having offered Lily nothing but disregard when she probably needed me more than ever.

We were talking about George into the early hours of this morning, and it sounds like she has done a brilliant job with him. She couldn't speak highly enough of the support her parents have provided – support I should have been providing had I known – and she showed me several pictures and videos captured on her phone. And he is a ridiculously cute kid. So, as well as the feelings of guilt for not being there, it's also a kick to the gut to see how well he's doing because I'm not there spoiling everything.

I sit up, not wanting to disturb Lily, but conscious that if anyone else catches me in her room in last night's suit and shirt they're going to leap to all of the wrong conclusions. She stirs as I carefully try to lift myself from the mattress.

'You don't need to sneak off again,' she says, her eyelids still closed.

And it's a slap to my face: a reminder of how cold I was the night after George was conceived.

'I wasn't... I was just—'

Her eyes ping open and a small smile breaks across her face.

'I was just kidding,' she says, but I'm not convinced she was.

'I thought I should get changed before anyone starts assuming that we... you know.'

She nods at this, swinging her legs over the bed and standing.

'That's probably for the best. I told Zoë about George last night as well, but... she doesn't know he's yours. With everything going on... it just didn't feel like the right time.'

I'm grateful for this admission. At least that's one other person who doesn't yet know just how much of a screw-up I am.

I collect my jacket from the edge of the bed. There is so much I want to say. I want to apologise for not being there, knowing that had I not avoided her for as long as I did, I would have learned she was pregnant a lot sooner. I want to thank her for not involving me in the decision about whether to keep the unborn baby or not. I want to ask her what the future holds in her mind. She said I can be involved as much or as little as I want, but I also think she needs to own those decisions.

I don't think it's yet sunk in that I'm now a dad. Most fathers would have had nine months to adjust to the idea before meeting their child for the first time, and it's not even been nine hours yet.

I don't know how much I want to be involved. I mean, I definitely do want to meet him and provide whatever support he and Lily need, but I don't think I have the right to demand to see him whenever I want, because I haven't been there. And given my current financial issues, I can't even afford to support either of them. All I can offer is my time right now, but that feels desperately short of what they deserve.

'We have a lot to talk about,' I say, wanting the time to compose my words, so I can try to convince her that I'm not always going to be this loser.

If I can get the house on the market, clear my debt and get Mam somewhere she'll be properly looked after, maybe then we can talk about the future and how I can help as much as they want. My gut tells me that I want to secure their future in any way I can, but I need her to tell me what works for her. I don't think she's asking for a romantic relationship with me – and I don't blame her – but it breaks my heart thinking that I'll miss any more of my son's big moments. I didn't witness his first steps or first word, but I want to be there for the rest of those key milestones.

'Maybe we should meet for a coffee or something one day this week,' she replies after some thought. 'Let it all sink in a bit, and then we can see where the land lies.'

I'm about to say that sounds like a plan when my phone bleeps at me. For once it's not a battery indicator, but when I check the screen I see a message from Rod asking me to meet him urgently, as there's something he needs to talk to me about.

'We'll definitely do that,' I tell Lily, 'but I'd better go get changed. I guess I'll see you at the ceremony later on this morning?'

She nods, stretching her arms over her head as she heads into the bathroom, and I just stare as she glides across the room. What could have been, had I not been such a dick.

I leave the room, and given the urgency of the message tone, head in the opposite direction to my room in search of Rod. He hasn't said where to meet, but given we were in the basement garage last night, I head there first, but there's no access through the security door, so I head back upstairs in search of Belvedere. There are caterers and decorators milling about the place, but no sign of any of the staff who work in the house, and so I find myself heading along the corridor in search of Rod's room once again. And when I get there I have a flashback to the last time I was standing here, eavesdropping on Bella.

They still think they're here to witness this sham of a wedding, but they'll know the truth soon enough.

Having been set upon by Glynn as I hurried from the room, I'd almost forgotten about what I overheard.

The door to the room is open, and so I push it wider and poke my head through. I'm surprised not to find Glynn and a team of police standing inside waiting to arrest me because he knows what I did. But the room is empty. The bed doesn't look slept in. I head inside and close the door behind me, figuring it's as good a place as any to wait. There's a single chair beside the dressing table so I pull it out and sit, trying to compose and settle the thoughts whizzing through my mind right now.

I should phone Jem and check how Mam is doing today. Since the dementia took hold, she has good days and bad. Some days she seems just like the mam I remember, in a constant state of flux, busying herself with tasks around the house. I came home from work one day and found she'd pulled out the fridge and was behind it sweeping up crumbs and laying rat poison. But then there are other days when it looks as though she hasn't moved from her armchair all day. It's as if she is a wind-up toy and sometimes she is at full pelt, and the others, she's run out of spin.

My thumb hovers over Jem's number in my phone when I hear another phone ringing nearby. Assuming it must be Rod's and that he is behind the closed bathroom door, I head over and knock, but open the door when there's no response, and he isn't inside, nor is the source of the ringing.

I should just ignore it. It's not my phone. But as I sit back on the chair, the muffled ring sounds closer, so I turn and open the drawer of the dressing table and start as I see an image of Saul's face staring back up at me. It's so unexpected that I gasp. The framed image is one of him wrestling Rod in a garden some-where, but the pair of them are smiling, so it looks relatively play-ful. It's been years since I saw this face in a photograph, and it instantly takes me back to the last time I saw Saul, eyes closed and at peace in his coffin.

The ringing phone inside the drawer stops, and a missed call message flashes on the display. I lift it out, assuming it must belong to Rod. It's fairly modern but it's an Android phone, when I'm sure Rod said he has an iPhone. I suppose he could have two phones, though I can't think why he'd need two, given his lack of formal employment.

I start as someone barges through the bedroom door, but Zoë is the last person I'm expecting to see.

'What the fuck are you doing with that phone?' she yells, rushing across the room and snatching it out of my grasp.

'Hey,' I snap back, standing. 'What the hell?'

She's panting and I see she's holding her own phone as well, and presses redial. The second phone starts ringing again, and her eyes snap up to mine, and she takes several unsteady steps backwards.

'W-why do you have Evan's phone?'

'What?' I say, confused by the question. 'I found that phone in the dressing table.'

'What are you doing in here? Where's Rod and Bella?'

I don't like how scared she looks, and I don't understand what is causing such distress.

'Rod messaged me to meet him, but he isn't here. I don't know where either of them are.'

She continues to walk backwards, increasing the distance between us. 'Is it you? Are you the one who's been messaging me?'

'I don't know what you're talking about. I swear to you, Zoë, I don't know whose phone that is, but it was ringing, which is why I searched for it. I assume it's Rod's given where I found it. But I also found this.'

I extract the framed photograph and hold it up.

The blood drains from her face in an instant. She looks from the picture to the second phone and then back again, her face blank as her mind processes what she's seeing.

'Why do you have Evan's phone?' she asks again.

'Wait, do you mean that guy you were telling me and Lily about last night? The arsehole sending you nasty messages?'

She nods, her eyes narrowing as she continues watching me.

'Why do you have his phone? Is he here now? Have you been working with him to try and scare me into confessing about Saul?'

Her mind is making crazy leaps, and I take a step forward to try and comfort her, but she shuffles backwards, in obvious fear, so I stop and offer out a hand.

'Come on, Zoë, you know me. Look at my face: I don't know

who this Evan guy is, nor why his phone is in Rod's room. Yesterday, I did overhear Bella talking to someone about us and they
said this whole weekend is a sham. I'm taking a guess here but
maybe this Evan person is who I heard her talking to.'

She looks back at the phone, and then up at me.

'I swear to God, Dan, if you're lying to me I will fucking kill
you.'

40

ZOË

I so desperately want to believe what Dan is saying to me, but I know he's lied before. He should have been parked up outside the school, waiting for me to come out so we could make a quick escape if something went wrong. But I was there watching and Dan didn't appear where he should have been. So, when Saul came rushing out, the alarm wailing and being pursued by security, he didn't know which way to turn. And yet later that night when the three of us convened in the woods, Dan claimed he'd been there and watched the whole thing. He claimed Saul had turned the wrong way, into the onrushing car. I didn't call him out on his bullshit then because of my own overwhelming guilt at letting Saul take my place, and because I fucked up silencing the alarm.

Twenty-four years later and I've caught him holding Evan's phone. What does this mean? Does he know Evan? Have they been complicit in trying to get me to admit how I messed up with Saul?

I can't see answers to those questions in my head. I can't imagine a world where Evan's and Dan's paths would ever have

crossed. The last time I saw Dan before Friday morning was the
night of my surprise party, but even then the meeting was fleeting. And I didn't know Evan back then, so he wasn't in atten-
dance. Even if they had met that night, I can't see how the two of
them would have started talking or reached an agreement to
disrupt my life. Evan joined the firm eighteen months ago, but
nothing happened between us for the first year, and the harass-
ment only started when I ended things a few weeks ago. My mind
is all over the place and I just want someone to cut through all
the bullshit and explain to me what is going on here. Why does
Dan have Evan's phone, and where the fuck is Evan?

The only thing that's lending Dan's story any credence is the
framed image of Saul and Rod wrestling in a garden that he's
holding. It isn't a picture I ever remember seeing before, and I
don't know why Dan would be carrying that around the house
with him. It's too big to hide in a pocket.

'I'm not lying, Zoë,' he says now. 'Come and look in the
drawer and I'll show you exactly where I found both items. Don't
forget this is Rod's room.'

I take several uneasy steps forward, straining my neck until I
can see into the open drawer of the dressing table. Dan is
pointing to the right half of the drawer.

'It was just here. I pulled out the ringing phone, trying to
work out whose it was when I saw the picture. I pulled them both
out and then you barged in.' He pauses and frowns with more
than a hint of suspicion. 'Wait, why were you coming in here
anyway?'

'I was following the ringtone,' I answer. 'I received a message
from the withheld number and, thinking it was from Evan, I
dialled the number I have for him, and that's when I heard it
ringing.'

He passes me the phone.

'You're sure this is his?'

I nod and tap the screen ready to type in Evan's PIN, but the screen immediately opens.

'Wait, something isn't right. Evan's phone has a PIN to unlock it in case his thumbprint doesn't work, but someone has amended his security settings.'

I open his recent calls list, and hold the screen out so Dan can see my name and number listed on both incoming and outgoing calls. In fact, what's scariest is that mine is the only name and number listed for the last two weeks. Eventually I find Mae's number towards the bottom of the list.

I next flick to the photo gallery app, ready to show Dan the compromising images he has of us both, but stop when I see the image of the five of us in the car with me passed out behind the wheel. I think I'd already deduced that he might have been the one to give the printed picture to the barmaid, but seeing it confirmed is still a shock. Dan must sense my unease as he circles around so he can also look at the screen.

'So he was the one who took the photo of us and gave it to the barmaid,' he says. 'Who is this guy really? Why is he here?'

I'm not listening to Dan, continuing to scroll through the photographs, seeing more images of me. There are other pictures of me and Lily at the party, images of us arriving at the village pub the night we arrived in Scotland, pictures of me at Southwaite Services where we stopped on the outskirts of Carlisle. Then there's a photograph of me standing by the side of the road waiting to be collected by Lily.

Fucking hell, he's been following me for ages.

There are more photos from the days leading up to the trip away. Pictures of me leaving my house; images of me arriving at work; shots of me talking with clients in my office. I hadn't realised just how obsessed he was. And then I reach the screen-shots from the firm's security system, and I quickly lock the screen before Dan can see any of those.

'Who is this guy, Zoë, apart from someone who's clearly been stalking you for ages?'

'He's just...'

I can't complete the thought as I try to remember exactly how the two of us met, and whether it felt natural or forced in some way.

I couldn't understand how Evan could know anything about my involvement with Saul, but if he's been in contact with Rod, then maybe Rod said something. Again, right now I can't understand how Rod and Evan would have come into contact, but given the phone is in Rod's room, I have to just accept that they do know each other somehow. So, accepting that they're friends, could Rod have told Evan to try and seduce me so they'd be able to blackmail me to get to the truth about Saul? That feels too farfetched and like the plot hole in some lame movie.

'Who is he, Zoë? Why was he at the party on Friday night?'

'I... I don't know. I guess he followed me up here...'

My stomach rolls at the thought that he was waiting outside my house and followed as I went to the station and caught the train up to Mam and Dad's house on Thursday, and I had no idea he was there. All those pictures of me on his phone, I was oblivious that he was taking them. I shudder at the thought. It's such an invasion of privacy, and I almost want to forward them all to myself so I have the evidence to show Mae when I speak to her tomorrow. This kind of behaviour is absolutely unacceptable and I want it dealing with once and for all.

'Do you think he was the person who spiked our drinks?' Dan asks now, and it brings my mind back to the present.

'I... I honestly don't know. The pictures on this phone prove he was there so it's definitely a possibility, but I don't understand why he would spike all of our drinks other than to cause us to crash...'

Is that why he's been getting so close: I spurned him and now he wants me dead? There are so many other ways he could have killed me before now. He could have run me down in his car on any of the occasions he followed me from my house. Or he could have pushed me in front of the train at Winchester station. Or even slipped some kind of poison into my drinks at work. I don't understand why he'd follow me all the way up here and then spike our drinks.

'No, wait,' Dan interjects, shaking his own head in confusion. 'I was forgetting Rod said he was the one who had the GHB, so I don't see how this Evan guy would have got hold of it.'

'Maybe Rod gave it to him,' I say.

'But why would Rod want us all drugged?'

'Isn't it obvious? Don't you remember how obsessed he became after Saul's death? All the questions all the time. And now he drags us all together for this surprise wedding weekend and we all end up in this position.'

'Lily wasn't drugged, don't forget.'

'No, but she was drunk anyway, so maybe he figured he didn't need her incapacitated.'

Dan steps away, throwing his arms into the air, I'd imagine as frustrated by the lack of answers as I am. I still feel like we're missing something obvious that will neatly explain what is going on, but for the life of me I can't put my finger on exactly what it is.

I have a fresh idea, and unlock my own phone, calling Jasper. It's unlike him to take so long to source information on a client. He answers on the first ring.

'Any luck locating Bella Walker or Bella McDonald?' I ask him.

'No, nothing I'd say is concrete. I haven't found anyone with either name born in Manhattan in the decade between 1992 and 2002. I have widened my search to other states, but it's taking time.'

I switch the phone to speaker so Dan will be able to hear Jasper's gruff voice too.

'I think the American accent is false,' Dan says now. 'When I overheard her in this room yesterday, I swear I heard her lose the accent. I think she might be English.'

'What? Why didn't you mention this sooner?' I challenge.

'I thought I had?' he says, frowning.

'What about the marriage licence, did you find anything in Rod's name?'

'I'm sorry, I haven't managed to check that yet. Do you want me to prioritise that?'

'Please. But focus the search on Rod's name as it might be easier to find. And whilst you're doing that, can you see if you can find any connections between Rod Astor and a man called Evan Reinhold.'

I hang up the phone, and unlock Evan's phone again.

'What are you doing now?' Dan asks, looking nervously towards the bedroom door.

'If Evan has Rod's number in his phone then it proves they know each other,' I say, scrolling through Evan's list of contacts, but not finding Rod's name. 'Can you read me out Rod's number and I'll type it in and see if maybe he's listed Rod under another name, and whether the two have exchanged any messages?'

Dan pulls out his own phone and begins to read Rod's number while I type it into Evan's phone, but there's no record of it.

'Maybe they email instead?' Dan suggests, and I open Evan's email app and look at his sent folder.

There are no messages to Rod but I find two to the email

address of the village pub we were at yesterday, one of which includes the picture of the five of us in the car.

'You're not going to believe this,' I say next. 'Evan sent the picture to the barmaid via email, along with a message telling her to print it and take it up to the farm. Oh my God, it's all here. He's listed our names, and tells her to demand five grand in exchange for her silence. He says if we ask she should say he came into the pub in person, and to provide a vague description, but that she'd never seen him before. Oh my God, he set all of this up.'

My knees feel weak, and I have to grab hold of Dan's arm to support myself.

'So, Evan told her to demand five grand, knowing Rod already had the money in his case,' Dan says, leading me to the bed so I can perch.

'It would seem so.'

'And Rod told me to suspect you and Lily of conspiring so that we wouldn't trust each other enough to figure out what they've been up to. That son of a bitch. This whole nightmare is all to do with what happened to Saul. But why is he still so obsessed about it after all this time?'

'I don't know, but I don't think we should hang around here to find out. We should get Lily and then the three of us should just get out of here. We can try and find a taxi or a passing car and get back to the ferry. I don't like that Rod's been manipulating us from the very beginning.'

'We'd better put the phone and the picture back though,' Dan suggests. 'We don't want Rod to realise we're on to them.'

I agree, but take a picture of all the images of myself on Evan's phone so I can show Mae tomorrow. Dan returns the frame to the drawer and I carry the phone over, but something catches my eye as I place the phone in the drawer. I hadn't noticed it before, but there's a black leather wallet of sorts that I now find myself reaching for.

'We'd better go before Rod comes back,' Dan says, hurrying to the door, but I don't move.

I open the wallet and can't stop the gasp escaping as I see the police warrant card, and Bella's face on it.

41

DAN

I'm peering out from behind the bedroom door, certain Bella and Rod will return at any moment. The coast is clear and I'm about to head out until I realise Zoë isn't beside me. I check back and find her still standing beside the open drawer of the dressing table.

'What are you doing?' I say in a loud whisper. 'We need to get out of here before they catch us.'

But she doesn't move. I can't see what she's holding, but the blood has drained from her face and neck. I abandon my lookout spot and approach, ready to grab her arm and drag her away if necessary, but then I stop when I see the open wallet she's holding.

'Bella's in the police,' she whispers in disbelief.

I look closer at the warrant card inside the wallet and it's definitely Bella's face on the card, but the name reads as Louise Walker.

I recall the unfamiliar man's voice from last night: *I'm worried about you, Lou.*

I can't believe that Rod knows she's in the police and has lied to us.

'I feel sick,' Zoë says now. 'All this time she's been lying about who she is and what she's after.'

'What do you mean *what she's after*?'

'Isn't it obvious? She must be part of Glynn's team. He must have sent her in undercover to try and get us to talk about what happened to Saul.'

This thought hadn't occurred to me, but I can't see why the police would go to such lengths to solve a decades-old case. And I'd be shocked if they have the kind of budget to use an undercover operative in a cold case. It doesn't add up in my head.

And yet Glynn has already told me why he's at the wedding, and Lily said he'd already approached her before this weekend. If he's that convinced of our guilt, then maybe he has the ways and means to send an officer in to infiltrate the pack. But what I can't compute in my head is the accident on Friday night. Surely if she's a police officer, she should have arrested us for leaving the scene. In fact, at no point did she tell us not to run.

'I don't think we should change our plans, despite this new development,' I say, holding my hand out for Zoë to take. 'Please, let's get out of this room, back to Lily and then the three of us get out of this place.'

'What about Rod?'

'What *about* Rod? He has to be in on all of this. He told me yesterday he knew Glynn was reviewing Saul's hit and run, and if the bride-to-be is an undercover officer then there's no way Rod can't know about that. Let's just find Lily and go. We can figure out the rest once we've put space between us all.'

She closes the wallet, but puts it in her pocket rather than returning it to the drawer.

'I'm taking this to show Lily,' she says, and I don't have the patience to argue with her.

We cross back to the door, and I peer out, before we leave the room, and hurry along the corridor back in the direction of our rooms. The main reception area is crammed with flowers and ribbons, and I can't help but wonder what Glynn's and Bella's – Lou's – plan is here. If they are so certain of our complicity in the events leading to Saul's death, why haven't they arrested us yet? Why go to the lengths and expense of all this elaborate wedding set-up? Something just doesn't add up in my head about this whole situation.

'Hey, where are the two of you rushing off to?' Rod asks when I practically run into him as we turn the final corner.

'Oh hey, we um... just...' I look over to Zoë, who is also short of breath from the exertion of running, but I hope she can think of a reasonable excuse for our sprinting.

'We, uh, were out walking and suddenly realised the time,' she says, and I nod along in concurrence, although I have no idea what time it actually is.

'Yeah, so we were hurrying back to our rooms to get changed for the wedding,' I add, with a smile that I hope he can't see through.

'Did you get my message earlier?' Rod asks, now leaning closer to me. 'There's something urgent I need your help with.'

Oh God, is this his way of trying to separate us so he can lead me to Glynn, or is the plan to lead me one way while Glynn and Bella swoop in on Zoë? For all I know, they already have Lily in their clutches.

'Um, yeah, I did. I was actually looking for you when I ran into Zoë,' I say. 'Can it wait until after the wedding though? I need to change and don't want to be late.'

What I really mean is that I want to throw all my stuff and the twenty grand he gave me last night into a bag and hightail it out of here.

'Not really.' He takes my arm and leads me towards a closed door, but makes no mention of Zoë, so I take her hand and drag her with us.

Rod opens the door with a key, and leads us into what looks like a library of sorts. All the monotone spines are indistinguishable from one another in the floor-to-ceiling bookcases. There is no Glynn, Bella or team of police officers awaiting us. Rod waits until we are both in before closing the door.

'This is a bit awkward, but I'm just going to come out with it,' Rod begins, and it's only now I see how flustered he looks, his unbrushed hair poking out in all directions as if he's been clutching it. 'It looks like my best man isn't going to make it in time. His flight has been delayed, so I need a stand-in. And, given how long we've known each other, I thought... well, I wondered whether *you* would stand at the altar with me, Dan?'

'I, uh, don't know what to say,' I tell him and I genuinely don't. If he knows Bella is really an undercover police officer, then surely there isn't going to be a wedding, so I don't understand why he is asking me.

'Is that a yes?' Rod asks eagerly.

I look to Zoë for guidance, but she just raises her eyebrows in my direction.

If I tell him I can't do it, he's going to know something is up, and I don't want him disrupting our plans to get out of here. Yet, at the same time, maybe this is already his ploy to keep us where we are, and to prevent us from escaping.

'Yes, of course, I'll do it,' I say when I can no longer stomach the awkward silence.

Rod's face breaks into a huge smile, and he thrusts his arms around my shoulders, wrestling me into a bear hug.

'Thanks so much, mate. It means the world that you came all this way for my big day, and now you're helping me out last minute.' He pauses as he eyes Zoë's hand clasped in mine. 'This is an interesting development,' he says in a lewd manner. 'You two were just out *walking*, were you? Don't worry, your secret is safe with me.'

We immediately pull our hands apart.

'Oh, no, this isn't what you think,' Zoë tries to say, and I echo her words.

'What happens on Jura stays on Jura,' he says with an exaggerated wink. 'Dan, go and get dressed and then meet me down in the garage where I'll hand you the rings and we can chat through the order of service for today. You know, I never thought I'd be so excited to be getting married after all these years!'

He slaps my upper arm, and then crosses to the door, leaving the library and us behind.

'What do you make of all that?' I ask Zoë, and she simply shrugs, before heading out of the room.

I hurry after her as she jogs back towards Lily's room, knocking twice before entering with me in tow.

'Oh, hey,' Lily says, lowering the pair of GHDs. 'I was wondering where you two were.'

She's wearing an ankle-length silver gown which shimmers in the sunshine creeping through the window between the parted curtains. I've never seen her looking so beautiful and I rue the day I snuck out of her room without speaking.

'We need to get out of here,' Zoë says, lifting Lily's suitcase onto the bed.

'What? Why? What's going on?'

'Bella is not who she claims. Her real name is Louise Walker – Lou – and we believe she's an undercover police officer, presumably working with Glynn.'

Lily's stare snaps to me momentarily, maybe wondering whether I've mentioned the little tête-à-tête she told me about last night.

'Oh my gosh,' Lily says. 'You think she's also investigating what happened to Saul?'

'We found her identification,' Zoë says, offering the wallet, 'along with a framed photograph of Saul and Rod wrestling. Dan overheard her talking last night, describing this wedding as a sham. And there's another thing, we think Rod knows and is working with the two of them.'

'Wait,' I interrupt, 'do you really think Rod is involved? He just asked me to step in as his best man; would he need to do that if he's trying to set us up?'

'Yes, if he wants us to think the wedding is genuine.'

'I'm not so sure. He looked genuinely worried when he just collared us, and—'

'Think about it, Dan, do you really think the police would allow one of their officers to go through with a fake wedding without informing the groom? You've seen how this place has been decorated – no expense has been spared. And who do you think is funding all of that, because I can guarantee it isn't Glynn and his team.'

'But maybe they think Rod is involved as well. I know he doesn't know why Saul went into the school that night, but maybe Glynn and this Lou woman think he does. Maybe he's another fly they're trying to trap.'

'But we found Evan's phone and the framed picture in Rod's room,' Zoë argues.

'Rod *and* Bella's room. We don't know he knows they were there.'

Zoë sighs in frustration and it instantly takes me back to when we were in school and she'd become frustrated because I wasn't following her train of thought. Most of the time I would back down the moment she sighed just like that, but not today.

'Okay, Sherlock, well, tell me this,' she says, her tone testy, 'if Rod isn't in on the undercover scam, why wouldn't he be questioning why his beloved Bella hasn't slept with him yet?'

My brow ruffles.

'An undercover officer wouldn't be permitted to have sexual intercourse with a suspect; it's morally and procedurally wrong. And we all know what Rod is like: there's no way he would be marrying – let alone dating – someone he hasn't already had sex with. So, if she's not allowed to sleep with him, why would he be going through with this wedding unless he knows none of this is real?'

I see her point now, but I don't want to believe that Rod is that good of an actor to have lulled me into believing his lies.

'What about your office stalker?' I snap back, leaving her question unanswered. 'We found his phone in that drawer as well, and we know from the photographs that he followed you up here and was at that party. We also know that he paid that barmaid to blackmail us. But to what end? How does he fit into your master plan? And where the fuck is he?'

'I honestly don't know, but frankly, I don't care either. Coming up here was a stupid idea and I wish I hadn't come away. I should be at home with my husband right now, Lily should be at home with her son, and you, Dan, you should be sorting out your financial mess.'

My cheeks sting at the attack, but I can see how frustrated she is with all of these unanswered questions.

I take a deep breath, composing my thoughts.

'We know for a fact that Evan followed you up here. He observed us at the village inn and followed us to the party in that barn. While we were all there, someone spiked four of our drinks. Now, this may have been Evan, Bella, or Rod – assuming that none of us did it. And it may or may not have been with the missing GHB that Rod smuggled in from Amsterdam. For some reason Lily wasn't drugged, but Zoë and I definitely were. At some point between that and us waking yesterday morning, that homeless guy was hit by our car and killed. We also now know that Bella's name is actually Lou and that she's in the police. We also know that our old bully Glynn is also in the police and reviewing the hit and run that killed Saul twenty-four years ago. The two incidents could be totally unrelated, but there's too much coincidence for me to accept that. Our options, as I see them, are to hang around and wait to see how all of this plays out, or we get the fuck out of here and don't look back.'

Zoë holds up a finger as her phone bursts into song.

'Hold that thought,' she says, pressing the phone to her ear. 'Jasper, what have you got for me...? You're fucking kidding me. She's what?'

42

ZOË

My blood runs cold as I ask Jasper to repeat what he just told me.

'I located the marriage licence in Rod Astor's name, but the woman he is set to marry isn't Bella Walker, but *Louise* Walker. But Walker isn't her maiden name. This will be her second marriage, but she never changed her name back. Her real name is Louise Benedict. One of three children. Born on Christmas Eve in 1991, which makes her thirty-two years old. She has two older brothers, Reuben and Saul, though the latter died in 2000.'

I almost drop the phone as my muscles weaken.

She's Saul's sister.

Suddenly the fog of doubt clears before my eyes, and it's like I've just discovered the key piece in the puzzle.

'What is it? What's wrong?' Lily says, catching me as I fall into her arms.

'Sh-she's Saul's sister,' I whisper breathlessly.

Lily gasps but Dan stands frozen.

'No. Impossible,' he eventually declares. 'Saul's sister is... well, she's... she's a child.'

'That was twenty-four years ago,' Lily says quietly.

I barely remember Saul's sister, other than she would always interrupt us when we were hanging out in Saul's garden. We'd be talking or listening to music, trying to act all cool and like we had our shit together, and she was just this annoyance who would come over and ask what we were doing, and begging Saul to play with her on the Swingball set. Sometimes he'd cave and play one game with her and that would sate her curiosity, but other times he'd tell her to leave us alone.

Bella can't be that same girl, and yet the moment Jasper uttered the words I knew it to be true.

'Is there anything else you need from me?' I hear Jasper's voice crackle through the phone.

I can't find the words, but just as I'm about to hang up, I tell him, 'Can you see if you can find any connection between her and Evan Reinhold?'

'I already checked that. You mentioned his name in connection with Rod Astor but there's nothing to connect the three of them, save for the marriage licence.'

'And what about Saul's older brother Reuben. Any idea where he is right now?'

'Due respect, Zoë, but my expertise is following online trails. I'm not a facial recognition system.'

'Please, Jasper. See what you can find out about Reuben Benedict.'

'You do realise it's Sunday?'

'I'll pay whatever the rate. You know I'm good for it.'

He groans, before agreeing to help and hanging up.

'Do you think Rod knows who she really is?' Lily asks next.

I honestly don't know how to answer that question. Rod knew Saul better than any of us. They were friends since childhood. And whilst I can barely remember what Louise looked like, other than blonde pigtails, I certainly didn't recognise her as the woman the rest of us met on Friday morning.

'How can he not know?' I ask nobody in particular. 'They're supposed to be getting married, so he must have met her brother and parents – or seen pictures. He has to be in on it. He has to know who she is and what she is, and that's why he dragged her along for the road trip. Maybe the accident is all part of their plan to get us to tell the truth about that night with Saul.'

'That's ridiculous,' Dan snaps. 'There's no way they could have known that drugging us would lead to another hit and run accident.'

'But you said yourself it's too coincidental that the three of us being together for the first time in twenty-four years ends with the same result.'

'Are we sure the guy in the road was dead?' Lily asks, and it's like an electric shock to my spine.

'We all saw his face. He didn't have a pulse,' I reply dismissively.

'Didn't he?' Lily says. 'Rod was the one who checked and said he couldn't feel a pulse. But nobody else corroborated that.'

'You saw his face, right? It was all smashed up and bloody.'

'Who's to say that wasn't part of it all? You've seen how realistic make-up effects are in television and films these days. They can make it look like limbs have been severed, and guts are falling out. We don't know that they didn't plan to drug us so they could get all of that stagecraft in place so we'd *believe* we'd killed someone. We left the scene, and for all we know the victim then clambered back to his feet and went home.'

'What about the police finding the body and the report on the news?' I ask.

'If Glynn is also involved, maybe he used his position to put out a false story? And given Rod's wealth, maybe he slipped someone a bribe. I don't know, I'm just speculating. Can you think of any other reason the two of you were drugged?'

That remains a question I can't answer despite the recent revelations about Bella.

'Something doesn't make sense,' Dan says. 'Rod warned me about Glynn being in the police, and he's given me some money to help me get back on my feet. If he was working with Glynn and Bella, then why would he do that? If he knows they're planning to question and potentially arrest us for our involvement, then why would he give me the money? And why would he tell me about the GHB going missing from his case?'

'To throw us all off the scent,' I reply. 'He probably knew you'd confide in the two of us, and he's been trying to keep us on edge.'

'Rod's many things, but his acting isn't that good. I genuinely think he loves Bella, and you saw how he was earlier when he said his best man was held up. He looked genuinely frantic, and then he was so happy when I agreed to step in. I'm telling you both that I think Rod believes he is actually getting married this afternoon. Call it a gut feeling, but I don't think Rod is lying to us.'

'We could ask him,' Lily suggests. 'Get him alone before the wedding and tell him what we suspect. He won't be able to pull the wool over all of our eyes. And if you're right, Dan, and Rod doesn't know, don't you think he deserves to know the truth?'

I don't like the idea of hanging around here any longer than is necessary, but I also want answers.

'He told me to meet him in the garage when I'm ready,' Dan says, 'so let's go and find him there.'

Pocketing Louise's identification card and my phone, I follow the two of them out of the room, and Dan leads us along the corridor and to a descending spiral staircase, which seems to go on forever, until we come to a security door. Dan bangs his fist against the door, and we hear Rod call out four numbers from the other side, which Dan proceeds to type into the panel beside the wall. The secured door slides open and the three of us huddle through, the floor lighting as we proceed into the darkness.

'Oh, you're all here,' Rod says, sitting up on the couch he's been stretched out on. 'Like a reunion.'

'Yeah, there was something we wanted to...' Dan begins, but I cut him off.

'We know what you're up to,' I say, throwing the wallet into his lap.

'What's this?' Rod asks as he slowly opens it, his eyes widening as the penny drops. 'Wait, is this? No, it can't be, but...' He studies the image closer.

'When were you going to tell us that the wedding is a sham? Before or after the registrar asks for any objections?' I say, watching his face for any tics or signs of recognition, searching for any clues as to whether he's going to continue lying.

'I don't know what... I mean, I know she was born Louise, and that Bella is her chosen name – she said it's what her dad always used to call her and it just stuck – but I swear I didn't know she was in the police. Where did you get this from?'

Dan joins Rod on the sofa, his approach softer.

'It was in the dressing table in your room,' he confides.

'In *my* room? You were in my room?'

'And when were you going to mention that your fiancée is Saul's younger sister? Or did that just slip your mind?'

Rod's gaze snaps up to mine, but the look he gives is one of disbelief.

'Don't be ridic—'

'It's true,' Dan says calmly. 'Louise Walker was born Louise Benedict. She's Saul's sister.'

Rod laughs nervously.

'No, this is all some kind of joke, right? A prank to get me back for all the shit I did to you lot back in the day.' He laughs louder. 'Oh, you lot are good. This ID looks so real. For a moment you genuinely had me going.'

'This is no joke, Rod,' I say firmly, but he isn't listening.

'And which of you came up with the jape about her being Saul's sister? That's pretty sick, even by my standards. Phew.'

It's not the reaction I was expecting from him. I figured if he was in on it he'd vehemently deny the accusation, or maybe call out the others.

'Saul's sister,' he repeats with a hearty chuckle. 'You guys!'

I'm usually good at judging when people are lying to me; it's what makes me so good at my job during trials. But I'm starting to think Dan might be right and that Rod is as clueless as the rest of us.

'We think she's working with Glynn,' Dan continues. 'He's been asking all sorts of questions about the night Saul died, and he thinks that the three of us had something to do with it. The fact that Saul's sister is the bride-to-be is too much of a coincidence. Now's the time to come clean, Rod.'

Rod's expression changes, deep lines forming in his forehead.

'Enough, guys. It was a good try, but you can take a joke too far, you know.'

'This is no joke, mate. She's working undercover to try and get to the truth about what happened to Saul.'

'But she wouldn't... she can't be... we... no, wait, if she's in the police she wouldn't be able to sleep with me, would she? And we've had sex a lot. And I mean *a lot*. There are rules against that sort of thing, surely?'

He looks directly at me as he asks this, and I nod.

'So you're saying you and Bella have definitely had sex together?'

'Of course we have!'

'Well, that might actually help our case,' I say, glancing back at Lily. 'Procedurally, she's broken so many rules that any case brought to trial would be instantly dismissed.'

'You seriously expect me to believe that my fiancée has been faking for the last ten months? All to try and get access to the three of you?'

When he puts it like that, it does make our theory sound more farfetched, but it's the only conclusion that fits most of what we've learned.

'And why would she – why would Glynn, in fact – be so interested in you three? You all had alibis for that night, and claimed to know nothing about what Saul was doing at the school.'

He looks at each of us in turn, and as tempted as I am just to spill my guts, I bite my tongue.

'Because we were all there,' Lily says. 'I don't want to lie any more.'

'Wait, what's she talking about?' Rod says.

'Now isn't the time, Lily,' Dan tries, and I join him.

'Think about what you're doing,' I say. 'Think about George and what he would want.'

'I'm sorry,' she says, lowering her face, her eyes closed. 'I can't live with the guilt any more. Rod is an innocent in all of this, but he probably deserves to know more than anyone what we were all doing there that night. If it wasn't for Rod, none of this would have happened.'

43

DAN

They say the truth will set you free, but I've never felt more trapped and exposed my whole life. Lily told me last night that she's been desperate to tell our side of what happened to Saul, and whilst she's been able to accept her culpability, I'm not sure I'm ready to accept my own.

'What does any of that or any of this have to do with me?' Rod asks, and Lily looks from me to Zoë and then back again.

'We need to tell him,' Lily says, her eyes pleading for just one of us to concur.

'Tell me what?' Rod shouts.

Lily takes a deep breath, but I cut in before she can speak.

'Now isn't the time to do this, Lily. Okay? I think we have more pressing matters. Like where is Bella or Louise, or whatever her name is, and that other thing we discussed?' I narrow my eyes and mouth the word, 'escape' so that Rod won't see.

'I'm fed up of running, Dan. I have George to think about now, and what kind of mother will I be if I bring him up to be honest, knowing I'm not? I don't want to be a hypocrite.'

'This is different,' I reply. 'We swore that pact, remember?'

'Fuck the pact!'

She says it so forthrightly that I now see she has thought long and hard about this, and there's no stopping her.

'Rod, Saul was in that school because we wanted to get revenge on you and your dad.'

Rod's eyebrows drop in deep concentration.

'Revenge on me? For what?'

I turn my back, not wanting to watch the scene unfold, but also too involved to walk away.

'You were a real shit to most of us in secondary school. You and Glynn alike. All of your little pranks, and threats, and whilst you may have intended some of that to be good-natured, there are still nights when I relive some of those moments. Like the time you and Saul thought it would be hilarious to go into the locker rooms at the school swimming pool and steal all the girls' shirts. We were all forced to try and find something from lost property or wear our swimsuits for the rest of the day. Do you know how hard it was for me to see the better-developed chests and figures of the other girls, knowing I looked so different?'

'Oh, come on, you've developed now. You're a stunner, Lily.'

'I'm more comfortable in my body now, but aged fourteen I wasn't. I cried myself to sleep every night for weeks after that. And every time I was in school it felt like everyone else was looking over at me and thinking I was a freak. It dented my self-confidence and I've never managed to get it back.'

'We only did it for a laugh. We were planning to steal all the boys' trousers next time, but they started making everyone use the lockers and we couldn't get to them.'

'But even now, you're justifying your actions,' Lily says, frustration creeping into her voice, 'rather than actually understanding how horrific they were. You seem to think that it would have been fine if you'd messed with the boys as well, but it wouldn't have. It was a heartless thing for you to do, and I hated you for it. Do you remember, Zo?'

Zoë puts a reassuring arm around her.

'I certainly remember the humiliation of that day.'

'But it wasn't nearly as bad for you because you were at the same stage of breast development as the others. I used to envy your figure so much,' she adds, wiping her eyes with the back of her hand. 'All the boys fancied you, Zo. But me, I was just the gawky short-arse with glasses and unmanageable hair. That's why I used to follow you around and hang on your every word. I thought if I could cling to your coat-tails for long enough then people would think I was cool by association or something.'

'You were beautiful, Lily, and you are now.'

'I didn't feel it, and let's be honest, if we were both single in a bar right now, all eyes would be on you, not me.'

I want to speak up and tell Lily that she's wrong, and that I haven't been able to stop thinking about her since seeing her in that dress, but I sense she's not fishing for a compliment.

'Anyway, I've discussed all of this with my therapist, and I don't want to relive that experience yet again. My point is, Rod, that's just one example of how you made our lives a living hell in secondary school, and yet nothing ever came back your way. I mean, Jesus Christ, you actually burned down the chemistry lab at one point – and *everyone* knew it was you – but you didn't even get suspended. Because your dad was the head teacher, it was like you had a "Get Out of Jail Free" card in your back pocket at all times.'

'So why did you come this weekend?' Rod says, with just a hint of hurt in his voice.

Lily sighs.

'I honestly don't know. I thought it would be fun to see the old gang together one more time. By the time we got to sixth form, your personal attacks had stopped, and your pranks were more widely targeted, but I still resented you for never giving a shit about anything or anyone else. I had to work so hard to make the grades I needed to go to university – I think we all did – but you used to just rock up having not completed the homework assignment, or claiming not to have revised, and you never failed. But you were less hard on me in sixth form, and I didn't want you to revert back to your old ways, so I played along like everyone else, and just tried to stay off your radar.'

Lily has a point here. Rod was less of a personal bully after our GCSEs, and so when Saul would ask to bring him along to things – parties, barbecues, beach trips – we allowed him to come. But I had no idea just how difficult Lily found things back then. I wish I'd taken the time to check in on her. I'd assumed Zoë was doing that, and that as Zoë's boyfriend it wasn't really my place to ask, but I regret not trying.

'What did I ever do to the rest of you?' Rod now asks, defensive, his tone angrier than before.

'You used to throw gum in my hair in Year 9,' Zoë says. 'Do you have any idea how difficult that is to get out without cutting out huge clumps? You did it three times in the space of a week at one point, until I asked the teacher to be moved to the desk behind you. And then there was one time in school when you sent Dan a letter, pretending to be me, saying I wanted to break up with him as I was a lesbian.'

'Yeah, but he knew it wasn't from you,' Rod says, again somehow justifying his own behaviour.

'Yeah, he didn't, but that didn't stop the rumour spreading. I was actually approached by several girls asking if it was true and whether I'd be interested in experimenting with them. It was so awkward for me and for them. I had to tell each of them that I was flattered but not interested, and you had no right to lull them into thinking it was okay to share something they were still exploring themselves. One girl actually left the school afterwards. And I reported it to the teachers and once again nothing happened to you.'

'Actually, I got detention for a week.'

'And you think that was an adequate punishment?'

He doesn't answer this challenge. I can feel my own frustration growing. Hearing Lily and Zoë sharing their stories is putting me back in that place. I remember feeling like this the day we decided we needed to get revenge. But getting Rod back just wasn't enough. His dad was his enabler, and it was me who said if we go for both it will have a bigger impact.

'And Dan, what did I do to you that was so fucking awful?'

I recall the feeling of dread that enveloped me when I ran into Glynn yesterday, and I don't want to relive that feeling, as it claws and scratches at my skin. Just thinking about it has my chest tightening.

'Does it matter?' I say. 'After all this time, it doesn't alter anything. We can't change the past, so we're better off not reliving it. You're clearly not the same person you were back then, as you proved to me yesterday with your generosity.'

I'm not prepared to kick a friend when they're down, and am hoping we can all just move on. But Lily isn't prepared to let it rest, it would seem.

'We decided we'd get you and your dad back once and for all,' Lily says. 'We spent ages thinking about ways and means of doing it. Scratching something into the paintwork of one of his beloved cars, but he'd be able to repair that. Someone suggested we write a letter from your dad condemning your behaviour and accepting accountability for your actions, but he'd be able to prove it wasn't real, and it would only confirm what everybody already knew. And then...' She pauses and I see in the reflection of the car's wing mirror beside me that she's looking in my direction. 'Then Dan suggested the best way to leave our mark.'

I spin on my heel so I'm facing the group again.

'Just think about what you're doing,' I warn Lily, but it falls on deaf ears.

'We decided we would get into your dad's office and leave hardcore porn in his desk for his secretary to find. Imagine the scandal: a head teacher with a distinguished career discovered to be a pervert. It's one of those accusations that sticks regardless of the legitimacy of it. His reputation would be in tatters and he'd have to leave education permanently. And you'd forever be known as the son of a deviant.'

Rod's mouth drops, and hearing it described this way shows just how cold an idea it was. It disturbs me that my mind could be so evil in its machinations, and when I first suggested it I was certain the others would reject the idea, but it was late and we'd been drinking in the afternoon sun in Saul's garden, and we all agreed on the plan. I remember going home that night and thinking the rest would come to their senses in the morning, but when we got together after school, it was like it had been set in stone.

'We went to the school that night to break in and plant the magazines and videos in your dad's desk,' Lily continues. 'We drew straws for who should do it, and Saul—'

'I should have been the one to go in,' Zoë interrupts. 'I drew the shortest straw, but I was terrified of getting caught. All the bravado I outwardly projected was a lie, and I was suffering with undiagnosed anxiety. Saul was supposed to cut the electrics to the alarm so that the security guards wouldn't know I'd got in. We met earlier that day so he could talk me through what he was supposed to do and so we could agree a signal for when it was safe for me to open the window. But I think he saw how worried I was and he offered to go in my place.'

I freeze as I hear this. I had no idea Zoë had drawn the short straw, I just remember the relief that it wasn't me. We weren't supposed to know each other's roles so that there'd be plausible deniability, so all these years I'd assumed Saul was the person who was meant to go in.

'He probably did that because he was madly in love with you,' Rod says.

'Wait, how did you know that?' Zoë asks.

'He used to go on about it all the time. He respected Dan too much to ever do anything about it, but he was crazy about you.'

I had no idea Saul's feelings were that strong, but I can remember catching him looking at Zoë for a little too long on occasions, and I remember hoping she didn't realise and pick him over me. I think that's why I went to buy the engagement ring that night. I wanted to show her how committed I was, and hoped that she'd reciprocate those feelings.

'He told me he loved me and that he didn't want me to feel so nervous,' Zoë resumes. 'He suggested we swap places and then he told me what I would have to do with the electronics. He wrote it on a piece of paper for me. But when we arrived at the school it was raining, and the words blurred on the paper until I couldn't make out what to do. I tried but within seconds the alarm was sounding. It's my fault that the security guards were chasing him down.'

Zoë buries her face in her hands, and Lily places an arm around her shoulders, gently rubbing.

'It wasn't your fault, Zo. I'm the reason the alarm went off.'

44

ZOË

I give Lily a confused look.

'How can it have been your fault? I was the one who was supposed to cut the power to the alarm. With the writing blurring on the page, I tried to remember if he told me to cut the blue wire or the red one, and in the end I cut neither. He wasn't supposed to open the window until I gave him the signal, but he must have thought I had and opened it too soon.'

But Lily continues to shake her head beside me.

'That's not what I meant.' She pauses, steadying herself. 'I phoned and reported the break-in anonymously.'

I blink several times, uncertain whether I misheard what she said.

'I hardly slept in the week leading up to that night. I assumed it was the stress of exams, but it was because I was so worried we'd be caught breaking in and then we'd get kicked out of school, unable to sit our last exam, and then we'd lose our places at university. I was having nightmares about us getting arrested, and what it would do to my parents to have a jailbird daughter.

Things were hard enough for them running the pub without me bringing trouble to the door.

'I kept hoping one of you would feel the same way and the whole thing would get called off, but none of you did. I didn't want to be the odd one out, so I played along, but I then had this idea. I thought if I reported the crime *before* it happened, then the alarms would trigger, and you'd all panic and change your minds.

'But they didn't take it seriously, or whatever, so I threw a rock up at one of the windows. I didn't realise Saul was already over the fence and inside the grounds. So, when he came running out with security guards chasing him, I knew it was all my fault, and then when that car struck him...'

I can't believe my ears. I've lived with this guilt – the feeling that I don't deserve such a good life – and all the time it was Lily who caused the alarm to go off. I don't know what to say. I feel betrayed, even though I can see her intentions were right.

'When we met later in the woods,' she continues, 'I wanted to admit what I'd done, but I was terrified neither of you would ever speak to me again. You were the only friends I had and I couldn't afford to lose you. That's why I was so keen for us to tell the police, so then the truth would be out, but we'd all be in it together. But when Dan said we should lie, and you agreed, Zo, I knew I would have to agree as well. And so we swore that pact, and I never mentioned it to anyone. Well, not until—'

'Until what?' I snap, glaring at her.

She simply shrugs and looks to Dan for support.

'Glynn. He came to my parents' pub and started asking all kinds of questions about that night. He was implying that one of us was behind the wheel of the car, and I wanted to correct him. And then he threatened George. He said if I didn't come clean he'd report me to social services and they'd take George away from me. I panicked and told him the truth, but made it clear that none of us was driving.'

I think back to Glynn's questions at the breakfast table earlier. I sensed he knew more than he was letting on, but I never imagined this.

'So, you told the detective investigating the crime what we all did?'

'I'm sorry,' she says, wiping at her eyes again. 'I'm sorry, but I'm not prepared to lose my son over something so stupid. We made a mistake that cost Saul his life, but Glynn said if I testify to that, he will make sure George stays with me. What would you have done in that situation?'

'I would have stuck to the fucking pact,' I snap, stomping away, although in truth I don't know what I would have done.

'I can't believe I'm hearing all of this,' Rod now says, crossing to the small fridge in the corner, extracting a bottle of beer and taking a long drink. 'Have you all hated me this much for all this time? I thought we were friends. I invited you here to celebrate with me, but you've been plotting behind my back for years.'

'No, it isn't like that,' Dan says. 'This was all a long time ago. It was stupid – *we* were stupid – and a lot of water has passed under the bridge since then. Your dad retired the year after anyway, and we all went in different directions. The problem with burying a lie that deep is that when it eventually emerges it appears far bigger than you remember. And before the two of you start falling on your swords, you should know that I was late collecting Saul. Had I been there when I said I would be, he wouldn't have been wandering in the street searching for me.'

I turn my glare to Dan next.

'Why were you late?'

He pulls a strange face.

'If you really want to know, I'd gone to buy you an engagement ring. I was planning to propose to you straight after our last exam, but after Saul died, and with the police asking questions... it was just never the right time.'

I don't know what to say to this. I had no idea he was thinking about proposing. The moment Saul kissed me, I was ready to break up with Dan.

'So, the big secret you've all been keeping all this time is that you were planning to get even with me and my dad. That's why Saul was at the school that night?'

Dan's right: it sounds so petty now, but when we were immature eighteen-year-olds we thought we knew better. Had any one of us thought about it, and stopped the others, Saul wouldn't have been wandering in the street when that driver struck him.

'Ultimately, had we not sworn a pact of silence, it wouldn't have made a difference to the outcome of the case,' Dan says now. 'We lied because we were terrified of the repercussions that would come because ultimately our actions led to Saul's death, but it wouldn't have helped the police track down the person responsible for the hit and run. Even if we come clean to Glynn now, it won't help.'

'Are you so sure about that?' Rod asks. 'You know, for years I suspected there was something you were all hiding, but I couldn't figure out what it was. I actually thought one of you had pushed Saul into the road or something, and that's what had led to the accident. I couldn't work out why you were all lying, and now I guess I know.'

'So, now that you know, Rod, are you going to admit the truth to us?' Lily asks.

'What truth?'

'The truth about why we are all here in Scotland, and why you're pretending to marry an undercover police officer. This is what you wanted to achieve, right? Our sordid confessions. Well, we've told you the truth, why don't you tell us what really happened on Friday night?'

Rod looks at each of us individually.

'I have no idea what you're talking about.'

'You admitted to Dan that you smuggled GHB back from Amsterdam,' Lily continues, 'and you told him you thought I took it from your bag when we both know that was nothing to do with me. Your bag was already unzipped when I went looking for the charger, so someone else had been inside. I don't believe it was either Dan or Zoë. And if I had to guess, I'd say it was you that spiked Dan's water and then made sure the rest drank from it. One final prank to prove that you're the joker in the pack.'

'Don't be ridiculous,' Rod roars. 'Do you think I have a death wish? Why the fuck would I drug the designated driver?'

'Maybe because you were hoping to extract this confession from us,' I add. 'The thing is, I know a little about GHB and the effects it can cause. It's a party drug that is supposed to produce feelings of euphoria, confidence, relaxation and sociability, but what happens when people are in that kind of mental state? They're more honest. So, I put it to you, Rod, that you drugged us, hoping to extract the truth about why Saul was outside the school.'

'Well, that simply isn't true,' he says.

'So, why did you bring it back from Holland?' I press.

'Because I enjoy sex more when I've used it. Okay? There's no crime in that. And besides, I wouldn't have been stupid enough to give it to you and Lily, given you were both drinking alcohol. GHB and booze don't mix well, and you're more likely to end up in a coma. I never intended anyone to use it but me, and not on that night. It was supposed to be a wedding present for Bella. We were supposed to use it tonight, which is why I was so annoyed someone had stolen it.'

'And had you discussed this with her?' I ask.

'Of course I did. I'm not in the habit of spiking other people's drinks. What do you take me for?'

'So, Bella knew about the GHB,' Lily says.

'Well, yes of course she did, but why would…?'

Silence descends on all of us as we contemplate that very question.

'She'd lose her job and probably wind up in prison if it got out that she'd drugged us as part of her assignment,' I say for the group, and yet everything else seems to be slotting into place in my head. 'What if she drugged us to try and get us to admit what had happened to her brother, but she didn't realise we'd pass out. That would explain why she couldn't allow the police to find her at the scene of a hit and run.'

'Wait, I think you're all getting a bit ahead of yourselves,' Rod says. 'You're making massive leaps of judgement about Bella, and I don't think you should say any more without her here.'

We all turn at the sound of heels clapping against the tiled floor, and the lights slowly bring the emerging figure into sight.

'Oh, please don't stop on my account,' Bella says. 'You've all given me exactly what I was looking for, apart from one thing: the name of the person who killed my brother.'

45

DAN

I can't say I'm surprised she's not wearing a wedding dress. From what we've concluded in the last couple of hours, she never intended to marry Rod. She's dressed in navy jeans, ankle boots and a sports jacket. With the rifle beneath her arm, she looks like she's going on a hunt, only the barrel is pointed at us.

'Bella, darling, what are you doing?' Rod tries to ask, taking a step forward, but she adjusts the barrel so it's pointed square at his chest.

'This is loaded and I am prepared to use it if I don't get the answers I've spent more than two decades chasing. I want to know the name of the person who killed Saul and then the rest of you can go.'

I raise my arms, palms pointing outwards to show I'm not a threat.

'We don't know who killed your brother. We're going to tell Glynn everything we know in the hope it helps him, but the actual driver wasn't one of us. I was parked in my dad's van down the street, and I saw both Lily and Zoë at the side of the road.

And Rod wasn't even there. So there really is no need for the weapon.'

She swings the rifle in my direction next, and even though there's a good four metres' distance, any blast will do enough damage to at least require hospital treatment. I stretch my hands even higher in passive surrender.

'Do you have any idea how much my brother hated you, Dan? You can read all about it in his diary. He shares his views on all of you, and it was quite the eye-opener when I found it amongst his old things when I was clearing out my parents' attic last year. I bet none of you even knew he kept a daily journal. I had no idea but then I spoke to Reuben and he told me that Saul used it to control his anger management issues. It turns out we're all a little narcissistic in this room, aren't we?'

'Speak for yourself,' Lily mutters under her breath, but Bella hears and swings the barrel again.

'Big words from the one my brother called little lapdog Lily, hanging on Zoë's every word, so desperate for her approval that you didn't dare tell her how much of a bitch she was to you. I bet you'd still jump now if Zoë gave the word.'

Lily doesn't answer, her eyes glued to the rifle.

'Do you have any idea how long I've waited to have the four of you in a room together? My brother's unsolved murder is what drove me into the police in the first place. I was so desperate to find answers to what happened to him. I spent hours poring over the original case notes to try and figure out why he died. And despite begging my superiors, there was no appetite to reopen the case with no new evidence available. I tried to do my own digging, but was warned to leave it alone, and when I refused, they suspended and eventually dismissed me. Can you believe that? All because I wanted to find the truth. The criminal justice system is a joke in this country.

'Even when I showed them Saul's diary last year, and how complicit you all were in his demise, they weren't interested in digging up the past. They left me no choice but to kick over a few rocks of my own. The one common thread in all of your statements to the police was the apparent lack of awareness of what Saul was doing out on the street at that time. There was no mention of a break-in at the school, and there's only one person who could have kept the security guards at the school quiet, isn't there, Rod? But if you weren't aware of what the others had planned, why would your dad not report the break-in?'

All eyes turn on Rod. I had always assumed the police knew that Saul was running out of the school when the accident occurred, which is why the rest of us kept our mouths shut. But if none of us mentioned it, and Rod's dad stopped the school reporting it, the police would have no reason to suspect Saul had broken in.

'You'd have to ask him, only he's already dead, so you can't,' Rod replies nonchalantly.

'It's all there in Saul's diary; how your dad pulled all manner of strings to keep you out of trouble, Rod. He even paid for the school to have a swimming pool installed, so that the board of governors didn't insist on excluding you. The only conclusion I can reach is that your dad was once again covering for you.' She takes a menacing step forward, the rifle now trained on Rod. 'So, tell me, Rod, were you driving the car that killed my brother?'

The blood drains from his face.

'Saul was my best friend, I wouldn't do anything to hurt him. I didn't know what these fucks were up to, and if it wasn't for them planning to get revenge on me and Dad, your brother wouldn't have been in that street at that time on that day. So, if you're looking for culpability, aim at them, not me.'

She isn't persuaded by the argument.

'It's funny, he wrote about your willingness to throw anyone else under the bus to keep yourself out of trouble. Like the time you and he stole the shirts from the changing rooms and you blamed it on Glynn, who had nothing to do with it. That's what this is now, isn't it, Rod? You won't ever admit when you're in the wrong, so you deflect.'

'No, that isn't what I'm doing. I wasn't there.'

She smirks at this.

'Your dad's car was though, wasn't it? The Aston Martin. James Bond's car. I located a witness who placed it a couple of streets away from the school that night.'

I watch Rod closely for any sign of recognition or acknowledgement. We always assumed his interest in the events of that night was because he knew we'd been plotting against him, but could it be that his questions were to establish whether we could place him at the scene?

'Fine,' he says with a heavy sigh. 'My dad's car was there that night, and I was in it when the accident occurred, but I wasn't the one behind the wheel. Put the rifle down and I will tell you who was.'

She makes no effort to abide.

'Okay, very well, it's not like you're going to be able to charge him now that he's dead. I was at a friend's house stoned out of my mind on that night. I overdosed and someone called my dad to come and collect me, and he was driving me to the hospital to have my stomach pumped when he collided with someone in the street. I vaguely remember the impact, but I was so out of it that I didn't really know what was happening. He didn't stop because he wanted to save my life, and it was only weeks afterwards that he admitted what had happened. He blamed me for the accident, and he had the car transported up here where it could be repaired discreetly and at considerable cost. He never forgave himself, nor me, for what happened, and we barely spoke after that night. There, are you happy now?'

I can't read what's going on behind her eyes, but I also can't believe what Rod has just told us. All this time he knew that his dad ran Saul over and he could have told us and we wouldn't have had to live with this guilt hanging over us.

Bella stares blankly at him, barely blinking while the cogs in her head process the revelation. Somehow, I sense it won't bring her the peace she's been searching for.

'I'm sorry, my love,' Rod continues. 'I know I should have said something sooner, but I only had his word for it. I was so out of it that night that I only have his explanation to go with. You can check hospital records and you'll see what date and time I was admitted and the treatment I underwent. And I'm prepared to tell Glynn as much when I speak to him later. Please put the rifle down and let's get married.'

Her astonished laughter echoes off the low ceiling.

'I never intended to marry you, Rod. Are you fucking crazy? This was never real; just a means of getting to the four of you and getting the truth. That's why I slipped the GHB into your drinks on Friday night, but I didn't realise it would react so badly with the alcohol. We were supposed to get back to the Airbnb and then I was going to tell you all who I was and question you with your inhibitions lowered. But then this dick went and knocked someone over, and I had to improvise.'

She's looking at me as she says this, and my heart sinks. So, it wasn't just coincidence that I woke in the driver's seat.

46

ZOË

Dan looks crestfallen at the news, and as I watch his world slowly falling apart, I feel equally heartbroken. I'd actually started to believe that somebody was trying to set him up to take the fall. And as his friend, I will do my utmost to make sure that he has strong representation. The fact that Bella has admitted to spiking our drinks with GHB means Dan can't be held wholly responsible for what happened on that road.

It's a shame there's nothing I can do to help ease the guilt he's going to feel with each passing day.

Rod also looks like someone who's had the rug pulled from beneath their feet.

'So you never loved me?' he says, and I can hear the stomach-crushing angst in his voice.

She tilts her head.

'I'm sorry for misleading you,' she says, 'but given you've protected your dad's secret from me and my family for all these years, you must be able to see why I had to do it? I created a fictional version of myself, someone I knew you'd fall for, because you were the only means of getting the others together. I tried coming at each of you as individuals, but you really did stick to that stupid fucking pact.'

'Wait, what do you mean you came for us?' I ask, not following this last statement.

She looks at me and narrows her eyes.

'I tried to instigate an affair with your husband, Tim, thinking you would have told him the truth about that night, but he had no idea who my brother was, nor what a lying cow you are. I wanted to threaten little lapdog Lily, but she never leaves her parents' pub, so I couldn't get her alone. And I was certain Dan would fall on his own sword when I instigated legal proceedings against him at the building site, but then I learned everything would be handled by solicitors and we would never get to meet. I was terrified Rod would recognise me when we first met, but he didn't, and it didn't take more than a little flattery to get him alone, but he didn't seem to know anything about that night either. And so then the plan started to form in my mind. I sensed you wouldn't be able to resist the prospect of reuniting one more time.'

'I think you can lower the gun though now, can't you?' I say, nodding at the weapon. 'You've got the answers you came for.'

A thin smile breaks across her face, and then she squeezes the trigger. Rod dives for cover, but there is no blast, just a vacant click, before she cracks the weapon open and reveals it was never loaded. Of course she was bluffing. With only two rounds in the chamber, she'd never be able to shoot all of us before someone overpowered her.

'I'd better head upstairs and let the guests know there won't be a wedding today,' Bella says, turning on her heel and heading away, discarding the rifle with a crash as it lands on the tiled floor.

'I guess we should go and pack,' Lily suggests, and I agree; I can't wait to get out of this place.

Lily loops her arm through Dan's and leads him away, but Rod remains sprawled out on the couch.

'Are you coming back upstairs?' I ask him, but he shakes his head. He doesn't look in the mood to be particularly sociable and given his fiancée has just called off their wedding, it's probably best to give him a bit of space.

I follow the others back through the garage, spying the Aston Martin on one of the plinths, and picturing Saul careering off the front of it. I can't help wondering whether Bella will use this new information to demand a forensic examination of the vehicle, or whether she'll just be satisfied with the truth.

What I still don't understand is how Evan's threats fit into this. Was he also part of her ploy to try and get the truth out of me? Did she somehow manipulate him into seducing me, and then planned to use the threat of exposing the affair to make me talk? That doesn't explain how she knew him, nor why he'd go along with her plan. It also doesn't explain why his phone was in the drawer of her dressing table, when I've not seen him anywhere in the house.

Something doesn't add up, and I hurry forwards to try and get to Bella, but by the time I catch up with her I see her in conversation with Glynn and another man I now recognise as Reuben, Saul's older brother, who gave me my first ever puff of a joint. He seems taken aback when our eyes meet, and I recall that intense stare that always made me feel as though he was trying to undress me with his eyes.

I just catch the end of Bella relaying the conversation to the two of them. Glynn looks at me.

'Is all of this true? You were there when Saul died?'

We could all deny the truth again, so it would be Bella's word against ours, but there's no point after all this time.

'We were all there. But Saul's death was an accident.'

'Did you witness Rod's dad collide with Saul?'

When I close my eyes, I can still see Saul's body being flung into the air, but it was so dark that I barely saw the silver car. It didn't stop for long enough for the make or model to register in my memory.

I nod, though, to give Bella the peace of mind she's been desperately searching for.

'Perhaps we should go somewhere quiet where you can all make your statements,' Glynn says, nodding towards the room where he was eating breakfast earlier.

'I want to speak to Evan first,' I say, just to read Bella's reaction.

'I'm sorry, I don't know who that is,' Glynn says, glancing at Bella to see if she will answer, but she also shakes her head.

'Who is that, sorry?'

'Evan. The guy at my work who's been stalking me.'

'Oh, him? He's not here,' Bella says so matter-of-factly that I instantly sense something wrong.

I reach for her arm.

'I know he's here. I saw his phone in the drawer of your dressing table. He was the one who asked the barmaid to black-mail us. Why would his phone be here, if he isn't?'

Bella wrenches her arm free and proceeds into the room, taking the seat at the head of the table.

'I don't know what you're talking about,' she says, but can't meet my stare.

I slide into the seat beside her.

'It's okay; I know he was working with you. It's just his Aunt

Mae hasn't heard from him in a few days, and I told her I would ask him to get in touch once I caught up with him.'

'I don't know what you're talking about,' she grizzles through gritted teeth, but I'm not buying her bullshit.

I pull out my phone and search for a picture of him, finally finding one of the two of us holding cocktails in a selfie. I slide the phone across the tablecloth so she can see the screen, but she gives it one glance, before shaking her head.

'I've never seen that man in my life before,' she says, sliding the phone back to me as Lily drops into the chair beside me.

'Oh my God, I remember this guy,' Lily says, her neck craned so she can see the screen.

'Wait, what?' I ask. 'You know Evan?'

I can barely see Lily's eyes as she pulls a confused face.

'I recognise him from somewhere, but I can't think where...' She closes her eyes, trying to recall the memory, but then her eyelids snap open, and she snaps her fingers together. 'He was there,' she says, staring at Bella. 'I have this memory of the two of you speaking. The window was down, and he was speaking loudly, but I can't remember what he was saying...'

'When was this?' I ask Lily. 'When did you see Evan? Here at the house?'

'No, no, on the night of the party. I think I must have come to at some point and yeah, I definitely saw him leaning in through the driver's window, and...' Her hands shoot up and cover her mouth as she gasps. '*You* were in the driver's seat, *not* Dan.'

Bella quickly looks away and calls Glynn over.

'I think you should take them out one by one to make their statements so we can get each version of the truth, instead of a corroborated story.'

'It's all coming back,' Lily says. 'We were pulled over, and I woke with Rod and Zo passed out beside me. Bella was in the driver's seat, and this guy was leaning through the window. He was shouting something and then Bella, you started the engine, and tried to pull away, but he jumped in front of the car. I think you tried to change gear, but the car shot forwards again, and...'

Lily covers her mouth again, and suddenly her words weigh heavy on my mind.

For an instant I'm back on the side of the road where Rod is feeling for a pulse. The body shifts and rolls towards us so that the man is on his back, but I don't recognise him because his face is a mangled mess of blood and bone where it's been squashed.

'Evan is the man who was run over,' I say, my voice barely a whisper.

That is why he hasn't been in touch with Mae for the last few days. But that also means if he is dead, then he wasn't the person sending the messages telling me to come clean about Saul. It also means he wasn't the one who emailed the barmaid.

'You killed him,' Lily says, pointing a trembling finger at Bella.

'I don't know what you're talking about,' she says airily, but the guilt in her eyes is so obvious to me now.

'How do you explain his phone in your room then?' I challenge, as if I'm in court and she's in the witness box.

'Dan, you weren't driving,' Lily says excitedly as he enters the room, looking bewildered. 'Bella killed him, not you.'

Glynn raises his eyebrows at this, but it's Reuben who speaks.

'Oh, shit, Bella, not again.'

'I don't know what they're talking about,' she says desperately. 'They're just trying to shift the focus. They're the reason Saul was run down by Rod's dad. That's what we came here to find out. Now, Glynn, do your fucking job and arrest them.'

But there's a look of shame that Reuben is now sharing with his sister.

'It wasn't my fault,' she says quickly. 'Dan was all over the road, and I had to force him to pull over. He must have drunk too much of the water and the drugs took effect too soon. He was going to kill us, so I made him pull over so we could swap places. But then this guy appeared at the side of the car. He said he was a friend of Zoë's, and he wanted to speak to her. He started banging on the window, so I lowered it and told him she was too drunk, but he said he saw me slip something into her drink, and was going to phone the police if I didn't pass her over to him. I told him I was with the police but he didn't believe me, and so I told him to fuck off. He was trying to ruin everything.

'So, I tried to pull away, but then he jumped in front of the car. I tried to reverse but the stupid gear lever slipped and it went forwards instead of backwards. The stupid idiot shouldn't have been there in the first place. It wasn't my fault. I wasn't to know he'd follow Zoë to Scotland. It's not like last time, Reuben, I swear. It was an accident.'

I lace my fingers together on the table, willing the cloud of emotion in my head to stay back. I can't believe Evan is dead, and yet I believe every word of what Bella has just said. I don't doubt it was an accident, but she was ready to let Dan take the blame, and that doesn't sit well with me. I also don't like the fact that both she and Reuben have suggested this isn't the first time she's killed someone. I'm suddenly very aware of the sharp carving knife in the centre of the table.

But Reuben must be reading my mind, because he stretches and picks up the knife, sliding it out of Bella's reach.

'I think we need to go and speak to Dr Nye again,' he says to her, in a calm voice, slowly moving closer, and placing a delicate arm around her shoulder.

'It wasn't my fault, Reuben,' she says, tears now flowing freely, as she allows him to lift her to her feet.

He leads her away from the table, stopping only to ask Glynn to contact the police on the mainland to report what has happened.

EPILOGUE
DAN

It's been a month since we returned from Scotland, and I still haven't come to terms with how that road trip down memory lane ended. I am still not sleeping properly, seeing glimpses of things I don't remember in my dreams. I don't know if I'll ever recover all the memories lost while under the influence of the GHB.

Once the police arrived, and we all gave accounts of the long weekend, and made our statements to Glynn about the night Saul died, Reuben revealed that Bella – Saul's nickname for her – had been receiving treatment for her mental health since she was dismissed from the police. It turned out that Glynn had no idea who she really was, and she wasn't part of his case review team.

Reuben told us he thought she was fine, oblivious to the persona and trap she'd set for us all. Apparently, he'd approached Zoë's husband on Friday to warn her about Bella's obsession, only to learn that we were already on our way to Scotland. It was only when he tracked his sister's phone on Jura that he figured out that she was somehow involved, and began to fear the worst.

Glynn has now formally closed the case on Saul's hit and run, though it will never be prosecuted. And thankfully none of us are facing charges for perverting the course of justice. I deeply regret the pact we made that night. And whilst we would have faced punishment for trying to smear Rod's dad's name back then, I can't help but think that things would have worked out better for all of us if we'd just told the truth. Living with guilt for that long does have a significant impact on your psyche. It certainly did mine. I always felt like I had to make up for doing the wrong thing, and have spent my life living in my dad's shadow, and never quite measuring up. I've always assumed I don't deserve a happy ever after, because of that one act, and I've been subconsciously spoiling my own future as a result.

I received an offer on the house the day after it went on the market, and a small bidding war means I should be able to settle my debts, pay for Mam's full-time care, and I'll be investing the rest in a new business that will certainly keep me busy. I know next to nothing about running a pub, but Lily's dad has agreed to show me the ropes for my 50 per cent share, allowing him and Lily's mam to semi-retire.

I don't know that anything romantic will ever blossom between Lily and me – probably way too much water has passed under that bridge – but I'm loving being a dad to George. I'm waking every day with a renewed sense of purpose, and I plan to spend every day teaching him not to follow in my footsteps.

I certainly didn't realise I would see the others again so soon after the last reunion, but it was Lily who suggested we convene at Saul's graveside to say a proper goodbye. Zoë says she and Tim are making progress with marriage counselling, but it's still too early to say if things will last. I still care for her, despite everything, and only want to see her happy. And Rod says he is ploughing on with his charitable trust.

Rod pops the cork on the bottle of Jura single malt and adds a splash to each of our glasses, raising his into the air.

'To our dearly departed brother, Saul. You brought us together, and passed way too early. We promise to make the most of our remaining years in your memory.'

ACKNOWLEDGEMENTS

Thank you for choosing and reading *The Reunion*. I hope it kept you gripped and entertained. Please do tell your friends and family (and any other person who will listen) how much you enjoyed it. And please do get in touch with me via the usual social channels to let me know what you thought about it (remember to be kind).

Since my recent autism diagnosis, I've spent a lot of time reflecting on my life and the key moments and experiences that have led me to where I now find myself. On the whole, I'm pretty happy with my lot, and I love that I've found writing as a means of indulging my overactive imagination and passion for story-telling.

But that isn't to say there haven't been low points, and when I reflect on the people who have entered and exited my life in the last forty-three years (gosh am I really that old?). I can't help lamenting the loss of some of those relationships. There are only two people in my life I consider true friends, i.e. people I feel comfortable being myself around and who I know I could trust with my deepest fears and darkest secrets. And it was with this in mind that I embarked on the story of four former close friends who reunite many years later and have to adapt to how much each has changed. I wanted to examine what would happen to this once tightknit group if pressure was applied.

What did you think about the intricacies of the relationships, and were you surprised by how each handled the pressure of the second hit and run? And in your close circle of friends, which would you trust with your darkest secrets, and which would you not?

I should probably clarify at this point that none of the characters that appear in this book are based on anyone I know/have known. The benefit of having an overactive imagination, is that these voices often appear in my head with no explanation as to where they've come from, nor why they've decided to speak up now. Even as I type this acknowledgement note, I have four new voices shouting to be heard as I work through edits of my next book (coming March 2025).

As always, I'd like to thank my inspirational agent Emily Glenister at the DHH Literary Agency, who is always only a phone call or email away when I'm struggling and need her to remind me that I'm a far better writer than I ever give myself credit for. It means so much having someone to champion my books and I'm indebted to her honesty and support.

Thank you also to my eagle-eyed editor Emily Yau who pushes me to make my stories the best they can be. And the whole team at Boldwood Books deserve huge credit for the work they do in producing my books in the array of formats available. From line and copy editing, proof-reading, cover design, audio-book creation, and marketing. The fact that you're reading this acknowledgement is testament to the brilliant job they do.

My children are an inspiration to me every day, and as they continue to grow so quickly, I am eternally grateful that I get to play such an important role in their development. They continue to show one another affection, patience and kindness, and make being their dad that bit easier. I'd like to thank my own parents and my parents-in-law for continuing to offer words of encouragement when I'm struggling to engage with my muse.

It goes without saying that I wouldn't be the writer I am today without the loving support of my beautiful wife and soulmate Hannah. She keeps everything else in my life ticking over so that I can give what's left to my writing. She never questions my method or the endless hours daydreaming while I'm working through plot holes, and for that I am eternally grateful.

And thanks must also go to YOU for reading *The Reunion*. Please do post a review to wherever you purchased the book from so that other readers can be enticed to give it a try. It takes less than two minutes to share your opinion, and I ask you do me this small kindness.

I am active on Facebook, Twitter/X, Instagram, and now TikTok, so please do stop by with any messages, observations, or questions. Hearing from readers of my books truly brightens my days and encourages me to keep writing, so don't be a stranger. I promise I *will* respond to every message and comment I receive.

Stef (a.k.a. M.A. Hunter)

ABOUT THE AUTHOR

M.A. Hunter is the pen name of Stephen Edger, the bestselling author of psychological and crime thrillers, including the Kate Matthews series. Born in the north-east of England, he now lives in Southampton where many of his stories are set.

Sign up to M. A. Hunter's mailing list here for news, competitions and updates on future books.

Visit M. A. Hunter's website: stephenedger.com/m-a-hunter

Follow M. A. Hunter on social media:

𝕏 x.com/stephenedger
facebook.com/AuthorMAHunter
instagram.com/stef.edger
bookbub.com/authors/stephen-edger
goodreads.com/stephenedger

ALSO BY M. A. HUNTER

THE

Murder

LIST

**THE MURDER LIST IS A NEWSLETTER
DEDICATED TO SPINE-CHILLING FICTION
AND GRIPPING PAGE-TURNERS!**

**SIGN UP TO MAKE SURE YOU'RE ON OUR
HIT LIST FOR EXCLUSIVE DEALS, AUTHOR
CONTENT, AND COMPETITIONS.**

SIGN UP TO OUR
NEWSLETTER

BIT.LY/THEMURDERLISTNEWS

Boldwood

Boldwood Books is an award-winning fiction publishing company seeking out the best stories from around the world.

Find out more at www.boldwoodbooks.com

Join our reader community for brilliant books, competitions and offers!

Follow us
@BoldwoodBooks
@TheBoldBookClub

Sign up to our weekly deals newsletter

https://bit.ly/BoldwoodBNewsletter

Printed in Great Britain
by Amazon